PENGUIN BOOKS

THE NIGHT SKY

Ann Lauterbach was born and grew up in New York City. After college (University of Wisconsin, Madison), she attended Columbia University on a Woodrow Wilson Fellowship, but moved to London before completing her MA in English literature. She lived in London for seven years, working variously in publishing and arts institutions. On her return, she worked for a number of years in art galleries in New York before she began teaching. She has taught at Brooklyn College, Columbia, Iowa, Princeton, and at the City College of New York and Graduate Center of CUNY. Since 1991 she has been Director of Writing in the Milton Avery School of the Arts at Bard College, where she had been, since 1999, Ruth and David Schwab II Professor of Languages and Literature. Lauterbach has received a number of awards and fellowships, including a Guggenheim Fellowship in 1986 and a John D. and Catherine T. MacArthur Fellowship in 1993. She is the author of seven collections of poetry, including *Hum, If in Time: Selected Poems 1975–2000, On a Stair, And for Example*, and *Clamor*, and she has collaborated on several books with visual artists. She lives in Germantown, New York.

THE NIGHT SKY

WRITINGS ON THE POETICS OF EXPERIENCE

ANN LAUTERBACH

PENGUIN BOOKS

PENGUIN BOOKS

Published by the Penguin Group

Penguin Group (USA) Inc., 375 Hudson Street, New York, New York 10014, U.S.A.
Penguin Group (Canada), 90 Eglinton Avenue East, Suite 700, Toronto,
Ontario, Canada M4P 2Y3 (a division of Pearson Penguin Canada Inc.)
Penguin Books Ltd, 80 Strand, London WC2R 0RL, England
Penguin Ireland, 25 St Stephen's Green, Dublin 2, Ireland (a division of Penguin Books Ltd)
Penguin Group (Australia), 250 Camberwell Road, Camberwell,
Victoria 3124, Australia (a division of Pearson Australia Group Pty Ltd)
Penguin Books India Pvt Ltd, 11 Community Centre,
Panchsheel Park, New Delhi – 110 017, India
Penguin Group (NZ), 67 Apollo Drive, Rosedale, North Shore 0632,
New Zealand (a division of Pearson New Zealand Ltd)
Penguin Books (South Africa) (Pty) Ltd, 24 Sturdee Avenue,
Rosebank, Johannesburg 2196, South Africa

Penguin Books Ltd, Registered Offices:
80 Strand, London WC2R 0RL, England

First published in the United States of America by Viking Penguin,
a member of Penguin Group (USA) Inc. 2005
Published in Penguin Books 2008

Some of the essays in this book were previously published.
Acknowledgments to the original publishers appear in the introductory
notes to the selections.

Page 262 constitutes an extension of this copyright page.

Cover art by Joe Brainard, © 1978, 2005

ISBN 0-670-03410X (hc.)
ISBN 978-0-14-303737-8 (pbk.)
CIP data available

146028962

Life, as the ultimate unity, lies at the basis of the poeticized.

—Walter Benjamin

To Joan Richardson and Michael Brenson

CONTENTS

Introduction / 1

Use This Word in a Sentence: "Experimental" / 8

Inventing Unreality / 12

Uncle Edgar Was Watching / 19

Disobedient Choices: On the Eve of Exile / 23

Is I Another? A Talk in Seven Beginnings / 31

As (It) Is: Toward a Poetics of the Whole Fragment / 40

The Night Sky

    I. "There Is No Topic Sentence" / 46

    II. "Green (thought, shade)" / 64

    III. "Peace" / 80

    IV. "Action" / 95

    V. "Ragged" / 114

    VI. "On" / 131

    VII. "There Is No Topic Sentence" / 152

What Is the Grass? Notes Leading up to and away from
    Walt Whitman / 165

Slaves of Fashion / 176

Three Introductions

    Fanny Howe / 181

    Michael Palmer / 184

    Rosmarie Waldrop / 187

Barbara Guest: Architect of Air / 189

On David Smith's Language: The Poetics of Identity / 197

Gerhard Richter: "The Enigma" / 207

John Currin: Pressing Buttons / 211

Remembering Joe Brainard / 217

9/11

    What Is a Day? / 225

    After the Fall / 231

After Emerson: Of General Knowledge and the Common Good / 235

Acknowledgments / 249

Notes / 251

Index / 257

INTRODUCTION

What compels a poet to write prose? The answer is in each case unique, but since the Renaissance, Western poets have elaborated and augmented their genre in prose writings. The ecclesiastical English metaphysician John Donne wrote sermons and meditations; his great lines "No man is an island, entire of itself; every man is a piece of the continent, a part of the main" are found in his "Meditation 17." In "A Defense of Poetry" the Romantic revolutionary Percy Bysshe Shelley asserted, famously, that poets are "the unacknowledged legislators of the world." Charles Baudelaire's essays on writers, artists, and art were central to many modernist thinkers, notably Jean-Paul Sartre and Walter Benjamin. W. B. Yeats practically *invented* the New Age with his occult cosmology *A Vision*. Up until the Internet hit town, poets' letters and journals lent archival grist to biographical and interpretive mills. John Keats's trenchant formulation of a poet's necessary disposition, "negative capability," was in a letter, as was Arthur Rimbaud's prescient "Je est un autre" (I is an other). Emily Dickinson's *Master Letters* spawned a small industry of distracting speculation about her amorous life. Rainer Maria Rilke's *Letters to a Young Poet* still inspires a call to write poems. Each of these examples, and there are countless others, is at least in part animated by a belief that poetry, as old as the human voice itself, is integral and necessary to the human conversation; that it helps to construct the infinitely various linguistic bridge—the beautiful contingency—between persons and their worlds.

Many twentieth-century American poets brought to their practice a critical engagement with other arts, as well as a new experimentalism, often informed by unprecedented rapid changes in international culture, both at the level of shifts in the language of form and in circuits of production, distribution, and reception. Poets wrote essays and reviews, letters and manifestos; they edited magazines and critiqued each other's works. Many wrote novels, plays, and short stories as well as poems. Some undertook to undermine the strict separation between genres; some collaborated with artists in other fields. In my own generation, poets have extended these connections, helping to reconfigure American poetics into the communities of world literature and to bring a charged and rigorous articulation to discourse between practice and theory. These poets have engaged with, and argued for, a radical ambition for the place of the poem in cultural life. In these pages, I add my voice to theirs.

When poets are connected to the times in which they live, the forms they explore give us keys to the construction of meaning. Gertrude Stein made this point most succinctly: "Nothing changes from generation to generation except the thing seen and that makes a composition," she wrote in "Composition as Explanation." Stein believed, and I agree with her, that humans share the same essentials in their "existing," but what changes is the emphasis, the "insistence," as she called it; "the thing seen." Artists, she believed, are responsible for portraying this shifting emphasis; that is, for finding forms that reflect the movement of time, as neither historical narrative nor descriptive mimesis, but as immediate engagement and response: "And each of us in our own way are bound to express what the world in which we are living is doing," Stein wrote in "Portraits and Repetition." Ezra Pound wanted poetry to be "news that stays news," condensing and codifying the double-edged desire for poetry to be in and of its present, while simultaneously turning that immediacy into a lastingly fresh apprehension—"petals on a wet black bough." This tension between ideas of endurance and ideas of immediacy characterizes much of modernist poetics.

In these writings I explore the proposition that poems, and artworks in general, are not only pleasant distractions, entertainments; not just icing on the cake of life. I don't want to claim that *poetry is good for you* the way walnuts are. But good poems reconfigure the place between acts of perception and response, mental conception and material structure, in sets of particulars that keep the new(s) from shredding existence into repetitious and interminable platitudes. Yet poetry in America is in, at best, a marginal relation to mainstream culture, even mainstream academic culture. Why, I have often wondered, do so many persons want to write poems, if the culture at large disdains to include them in its self-picturing? When poet and publisher Sam Hamill declined an invitation from Laura Bush for tea at the White House in the fall of 2002, because he did not wish to be seen, even implicitly, as in support of the imminent war in Iraq, he set off a cascading reaction, gathering literally thousands of poems on his Web site. This eruption of support led to a reading at Lincoln Center's Avery Fisher Hall in New York on February 17, 2003, organized by Not in Our Name and hosted by writer/actor Wallace Shawn and writer/actor/director André Gregory. I was happy to be included among those who read that night, a night in which the city was muted in deep snow. We did not expect much of an audience. But the hall filled, and when we walked onto the stage, the audience stood to applaud before a word was spoken. Why, at that moment, did "the public" want to listen to poems? They had, many of them, gathered a few days earlier, in silent protest. They wanted, I thought, their unity as a crowd to find individual utterance; they wanted to be, somehow, represented. The anonymity of poetry and the anonymity of the crowd shimmied into focus, into persons, faces, voices.

To write poetry in America is *in itself* a subversive act, a refutation of, and resistance to, certain assumptions about what constitutes "the public" and its interests.

Poetry protects language from serving any master.

One can see better from the periphery than from the center.

I begin with an assumption, perhaps too obvious for statement: that what I know is always a fragment of what there is to be known. There is a second assumption, perhaps less obvious: that what I know is sometimes a defense against what there is to be known. This defense can realize itself as fear, as contempt, as doubt, as ideology, as polemics—the desire to fasten one's partial knowledge and conviction onto universal value.

My fear is that my fragments of knowledge are just bits and pieces with too many unbridgeable gaps between them.

And so, in defense, I have come to celebrate *the whole fragment.*

This fear of insufficiency has rarely abated. I suppose it originates with memory, or, more exactly, with forgetting. I forget what I know or what I knew. I think I wanted to forget specific, concrete things from my early life in order to have a present life that is not simply one of reaction. Or to put it another way: by forgetting I have found a method by which the materials of the actual become materials for the possible. These issues, one way or another, beset all writers, which is at least one reason why we write. (Samuel Beckett claimed that Marcel Proust had a poor memory.) Poets, perhaps more than other writers, need to solve the riddle of memory in relation to language, because everything we write is, in a sense, experienced as an event.

Knowledge of what? Well, in the first place, of language. The registers of this knowledge are multiple: vocabulary, syntax, punctuation, grammar; diction, rhythm, cadence, tone, measure, scale, and so on. To write well, one needs to love these forms of knowing, to find in them, through them, sources of pleasure. Not just the immediacy of sensuous pleasure, but a kind of exalted curiosity about the most minor decisions: Should I use "the" or "a" with that noun, and what is the basis for the choice? Does this line range left, or does it jump into the white space of the page, rupturing the expected template? I have written this word, "experiment": I wonder what its etymology is.

The pieces collected here are for the most part occasional, written in response to a request: to give a talk, participate in a symposium, contribute an essay, introduce a poet. The earliest dates from the late 1980s, when I was in the midst of changing my means of livelihood from working in art galleries, writing now and then about visual arts in New York, to becoming a full-time teacher. Writing for me is associative, meditative, and digressive. Often I use material from my personal life to propel an idea, establish a perspective or perception, but I do not think of these as personal essays. "I" is a powerful character in our linguistic life but, as many have observed, it is no guarantee of either authenticity or transparency. Nevertheless, I have a desire for a *practical aesthetics,* wherein connections to the making or appreciation of forms have direct application to daily life, and daily life in turn inflects and conditions how to relate to the forms, artistic and otherwise, of the world. This shifting reciprocity is central to these writings. As you might expect, there are repetitions, recurring motifs, themes, and citations: Emerson's writings, whole fragments, choice, aesthetic gladness, progressive pragmatism, as well as such personal tropes as my father's early death and my mother's alcoholism. Writing is at least in part an act of trust in the fundamental capacity of language to inscribe paths, however circuitous; these paths are ones that we take more than once, sometimes to new observations, new destinations. Thoughts take on different meanings depending on where they are situated (otherwise, we would cease to read and write) just as we take on different aspects depending on with whom we are conversing.

We make music, painting, sculpture, films, novels in order to mediate our mortal visiting rights: a specifically human wish to intercede, to punctuate the ongoingness of time and the seemingly random distributions of nature. This punctuation is called history or, more precisely, culture, or, more precisely still, history of culture, now understood as a great plurality: histories, cultures. It turns out they—the *its* of history and the *its* of culture—are multiple and various, not linear and single. And so "the night sky" is a simple overarching rubric, a way of naming this variation and multiplicity, and to suggest that the way words make sentences and sentences paragraphs is also a kind of constellating, where imagined structures are drawn from an apparently infinite fund: *words, stars.* To look up into the sky and to see *objects;* to invent, as Greek mythology, as Ovid did, whole *stories* which somehow explain the panoply of lightspots in the night sky—these acts of narrative and imagistic invention were surely compelled by the inexhaustible human desire to transfigure the incomprehensible into intelligible form.

These writings are not formal essays; even those that address specific subjects are closer to meditations than to strict expository examinations or arguments. I have no set of ideas to promulgate, no specific intellectual terrain to explore. I am too impatient by temperament, too eclectic in my tastes, to be a scholar. My personal library reflects a preponderance of poetry and prose nonfiction—philosophy, cultural and political commentary, art and literary criticism. These nurture and comfort me; often in my writings I include quotations from authors I admire in an eagerness to share their voices, to create colloquy or dialogue, rather than to support an argument. Certain key passages recur; they steady the pursuit, anchor the habit of wandering.

Digression is for me one of life's pleasures; I rarely get from point A to point C without wandering through patches of Z or thickets of S. When I was young, I often fell asleep listening to a recording of John Jacob Niles singing the haunting spiritual that begins, "I wonder as I wander out under the sky / Why Jesus our Savior was brought forth to die." I remember feeling a kind of pleasurable fear in these lines, with their rhyme of "why" and "die" and the curiously close affinity between "wonder" and "wander." Perhaps these became twinned in my consciousness, separated as they are by only a single vowel. The fact that "wonder" flickers between awe and doubt, and that "wander" contains the magician's wand as well as the possibility of a lost destiny, might serve as an example of my mind's desire to bear witness to the fluctuating boundaries and nascent discoveries of language.

In any case, I do like to wander in language to the point of getting lost, to follow the lead of the sentence to see where it will take me: call it, if you like, a search for a quotidian sublime. This habit of mind is predicated on an odd empiricism, by which the terms of conclusion, the statement, emerges from as indeterminate and inclusive a ground as possible. Revision necessarily shadows this method. Linear argument, where one thing leads ineluctably to another, is of profound practical and rhetorical value, but necessarily it discourages vicissitude and ephemera, ambivalence and dead ends, *ruminations* that suggest a different mental economy, one that could affect conclusions beyond the restraint of reasoning logic. Such disparate discourses as, say, jurisprudence, medicine, and poetics share an interest in the observable world. But, as we have become increasingly aware, for each of these, objective knowledge and judgment are inevitably colored by subjective predilections, cultural traditions, personal desires, ideological constraints. Perhaps the greatest agon of our time will be understood once again to be the one that animated the Enlightenment, between structures of faith and structures of reason. Surely one of the most profound questions to arise in the wake of September 11th is how to bring an enlightened skepticism into alignment with what William James called "the will to believe." One cannot imagine a democracy without a belief in its secular institutions; one cannot imagine a democracy without a separation between church and state; one cannot imagine a democracy without a sense of personal accountability.

When I read, and reread, Emerson's essay "Experience," I locate a central tenet: a belief in the active *power of doing* over the passive *power of fate*. Emerson demonstrates how writing can be a reforming experience; how linguistic resources can merge acute affective registers with reason's solace, and so alter our deepest alignments and assessments. Clearly, it is disingenuous to claim I have no ideas to promulgate. I do have ideas attached to beliefs that are attached to personal, aesthetic, and political convictions. Experience would be a good example of something to which I attach value: I believe we learn to know by doing what we care about, and that this *doing* is the best route to a life well spent. The relation between doing, knowing, and caring is embedded in reciprocity; and reciprocity is contingent on receptivity. But listening, taking things in—what others say, how they think, what they do—these seem endangered in our culture of personal enterprise and one-way conversations with screens, monitors, cell phones.

In the urgencies of the world's climate, the answer to the question "Who is speaking?" is of as crucial consequence as "What is she saying?"

But perhaps it is already a paltry cliché to say that experience itself is threatened by our culture of mediated distraction. Now we are faced with the task of asking what constitutes an experience that is not, in Jean Baudrillard's chilling diagnosis, a "simulacrum." To privilege "experience" at a time when it is contested as a viable descriptive referent (especially within contemporary experimental poetics) is perhaps perverse, and yet I want to imagine that the ways in which we come to trust each other, to value our perceptions and interpretations, still owes something to how we think about what we love and what we abhor, to the events in our lives that give rise to our commitments. The crucial job of artists is to find a way to release materials into the animated middle ground between subjects, and so to initiate the difficult but joyful process of human connection. This is not only the relation of a given self to a given other, but to show how that relation might move further to a consciousness of persons and publics beyond our familiar horizons.

Artists choose their materials and from these decide how to put things together. All artworks are, at the most basic level, simply an accrual of relationships that are the result of choices: *this, not that.* Form is the result of the convergence of *subject matter* with the limits of material and the artist's choices regarding that material; this convergence of subject matter with form releases *content.* Meanings arise when persons—the reader, the spectator, the audience—engage with this content; meaning occurs in the mind and heart of the person who reads the poem, studies the picture, listens to the sonata. It is important to acknowledge this elastic space of meaning, where what the artist or writer *intends* and what the reader or spectator *apprehends* are not necessarily in perfect alignment. It is perhaps even more important not to confuse subject matter with content; this habit, reified by journalism, threatens to obliterate the power of form to both instruct the imagination and animate our critical discernment beyond the reductive literalism that has come to dominate our lives.

But it seems to me that there is another, perhaps more urgent, site of meaning that informs our experience of art. When we are moved by an aesthetic object, a poem or a piece of music or a painting, we experience a dual gladness: that the artist has made these choices and, by extension and analogy, that we, too, are capable of making choices. This second sense is not always (perhaps only rarely) conscious, but I think it contributes to the power art has to change our senses of ourselves as agents in the world; how we might shift from passive spectators or consumers to active participants, interpreters, innovators. Art serves no practical purpose, but to engage with it fully is to acknowledge the (pleasurable, if often difficult) consequences of choice at the crux of human agency. I want to suggest that artworks can disrupt the degradation of *choice* as the site of, and synonymous with, commodification (consumer preference) and (re)align it with the rewards of independent determinations of value—processes of aesthetic discernment and critique seen as part of a continuum across individual, social, political terrain. Choice confined to the marketplace endangers the very core of participatory democratic processes.

At the heart of these pages is a belief—call it a desire, a hope—that persons who are not poets, not artists, can *choose to make forms* that imbue experience with experiment, and so come to know the gladness of making "it"—life—anew.

USE THIS WORD IN A SENTENCE:
"EXPERIMENTAL"

In May 1998, the critic Michael Brenson organized a symposium at the Rockefeller Foundation in New York at which a number of people in the arts were asked to consider certain words. My word was "experimental." This is a somewhat revised version of that talk. It was published subsesquently in By Herself: Women Reclaim Poetry, *edited by Molly McQuade (Minneapolis, Gray Wolf Press, 2000).*

Many years ago I read something by Noam Chomsky in which three disparate words—"Constantinople" was one—that seemed to have nothing in common were brought together in a sentence. Chomsky wanted to show how context and syntax—that is, the structures of linguistic meaning—are as malleable as they are unpredictable.

In the language game called the dictionary, the word path begins at "expenditure," moves through "expense accounts" and "expensive," ascends to the rose of "experience," in all its variants, and then on to the secret garden itself: "experiment." The two words, "experience" and "experiment" share an etymological root; they are the flora of *experiri*, to try, and related to *periculum*, which includes the ideas of both attempt and peril. The path proceeds on, somewhat perilously, to "expert" and then to its final nettlesome destination, "expiate."

Recently, I was introduced as an "experimental poet." The adjective was uttered with mild disdain; I felt I was being damned with the faintest of praise. In the world of poetry, to be experimental is sometimes taken to mean you have, as the poet Charles Bernstein has remarked, an aversion to form, rather than an aversion to conformity.

I went to a small progressive school founded on John Dewey's pragmatism, and now I perceive that the etymological root shared by "experience" and "experiment" formed its pedagogical ground. Put most simply, the idea was that doing something is the best way to truly understand it. This notion was, in turn, the basis of an ethical vision, where individual engagement would extend outward into social, public realms, fueled by a practical curiosity. "Difference" or "otherness," that is, the unknown, would arouse curiosity rather than fear; problems would elicit a desire to find solutions. In this climate, cultural products, especially works of art, were viewed as essential and necessary; aesthetic experience was linked to a vocabulary of social accountability, response, and change.

Emerson uses the phrase "this new yet unapproachable America." The spirit of this—the new and the unapproachable—begins to depict the space in which experimentalism exists. It is the gap that Sacvan Bercovitch names when he talks about the American Jeremiad in his book of that title.

> But the American Puritan Jeremiad . . . made anxiety its end as well as its means. Crisis was the social norm it sought to inculcate. The very concept of errand, after all, implied a state of unfulfillment. The future, though divinely assured, was never quite there, and New England's Jeremiahs set out to provide the sense of insecurity that would ensure the outcome. Denouncing or affirming, their vision fed on the distance between promise and fact.

I take this gap between *promise* and *fact* to be akin to the one between rhetoric and practice, between the positivist language surrounding the creation of the euro, for example, and the economic competition that that new currency will unleashes, approves, and augments. It is the apparently insoluble gap between Israel and Palestine. Between promise and fact, between new and unapproachable, known and unknown, the experimental is always between, like a hinge. The risk, the peril involved is that you may not make it across the suspension; the experiment may fail, but a willingness to risk failure, to make mistakes, seems essential to turning promises into facts.

To risk failure one needs a sense of unfettered play, the play that would allow a failure to become useful for the next attempt, that would, in a sense, recycle the disaster.

Nuclear waste cannot be recycled. Perhaps it is the result of an experiment that should not have been undertaken.

I think perhaps science undertakes cool experiments and art undertakes hot experiments.

By "hot" I mean the kinds of formal discoveries that serve affective or spiritual needs; when the affective space is averted, the result is often experimentation for its own sake, self-conscious and self-referential, the aesthetic equivalent of narcissism. One way to avoid arid experimentalism is for artists to draw their ideas from a variety of sources, not from a single art form and its tradition. The tradition of the new is a dangerous precedent. The tradition of the old can be very useful. Years ago, I went to a young artist's studio. Just out of art school, he was working with an acrylic, a matte opaque gray mucous color, which he had fashioned into grids. Everyone in those days was making grids. I felt a sense of entrapment and violation, looking at this inert work and listening to the young man natter on and on, giving a critique; he had no idea what the actual effect of his work was. At last I said, "You are working in an exhausted iconography."

"Comforting art is art that you can make instant judgments about, that confirms your view," Sister Wendy, talking to Bill Moyers, remarked.

The poet Stacy Doris says she is meeting a lot of young people in their twenties who seem to have an extraordinary amount of knowledge about a lot of things; she takes this to be a result of the information age we are in, the fact that information is so easily accessed, at least by some.

I am interested in the relation between information and knowledge, the ways in which experience and experiment might link them, so that facts are converted into what Gertrude Stein called "useful knowledge."

We need to be careful not to mistake new technology for new knowledge.

To experiment means you must put what you know at risk to what you do not yet know.

I began to give up a conventional use of syntax, the logic of cause and effect, an assumed relation between subject and object, after my sister Jennifer died. The assumed narrative (she would live on into old age) had been ruptured, and I needed the gap in it to show. As these gaps began to occur, a new sense of isolated wholes, of complete gestures, began to replace old ideas of a constructed, even coerced, coherence. Instead, the figure of a mobile, moving in time and space, its components shifting in perspective and animated by potential contigencies, began to emerge, so that the natural narrativity of language gave way to a more problematic relation between cause and effect.

In this new dispensation, the hinges or places of contact became the most important location of structural relevance, as in music and in some abstract art. This seemed both more true and more natural to me. Prepositions, which show the relation *between* one thing and another, captured my attention. There are seventeen prepositions in English.

Art is not sufficiently understood as a meaning-making structure which might provide a given culture with nonviolent introductions to alternative modes of thinking about our world, and which, furthermore, might offer forms of redemption, solace, compensation, and critique for individuals that inhabit that world.

As the values of the free market consume the world economy, as entrepreneurship becomes rampant, as mergers beget mergers like rabbits in Paradise, our cultural institutions appear to be weaker and weaker, less and less willing to embrace works that propose or pose questions rather than provide answers.

It is the pressure of experience, the fact of attention to experience, which leads to real—that is, authentic—experimentation; a willingness to adapt to contexts, in order to derive not so much new meanings as new ways of interpreting the unpredictable.

Those who view form as static and reified are doomed to repetition, historical as well as personal. The fragments among which we live are, in my view, cause for celebration rather than lament, an invitation to create new ideas of coherence, where boundaries are malleable and permeable, so that inclusion and exclusion are in unstable flux. The fragment offers a possibility of vitality and variety—multiple perspectives, disparate vocabularies. The fragment might lead to clusters, to molecular structures, collaborations, artifacts, and institutions which retain the curiosity and flexibility of youth without sacrificing the digested experience of maturity, so that generations and genders no longer see themselves as competitive with each other. Such clusters would be deliberate disturbances of classic or traditional categories, including, need I say, traditional and classic vs. innovative or experimental. The best experiments surely make use of, are derived from, the major as well as the minor, the conservative as well as the progressive. History has no use for these distinctions.

As long as we long for lost syntheses, master narratives, complete views, we will be unable to imagine how to shape institutions which can override greed, self-interest, and cruelty, all of which are ready to assert their prerogatives, at the expense of the experimental.

INVENTING UNREALITY

The novelist Rikki Ducornet asked me to contribute an essay on "the monstrous and the marvelous" for an issue of the American Book Review, *July–August 1998.*

The normal outcome is that deference for reality gains the day. Nevertheless its behest cannot be at once obeyed. The task is now carried out bit by bit, under great expense of time and cathectic energy, while all the time the existence of the lost object is continued in the mind. Each single one of the memories and hopes which bound the libido to the object is brought up and hyper-cathected, and the detachment of the libido from it accomplished. Why this process of carrying out the behest of reality bit by bit, which is in the nature of a compromise, should be so extraordinarily painful is not at all easy to explain in terms of mental economics. It is worth noting that this pain seems natural to us. The fact is, however, that when the work of mourning is completed the ego becomes free and uninhibited again.

—Sigmund Freud[1]

1.

Reality had no fixed address. I could not keep it in a frame, it drifted, toward and away, accumulating as fast as it dissolved, a mercurial temporality that argued against the ordering sequences on which it was, ostensibly, founded. Temporality and chronology were antagonistic, sequences of possibility and probability were misaligned. What I desired began to separate, like a shadow from its object, to drift into scenarios of salvation and promise, installed on a phantom.

2.

The household, its slippery incipience, meant that one was obliged to invent.

3.

I was given some colored oil crayons. I made winged things whose radiant vitality surprised me. They seemed somehow beyond me, outside of anything I knew, a fiction whose purpose was to embody a truth. They appeared to inhabit more than one epistemology, more than one narrative.

4.

The poem makes a claim. It claims to know something about having been being. It acknowledges an oscillation between stillness and motion, recovery and discovery, difference and sameness. It is a search for the form of this different sameness, a recognition that transforms back to cognition.

> *that the poem is a toy*
> *with the structure of insomnia*
>
> —Norma Cole[2]

As if you could write *away from* and *into* simultaneously, so that the temporal articulates only presence. Yet there are instants so hard as to be gems, refracting and reflecting any new proximity.

5.

I have told myself that on the day my father was carried out of our house, not on a stretcher but on a chaise longue he had assembled from a kit (black cloth straps over blond wood) to be taken to hospital, he looked up at me, standing by the front door of our apartment, in the hall, on the black floor, my head quite near his, and said:

"Don't worry, I'll be back."

Did he say these words or did I rob another, earlier memory, when he was about to depart again for one of his assignments to the place called, mysteriously, *The Far East,* not lying sick on a self-made chair but standing in his tan raincoat, his typewriter in one hand, bending down to me:

"Don't worry, I'll be back."

A child tells herself a consoling fib; borrows a piece of reality. This fib enters the dream space.

At night, further scenarios were composed, shoots off the fiction of the return. A party, for example, in which he would say some coded something, to let me know he was himself, only *disguised.* He would give a sign. His death was a covert *trick,* a dissembling; he had been sent on a mission which demanded that his identity be obscured.

6.

Things are not outside of us, in measurable external space, like neutral objects (*objecta*) of use and exchange; rather they open to us the original place solely from which the experience of measurable external space becomes possible. They are therefore held and comprehended from the outset in the *topos outopos* (placeless place, no-place place) in which experience of being-in-the-world is situated.

—Giorgio Agamben[3]

On my eighth birthday, a few days after my father died, something occurred. I was not allowed to have a birthday party with children my age, as I was quarantined for polio, but several of my father's friends came by. (Friends came by all week; I do not remember if my birthday was singled out as an event within this murmuring current of mourning celebrants.)

A gift arrived, carried up the staircase that he had descended for the last time, in a large oblong white box. It came without a card.

7.

When my father returned from his trips he always arrived with presents: Chinese pajamas, black silk pants with white piping, a mauve silk jacket meticulously embroidered, tiny frog closures; a pale green chiffon dress whose floral print was a foggy Parisian park; for my mother, an engraved sandalwood fan, a painted Russian Easter egg; bolts of silk brocade, wrapped around themselves like huge ribbons; a small Chinese box in which there was a seal on a smooth nut which, when pressed into thick crimson paste, made a mark in indecipherable Chinese characters; a Samurai sword in a long sheath with a hidden button to open it; an immense black kimono lined in crimson, with green flowers, and another, pale yellow jacket, with black satin edging, in which my sister and I were enfolded and photographed, one sister to each sleeve, holding our infant brother in a swaddling blanket; a frail silver charm bracelet with a jade clasp; a helmet, festooned with gold dangling ear cups and orange tassels, that sat akimbo on the head of a carved wooden figure, its rich wood darkly gleaming, with an inscrutable face, neither baby, nor Buddha, nor old man, rounded belly protruding, eyes squinting, a mute incubus, country of origin and provenance unknown. Presents/presence.

8.

The teddy bear was not beautiful. It was ordinary, brown and cream, with shiny amber eyes. More silky than fluffy. I named it Beauty. Over the years, it became matted, dirty, and it lost its eyes: a blind old ugly thing. My father never became blind or old or ugly; had he lived out his life, he might by now perhaps be all those things.

History and magic oscillate.

—Theodor Adorno

9.

The essential relationship between language and death takes place—for metaphysics—in Voice. *Death and Voice have the same negative structure and they are metaphysically inseparable.* To experience death as death signifies, in fact, to experience the removal of the voice and the appearance, *in its place,* of another Voice (presented in grammatical thought as *gramma,* in Hegel as the Voice of death, in Heidegger as the Voice of conscience and the Voice of being, and in linguistics as a phoneme), which constitutes the originary *negative* foundation of the human word. To experience Voice signifies, on the other hand, to become capable of another death—no longer simply a deceasing, but a person's ownmost and insuperable possibility, the possibility of his *freedom.*

—Giorgio Agamben[4]

synchronic : structure : *langue* : myth : ritual
diachronic : event : *parole* : narrative : play

In the episode of the advent of Bear/Beauty, the distinction between reality and make-believe became indistinct, contingent upon one another: a real event gave rise to an invented cause. The object came with its own internal puns and permutations: *ear, be* (perhaps a *bee in its bonnet,* Bear Thinking), *re* (returns). In its nakedness (bare) and its inexplicable appearance (the beautiful), it became a tangible witness to, well, the *unbearable lightness of being.*

10.

At a time when everyone was concerned to give us prompt and reassuring answers, the doll was the first to make us aware of that silence larger than life which later breathed on us again and again out of space whenever we came at any point to the border of our existence. Sitting opposite the doll as it stared at us, we experienced for the first time (or am I mistaken?) that hollowness in

our feelings, that heart-pause which could spell death, did not
the whole gentle continuum of nature lift one like a lifeless body
over the abyss.

—Rainer Maria Rilke[5]

A boneless stuffed Thing, comforting icon of a vanquished wish, trace of the
other side of time, fragment that had miraculously escaped, catapulted like
the white badminton birdie that wheeled over the net with the mere touch of
a racket, making a slight blunt sound, *plunk:* a souvenir.

The souvenir . . . is an allusion and not a model; it comes after
the fact and remains both partial to and more expansive than the
fact. It will not function without the supplementary narrative dis-
course that both attaches to its origins and creates a myth with
regard to those origins.

—Susan Stewart[6]

I had wanted to be a painter. Maybe I would have been a painter, but a paint-
ing, an object in space, could not articulate the ontological vanishing point
between Bear and Beauty.

11.

Stepping from room to room, into places that no longer exist, have not ex-
isted for decades, as if never lifted from an essential nocturnal disposition, a
tunnel or throat. An obdurate secret, like a dream whose telling cannot
recreate the experience of the dreamer.

Besides, *death* is always the name of a secret, since it signs the ir-
replaceable singularity. It puts forth the public name, the com-
mon name of a secret, the common name of the proper name
without name. It is therefore always a shibboleth, for the mani-
fest name of a secret is from the beginning a private name, so
that language about death is nothing but the long history of a se-
cret society, neither public nor private, semi-private, semi-public,
on the border between the two; thus, also a sort of hidden religion

of the *awaiting* (oneself as well as each other), with its ceremonies, cults, liturgy, or its Marranolike rituals.

—Jacques Derrida[7]

12.

Into the gap between Bear and Beauty comes the differential play of language.

13.

> *Who is my father in this world, in this house,*
> *At the spirit's base?*
>
> *My father's father, his father's father, his—*
> *Shadows like winds*
>
> *Go back to a parent before thought, before speech,*
> *At the head of the past.*

—Wallace Stevens[8]

There was a back door which led onto the back stairs, situated at the juncture of the hall as it went around the room I shared with my brother, and turned down the long hall to the bathroom and kitchen. The young man who collected the garbage came up these back stairs from the sooty coal cellar, dragging with him an enormous burlap sack, and we could hear this sack thumping up and down the stairs as he came and went.

UNCLE EDGAR WAS WATCHING

This was written for the fall 1989 issue of New American Writing, *edited by Maxine Chernoff and Paul Hoover. I am including it here for the simple reason that my father, like so many others who die young, has been forgotten in almost all subsequent considerations of the times in which he lived and participated. "Uncle Edgar" is J. Edgar Hoover, director of the FBI from 1924 to 1972.*

*In memory of my father, and for his namesake,
my nephew Richard E. Robbins*

For reasons that I don't know and therefore cannot enumerate, I have few early memories; that is, memories from my early life. There is a sense of place, and an almost cinematic atmosphere, a weather, which I can retrieve, but actual events are blurred and elusive. Perhaps Wordsworth was right about those spots of time: holes in time's fabric that alter chronology while capturing duration; maybe Lyn Hejinian is right, writing is an aid to memory.

In the summer of 1950 my family (mother and father, sister and brother) had rented a small house in Bridgehampton, Long Island. It sat not far off a road that ran along Poxabogue Pond on one side and potato fields on the other. There was a long lawn that was sheltered by unkempt, ragged growth—wild roses, honeysuckle, grasses. Huge white lilies opened on the pond each morning; their heavy sweet scent made its way into the house. My father, a journalist, spent the weeks in the city and came out on Friday evenings on the train, the "Cannonball." He had spent the war years as a foreign correspondent for Time Inc., for which he was head of the Moscow bureau in 1943 and 1944. He had written three books on Russia, had been a Neiman Fellow at Harvard, and, since leaving Henry Luce's emporium, had worked for the journals *PM* and the *Star*. He had helped to reinvent

Scientific American with his friends Gerard Piel and Dennis Flanagan. Now, with three children, anxious about his personal and professional future, he had embarked on a biography of Charlie Chaplin.

In the city, we lived in an apartment on East Eighteenth Street, in a building called "Stuyvesant's Folly" that had been built by the Dutch; it was known to us as "the second-oldest apartment house in New York," a phrase we reiterated proudly without much understanding of its import. A wonderfully generous edifice with a central lobby and courtyard beyond, two wings with wide mahogany staircases, and block-long apartments of seven rooms with at least one working fireplace. Ours was on the third floor of the east wing. My father, when he was home, had frequent visitors. It must have been in the previous winter, 1949, that we were told Charlie Chaplin was coming. I knew, of course, what he looked like: a small person with black hair, thick eyebrows, a mustache, who wore shabby billowing pants and walked with an odd, rocking, splay-legged motion. He had a hat and a cane. The day of his visit came and I was reasonably excited. Children are not immune to celebrity. I was seven. I think I was told to stay in the back of the house, in the kitchen, until invited to come up to the living room. Usually there was no such ceremony of exclusion when guests arrived, but clearly this was different. (Now I realize that my father was probably interviewing him.) At last we were summoned (although I have no recollection of either my sister's or brother's presence) up the long hall to the threshold of the living room. There, standing in front of the fireplace where a bright fire burned, was an old man with white hair wearing a gray suit. Children are most aware of fraud. I glared with indignation.

"You're not Charlie Chaplin."

Perhaps this outburst brought a surge of parental concern and reproval for my poor manners; I cannot recall. The visitor seemed amused. I think he asked me why I thought he was not Charlie Chaplin, and I responded, "Because you have white hair," which was only one of several good reasons. After that, I lose the thread, although I think I recall that, in order to prove he was himself, he walked across the red carpet in his inimitable walk and everyone laughed. This might be wishful embroidery. Perhaps I said nothing, but went silently and dutifully up to the impostor and shook his hand.

In any case, it was the following early September when a call came to the house in Bridgehampton to say that my father was ill with a fever. My mother decided that we should pack up and leave immediately for the city, some weeks before we had planned. There was a hectic frenzy that brought sudden closure to the barefoot, carefree days.

When we arrived in the city, my father was in bed. His bedside table was cluttered with used glasses, and these were washed separately. We were not allowed to enter his room. The phone rang; the doctor came. The house filled with an expectant gloom. My sister Jen and I knew the source of this dread; we knew about polio, the disease that had raged through the city that hot summer; we stood, one night, outside of our rooms and tried to do something like pray. After some days, it was decided that he should be taken to the hospital. He died a few days later, on September 20, 1950. He was thirty-six.

After his death, friends gathered and initiated the Lauterbach Award, to be given each year to a person who had contributed importantly to civil rights and civil liberties. It carried a cash prize. It went to Justice William O. Douglas, to the political cartoonist Herblock, and to the great editor of the *Atlanta Constitution*, Ralph McGill. After a while, the Award ran out of funds. I am not sure whom the other recipients were. I do know that a few years later, I came home from school to find my mother sitting in front of an open fire in exactly the place where Chaplin had stood. She was reading letters my father had written to her during the war, typed single-spaced on thin onionskin paper. After she read them, she put them into the fire. I think she might have been weeping. I was horrified. I could think of no reason to do such a violent thing. Every object that was connected to my father was for me *proof* of his existence. As long as they were around—his ties, his papers, his books—I was somehow reassured. My mother said:

"The FBI was here today. I have to burn these to protect our friends."

In his 1983 memoir, the journalist Harrison Salisbury wrote:

> I hadn't known Dick Lauterbach before Moscow. He was tall, dark, handsome, a Dartmouth man, spoke some Russian, and reported for the Luce publications. He was twenty-eight years old and brilliant. I envied him . . . I think of the eighteen of us who ended up at the Metropol in 1944, Dick was the one with the most talent, the most promise. I knew nothing of his background, but I thought he had the world before him—family, children, a super job, the kind of cool intelligence, judgment and enthusiasm that should take him anywhere. Dick and Tina [my mother] had traveled together in Russia in 1935. She was still at Smith, and Smith girls were not allowed to marry before graduation. So they married secretly in Moscow, very romantic, only a few knew it. I guess, from what friends have said, that Tina at some point joined

the [Communist] party; I can't see Dick as a party man, though. He was radical, but he possessed an iconoclastic mind; with his sharp wit, he was a better critic than claque. I can't see him following a party line, whether it was Communist or capitalist. He liked too much to disagree. That was one of his attractions . . . When I got my FBI files, I noticed with irony the entry: "in correspondence in Fall 1949 with Richard Lauterbach." I had written precisely one letter from Moscow to Dick, in October. Uncle Edgar was watching.

DISOBEDIENT CHOICES:
ON THE EVE OF EXILE

In the winter of 1995, I taught at the University of Denver. While I was there, David Rosenberg asked me to contribute to Communion, *a book he was editing on contemporary writers and the Bible. This piece, now somewhat revised, was my contribution.*

1.

    I begin this essay in Denver, Colorado, sitting in a strange room in a beautiful Victorian house, facing west, where I can see a scrap of the Rockies rising beyond the rooftops. It is early January. I have come here for a ten-week stint of teaching, but really to try to recover a rhythm of concentration and work which had evaded me in New York. I have made several such visits to American cities (Madison, Minneapolis, Iowa City), always with some ambivalence, as I pack up belongings and estrange myself from familiar surroundings. And yet I should be used to this, since New York is nothing if not a continuous shifting among and between the anonymous and familiar; where what is expected and what actually happens are inevitably, in Emerson's phrase, in a "stupendous antagonism."

As the stories we tell about ourselves condense over time, contracting not only from nuance of detail, but from an accurate reading of our original intentions, we treat them increasingly like familiar fictions to which we return. This return is not to recover something lost so much as to reinvent what is found, in a sense to move the past forward and so extend our present boundaries, the boundaries of our present. Our lives must finally accommodate and interpret the choices we have made, and what is recalled of those choices inflects how we proceed.

    Eve made a choice to eat the forbidden fruit. The serpent, she said, "beguiled" her.

    In graduate school, I had written a poem that ended with this stanza:

> *Call me indolent, self-indulgent. Ah yes, I crave*
> *an apple, peach and pear. I'll have them all*
> *and with each a slice of rare and aged*
> *cheese. That's the curse upon my sex, as*
> *someone said, we take an apple to our bed.*
> *I'll not deny the truth:*
> *I'm one with Cleopatra, Eve, and Ruth.*

Strong appetite was not something readily condoned in women then (it was the mid-1960s); women still felt constraints on their desire, intellectual as well as sensual. We did not want to appear too eager or too ambitious; our curiosities should stay, if not under wraps, at least within bounds. At Columbia University, entering students in the master's program in English were told not to attempt anything "creative" for a thesis; we were prey to a certain degree of patriarchal condescension. Wanting to be a poet, a namer of experience, I was told, in effect, that all things had already been named, and I should just put them in order. I felt, often, simultaneously overwhelmed and undersupported. My professor, Ted Taylor, a Milton scholar, told me I was "afraid to succeed." I didn't know where to begin, and so after the first year, I quit. The following September, I left New York for my first trip abroad, three weeks, starting in Dublin. Another professor, a Joycean, had drawn a chalk map of Dublin on the blackboard.

> 26 April: Mother is putting my new secondhand clothes in order.
> She prays now, she says, that I may learn in my own life and away
> from home and friends what the heart is and what it feels. So be
> it. Welcome, O life! I go to encounter for the millionth time the
> reality of experience and to forge in the smithy of my soul the un-
> created conscience of my race.
>
> —James Joyce, *A Portrait of the Artist as a Young Man*

Perhaps I could not fully identify with Stephen Dedalus's exalted vision of creative potency, but I was in thrall to the cadence of Yeats. Reading Yeats, it was easier to project myself into a landscape that might give itself up to multiple temporal braidings, where the mythic realm of the Fall could abide with a contemporary love story, Byzantium with old men.

I said, "It's certain there is no fine thing
Since Adam's fall but needs much labouring.
There have been lovers who thought love should be
So much compounded of high courtesy
That they should sigh and quote with learned looks
Precedents out of beautiful old books;
Yet now it seems an idle trade enough."

We sat grown quiet at the name of love;
We saw the last embers of daylight die,
And in the trembling blue-green of the sky
A moon, worn as if it had been a shell
Washed by time's waters as they rose and fell
About the stars and broke in days and years.

          —W. B. Yeats, "Adam's Curse"

My godfather, Tom Prideaux, who was theater critic for *Life* magazine, had taken me to see an early production of Beckett's *Waiting for Godot* and I had been stunned by the fact that within the human lacunae of *waiting*, of *delay*, a linguistic world of such mesmerizing invention could unfurl. Vladimir and Estragon, Lucky and Pozzo, marooned in Nowhere or Everywhere, in a post-apocalyptic Eden with a single unnamed tree, and no Eve.

Yeats, Joyce, Beckett.

I stayed away for seven years.

2.

I cannot think of any poetry which adequately expresses this yearning for the wild. The *wilde*.

          —Henry David Thoreau, *Journal*, 1851

In the beginning of Genesis, God creates each thing day by day, "after its kind," inventing as he goes. The days are counted; there is an orderly progression. Repetition brings solace: "And the evening and the morning were the first day . . . And the evening and the morning were the second day . . . And the evening and the morning were the third day."

The days of my childhood in Manhattan did not unfold with normal quotidian expectations, but with a heightened attention to the possible ruptures between what should be, could be, and what actually was; an atmosphere of protracted apprehension and alert. Nights brought episodes of mystery that threatened to, and sometimes did, erupt in violence. At night, sites of incipient danger were monitored for the least rip in the ordinary: tears, smoke, footsteps, doors, voices. There was the *stench* of chaos. Outside, the city contributed its harmonic: sirens, the Third Avenue el rasping along black tracks, cats, a distant foghorn, bells dividing the hours, planes overhead. The boundary between inside and outside was porous, leaky. I lay awake and imagined another reality, in which everything had a place.

There was an impediment to the order of things. One was told not to do something, but the person, my mother, who said *no* was herself the very embodiment of disobedience, of transgression. *Forgive us our trespasses as we forgive those who trespass against us.* The problem of obedience, of limit, was not an easy one to solve. I made up a second domestic world with my dolls, took them for strolls down the apartment's long corridors, inventing as I went, holding imaginary conversations with passing strangers. I made neat rows of the kitchen spice rack; at school, I was an ingratiating goody-goody, always volunteering. I painted pictures and played a violin, wanting to be distracted into focus, to be somehow lifted into the elusive structures of created order. Secretly, another, less dutiful, model formed: fantasies of exit—abduction, adoption, romance. Secretly, my psyche was a charged dominion of punishment and reward.

Or so I now think. January 10, 1995, Denver. The evening of the sixth day. One must be careful of the inertia of fixed stories. Floods in California. Begin to read Waiting for Godot *again and find it wildly funny. The mountains amaze, holding back the weather, or gathering it, as if winter could be kept in a huge rocky attic. How did it feel, to come across the country and see them for the first time, rising from the flat land, like vast beasts lounging on the horizon?*

The common etymological root shared by "exile" and "ecstasy" is in the prefix "ex," meaning "out of." "Exile" comes from the Latin *exilium*, banishment. "Ecstasy" combines "ex" with the Greek for "to place." Ecstasy: to leave stasis. Both exile and ecstasy cross boundaries—geographical in the first place, psychological or spiritual in the second.

In the second account of Creation, the one that we in the West have adopted as sacred iconography, there is a garden. "And the Lord God planted a garden eastward in Eden; and there he put the man whom he had formed." Most considerate Lord, to plant a garden prior to putting his creature in it! This garden had "every tree that is pleasant to the sight, and good for food; the tree of life also in the midst of the garden, and the tree of the knowledge of good and evil."

The night before I left on my journey, my friend Susan and I played a record of Paul Robeson singing the great "Jerusalem" hymn, in which Blake's lyrics portray England as a prophetic "green and pleasant land." I was sure I was going to die, Icarus-like, in a flaming crash, before I ever reached the other side of the ocean. The *fact* of this other shore seemed to me hypothetical, a fiction.

3.

> And out of the ground the Lord God formed every beast of the field, and every fowl of the air; and brought them unto Adam to see what he would call them: and whatsoever Adam called every living creature, that was the name thereof.

The considerate Lord, having given Adam a garden to tend, realizes that he will also need "a help meet for him." So He forms animals and birds, and brings them to Adam "to see what he would call them: and whatsoever Adam called every living creature, that was the name thereof." So there it was, the primordial, original act of authorship: *this thing, what shall I call it? A heron, a rose, an apple.*

> And Adam gave names to all cattle, and to the fowl of the air, and to every beast of the field; but for Adam there was not found a help meet for him.

And so the Lord put Adam to sleep, took one of his ribs, and "made him a woman."

> And Adam said, This is now bone of my bones, and flesh of my flesh: she shall be called Woman, because she was taken out of man.

Adam births a woman. The *first* immaculate conception.

4.

'Tis the best use of Fate to teach a fatal courage.

—Emerson, "Fate"

When I arrived in Dublin in September 1967 I was ecstatic—a manic joy descended. I felt as if I had been transported out of the actual into the imagined, as if the texts I had pored over in my tiny Columbia rooms had magically *devolved* from language to landscape. The scale shifted; time slowed; the light was sheer, radiant, sudden. I seemed to have escaped the present altogether and fallen into a future that resembled a new past. Everything beguiled me. Women carried baskets to do their shopping along crooked narrow streets; in Saint Stephen's Green the green shimmered wetly; everyone talked, giddy with speech, as if, indeed, speech itself were action. I had the sense that my destiny, my life, would be only what I might now make of it, what I might tell of it. Enthralled by this powerful new incipiency, I barely noticed how isolated and lonely and obscure I felt. I wrote in a little room on Lower Hatch Street. By New Year's Eve, I left, destitute and fearful, and moved to London.

> Now the serpent was more subtile than any beast of the field which the Lord God had made. And he said unto the woman, Yea, hath God said, Ye shall not eat of every tree of the garden?
>
> And the woman said unto the serpent, We may eat of the fruit of the trees of the garden: but of the fruit of the tree which is in the midst of the garden, God hath said, Ye shall not eat of it, neither shall you touch it, lest ye die.
>
> And the serpent said unto the woman, Ye shall not surely die.

Sometime during my seven-year sojourn in London, I again became interested in Genesis, in the story of Eden, in the figure of Eve. I must have been thinking about exile, about being an expatriate in bad times; I felt a conflicted shame at forsaking the political extremity foregrounded by the

Vietnam War. In London, the counterculture was ebullient and theatrical: Carnaby Street, flower children, the Beatles, sex and drugs and rock 'n' roll. I was becoming aware increasingly of distinctions; the British are good at making distinctions, especially, I often found, between themselves and others. The American habit of quick familiarity, of presumed intimacy, was ameliorated by the cool wit of British reserve; friendships evolved slowly, over time, within parameters of social restraint. I became conscious of how an inherent class structure limits social mobility: obviously, no one but the Queen grows up to be queen.

The two trees in Eden were the Tree of Life and the Tree of the Knowledge of Good and Evil, not, as many assume, simply the Tree of Knowledge. Reading Genesis again, it seemed to me a fable of adolescence, about the awakening of sexual desire, but more specifically, about the discovery of difference. If the Tree of Life symbolizes Unity, Oneness, Wholeness, Sameness, then this other, dangerous tree surely represents cascading dichotomies, dualities, and oppositions through which we negotiate our practical and moral world. The Tree of the Knowledge of Good and Evil is the Tree of Discourse, and the serpent its delineated marker, boundary; the serpent, a wagging tongue, is the symbolic order of Language.

5.

This is the morning of the seventh day in Denver. I am up early, before eight, having been dreaming of multiple leavings; a dream where I am split between leaving and staying. I cancel planes, I seek advice, a veritable whirligig of anxious indecision. This dream imitates life. Before I go somewhere (before I came here, for example), a state of frenzy sets in that verges on paralysis; I feel I am being forced to leave, rather than that I want to leave. I want someone to implore me to stay.

And the serpent said unto the woman, Ye shall not surely die: For God doth know that in the day ye eat thereof, then your eyes shall be opened, and ye shall be as gods, knowing good and evil.

And when the woman saw that the tree was good for food, and that it was pleasant to the eyes, and a tree to be desired to make one wise, she took of the fruit thereof, and did eat, and gave also unto her husband with her; and he did eat.

The serpent does not exactly tempt Eve, it simply reassures her by contradicting God, explaining that the reason God has forbidden them to eat of the Tree of the Knowledge of Good and Evil is that they will become "as gods." Eve makes her decision out of a daring, courageous curiosity. She decides she is willing to risk everything, life itself, for the rewards of finding out about life—about pleasure and wisdom. It is one thing to name things, objects, creatures, as Adam had; it is quite another to have names for the relations between them, the distinctions and judgments those relations imply. No sooner have Adam and Eve eaten the apple than they are made to suffer the consequences: they will cease to be mere creatures of God's delight and will become *human*, entering the chronic, the temporal, finding themselves in a new relation to each other and to the world; they will know labor, and sorrow, and enmity; they will struggle with obedience and fidelity; they will notice difference. Existence, henceforth, will be marked by the contingent. The serpent, of course, was wrong. Adam and Eve will indeed surely die. Life and Death, Power and Necessity, Eros and Ananke, Freedom and Limit. They will be responsible for the form of their life; they will be moral agents.

> And Adam called his wife's name Eve; because she was the mother of all living.

Is her name Eve because she must anticipate, think about *the next day*? She would then embody the very notion of narrativity (which carries *nativity* within). Adam named *things*; Eve, the anticipator, pregnant with the future, begins the telling of stories, how we represent ourselves to ourselves and to the world, how we think about our acts and their conseqences.

> Therefore the Lord God sent him forth from the garden of Eden, to till the ground from whence he was taken. So he drove out the man: and he placed at the east of the garden cherubim, and a flaming sword which turned every way, to keep the way of the tree of life.

Scribble, scribble. The pen is mightier than the sword, or so we like to think.

IS I ANOTHER?
A TALK IN SEVEN BEGINNINGS

This piece originated as a talk given to my students at Columbia University in the spring semester of 1989 for a class called "Is I Another? Self and Other in Contemporary American Poetry." It was subsequently published in American Letters & Commentary, *a magazine started by Columbia students and edited by Anna Rabinowitz. I have made some revisions.*

In memory of Robert Towers

Beginning No. 1

The question to which I keep returning, or which keeps returning to me, is: why do so many intelligent persons want to write poems while, as everyone agrees, so few persons, intelligent or not, read them? This is a riddle the Sphinx might still think to ask. Each time I set out to teach aspiring poets, it comes to me as quagmire and quandary, threatening to undermine my desire to impart such knowledge as I might possess. I must conclude that the failure of poetry to attract an audience larger than the sum of its participants must be part of a slow eradication of a curiosity that centers on the relation between language and meaning; that is, which elicits from us a desire to know how language works. Poetry demonstrates new ways of thinking about how language works; it is a crucial source of this knowledge.

Whereas the other arts—music, dance, painting, fiction—seem to have penetrated the public domain, poetry remains an orphaned, homeless art. The public pays its respects in abstract idealizations, in the occasional NEA grant, in the growing number of MFA programs and small presses, but the fact remains that the audience for new poetry is made largely of small communities of poets.

Not long ago I sat with my nephew Jack in my kitchen on Duane Street in Lower Manhattan and had a protracted discussion about his future. Jack is a junior at Harvard and thinks he knows a thing or two, which he does. Our talk began with Jack telling me he wasn't sure he wanted to be an architect after all and that, in any case, he was sure he didn't want to graduate and go directly on to graduate school. "I want to be a generalist," he said. "I think it is better to know a lot about a lot than about one thing. Besides, I'm not sure that being an architect would reflect my sense of social commitment. I like the creative aspects, but I am not sure about the business." He worried that the "business" of architecture would dominate his life. I mentioned urban planning, which he agreed was a possibility, but he thought that would mire him even further in bureaucratic compromise and political snares. Our discussion heated up. I said it was important to cultivate individuality; that our sense in America of individual efficacy was being eroded. Jack said I had it all wrong, what is needed is not an increased sense of individuality but of a sense of social responsibility. Individuals, he said, always act in self-interest. He said his peers at Harvard seemed to have little desire to change the world; they seemed happy with the world as they find it. I kept insisting that in order for an effective social consciousness to arise, there had first to be a strong sense of personal commitments, and that once these were in place, they could be extended to the public sphere. We kept talking in this way, not quite understanding each other, as if the words each of us were using somehow missed the point. At last, exasperated and unsure of my ground, I said, "Read Emerson."

Here is Emerson:

> It is unhappy, but too late to be helped, the discovery we have made that we exist. That discovery is called the Fall of Man. Ever afterwards we suspect our instruments. We have learned that we do not see directly, but mediately, and that we have no means of correcting these colored and distorting lenses which we are, of computing the amount of their errors. Perhaps these subject-lenses have a creative power; perhaps there are no objects. Once we lived in what we saw; now, the rapaciousness of this new power, which threatens to absorb all things, engages us. Nature, art, persons, letters, religions, objects, successively tumble in, and God is but one of its ideas. Nature and literature are subjective phenomena; every evil and every good is a shadow that we cast. The street is full of humiliations to the proud. As the fop contrived to dress his bailiffs in his livery and make them wait on

his guests at table, so the chagrins which the bad heart gives off as bubbles, at once take form as ladies and gentlemen of the street, shopmen or barkeepers in hotels, and threaten or insult whatever is threatenable and insultable in us. 'Tis the same with our idolatries. People forget that it is the eye that makes the horizon, and the rounding mind's eye which makes this or that man a type or representative of humanity, with the name of hero or saint.

In Emerson's despairing solipsism there is a certain grandeur. "Nothing can bring you peace but yourself. Nothing can bring you peace but the triumph of principles," he writes, suggesting that those principles and that peace are what constitute "the horizon." Elsewhere, in "Self-Reliance," he writes: "The centuries are conspirators against the sanity and authority of the soul. Time and space are but psychological colors which the eye makes, but the soul is light: where it is, is day; where it was, is night; and history is an impertinence and an injury if it be anything more than a cheerful apologia or parable of my being and becoming." It is little wonder, given these ruminations, that Emerson's chief poetic interlocutor, Whitman, would take as his subject the self, and imagine an omniscient seer, a form of contingency without boundary: I-eye-horizon.

Beginning No. 2

Last spring I taught at the Writers' Workshop in Iowa City. There was a piece of graffiti inscribed in energetic large print on the tunnel wall through which I passed to reach the English-Philosophy Building: SUBVERT THE DOMINANT PARADIGM. Each time I read this imperative I felt peculiarly giddy. It seemed so *abstract,* both generic and sophisticated, not like END THE WAR NOW or YANKEE GO HOME. Of course I had no idea what the specific "dominant paradigm" was that should be subverted; I wondered if there was only one, or many, and should each and all of them be subverted? Could persons have a dominant paradigm? Would that be what I call the "first script," the one with which we enter the world, where choices have been made for us, our DNA, where we grow up, our economic status, all that? Or does it refer, the dominant paradigm, to something more universal? I began to think that the dominant paradigm in late-twentieth-century America is the individual.

One of the best known, most frequently taught poems is Wallace Stevens's "Anecdote of the Jar." Along with T. S. Eliot's "Love Song of J. Alfred Prufrock" and William Carlos Williams's "Red Wheelbarrow" and, perhaps, Pound's "In a Station of the Metro," this poem seems to have become a talisman of American modernism. The poem opens with a single declaration: "I placed a jar in Tennessee." The jar is, I take it, emblem for any cultural artifact. Placed on the hill, it makes "the slovenly wilderness / Surround that hill." The manmade object, distinct from the wilderness, allows the wilderness to be perceived as such. But the presence of the jar seems to expand, to "take dominion everywhere." "Gray, bare, tall and of a port in air," this object suddenly begins to feel like a subject, a figure. Like Whitman's "I," Stevens's jar has an obliterating expansiveness.

But what is arresting to me is the implicit sense of reciprocity that Emerson, Whitman, and Stevens suggest: the sense that the world and our perceptions of it are intimately interlocked. So when the kid on the bus, making a huge racket with his pals, is asked by one of the travelers to quiet down so others might read or sleep, and snarls back, "What's it to you? It's a free country," I begin to see what my nephew Jack was telling me. There is no social contract between eye and horizon, jar and wilderness. The kid will put a whole mess of jars, Coke cans, beer bottles, in Tennessee, or New Jersey, and never notice the wilderness until it is too late. He will take dominion everywhere.

Each year, *Time* selects an individual as Man of the Year. (Sometimes they have even selected a woman to be Man of the Year, but I cannot remember when.) This year, 1999, they selected neither man nor woman; they selected Earth. At first I thought, in that jaded way, how corny. Then it came to me: *Time* magazine just subverted the dominant paradigm.

Beginning No. 3

In a review of Philip Roth's novel *The Facts*, Vivian Gornick distinguishes between the fictive and the real; she points out that novelists use language in the service of the imagination, while nonfiction writers use it analytically. She adds that poets, also, are writers of the analytical real. Although I am a great admirer of Ms. Gornick, I don't quite agree with her. I think poets are more conscious than most writers of the way language constructs much of what we take for "reality," and that it is precisely this fact that often compels us to write poems. Poets do not confuse the real with the true, terms which our litigious, empirical culture tends to conflate. It seems to me that truth cannot be understood as other than a "supreme fiction," one that informs and animates our knowledge of the real, but which cannot be reduced *to* the real. If we look at the negative of each of these, we can quickly see that truth is a moral idea, the opposite of falsehood, mendacity, lies. The real, on the other hand, is opposed by the unreal, let us call it the fictive or imagined. The true is a category of moral thought; the real belongs to empirical observation. Works of imagination—say George Orwell's *1984*—often are more "true" than a documentary. "Tell the truth, but tell it slant," Emily Dickinson wrote. Emerson, in one of my favorite passages from "The Poet," says that a poet cannot rely solely on "the energy of his possessed and conscious intellect" (Gornick's analytic) but must allow himself to "unlock, at all risks, his human doors" and submit to another energy: "As the traveler who has lost his way throws his reins on his horse's neck and trusts to the instinct of the animal to find his road, so we must do with the divine animal who carries us through this world."

Beginning No. 4

Yesterday I heard a young salesman in J&R Computer World tell a customer, "The way they have taught it to think . . ." He was referring to a small gray object. I could hear the old Cartesian formula "I think, therefore I am" come unstuck, the "I am" sundered from the "I think, therefore." Descartes was interested in the difference between mind and matter. He may have accommodated the computer simply by calling it an *extension*, but of what? Mind or matter? And for that matter, what exactly is language? The instrument of thought's "I am," but once written down, more matter than mind; the matter of the mind. Well, I cannot follow this into anything but a further wilderness over which I have no dominion. My confusion only grows when I try to answer the question about feelings. We know that the young man at J&R will not be able to utter the phrase "the way they have taught it to feel." There it is: the lurking, persistent dichotomy into which enlightened reason drives like a fully loaded Ford into a snowbank.

An old notion, that imagination finds forms for the alignment of affect with reason and thus gives us access to what might be true. This elided space is possible because language is capable of making an elaborate webbing between subjects and objects. In his most infamous and perhaps least understood essay, "What Is an Author?," Michel Foucault wrote:

> Since the eighteenth century, the author has played the role of the regulator of the fictive, a role quite characteristic of our era of industrial and bourgeois society, of individualism and private property . . . I think that, as our society changes . . . the author function will disappear, and in such a manner that fiction and its polysemous texts will once again function according to another mode . . . All discourses, whatever treatment to which they will be subjected, would then develop with the anonymity of a murmur. We would no longer hear the questions that have been rehashed for so long: Who really spoke? Is it really he and not someone else? With what authenticity or originality? And with what part of his deepest self did he express his discourse? Instead, there would be other questions, like these: What are the modes of existence of this discourse? Where has it been used, how can it circulate, and who can appropriate it for himself? What are the places in it where there is possible room for possible subjects? Who can assume these various subject functions? And behind these questions, we would hear hardly anything but the stirring of an indifference: What does it matter who is speaking?

One can feel the dominant paradigm cracking, like an egg in a desert out of which ride so many polysemous texts like fledglings. The "author," our culture's *signature* individual, is now to be a thing of the past, consigned to the dust heap of bourgeois capitalism in its waning days. We are of course already inside a world of authorless texts that freely circulate—advertising, obviously, with its endlessly unauthored jingles and logos. Equally obvious, although more problematic, President Ronald Reagan, B actor and front man for General Electric ("where progress is our most important product"), who embodied our myth of masculine American individuality (rugged, self-made, honest, friendly, optimistic, and so forth). But, as Michael Deaver pointed out, Reagan was also the most *malleable* of subjects, a vessel into which his Party could pour their ideas and have them "come out" as sincerely as a child reciting prayers. Reagan was known as the "Teflon president," because the consequences of things that happened while he was in office didn't seem to stick to him. Perhaps the reason for this is that the public understood that he was in some sense not entirely responsible. He was, after all, an actor. The violent campaign of Reagan's successor, George H. W. Bush, was conducted around key ideas and phrases that were targeted toward certain parts of the electorate but which, we were subsequently told, had little to do with "the real" George Bush, who is "kinder and gentler." Who authored Ronald Reagan? Who authored George Bush? Does it matter? What does all this have to do with poetry?

Beginning No. 5

This Beginning will begin with a quote from a study by Milton J. Bates, *Wallace Stevens: A Mythology of Self* (1985):

> Stevens disliked explaining because he feared that readers would lose interest in poems they could comprehend fully. It was not a question of mystification. Rather, he understood that pure poetry succeeds when it detaches the reader from reason and reality and lifts him by the most tenuous threads to another plane of existence. To explain is to make the reader overly conscious of those filaments and so to subvert their function.

When I was taken as a child to see the play *Peter Pan*, the woman seated behind my mother and me, when asked by her young companion about the figures flying through the air, pointed out the wires glinting in the light. (My mother was furious.) In any case, this "other plane of existence" has been seriously usurped in recent American mainstream poetry by an allegiance to that very reality that Stevens sought to simultaneously undermine and sanction through the imagination. Questions arising from such dichotomies as real and imagined, rational and irrational, reason and faith, have been part of the texture of American culture since its inception. Stevens moves me, because he comes to the very brink of transcendent vision, only to subvert it through a kind of alchemical pragmatism, where sequels of flamboyant mediation lead him back to the "ordinary" and even beyond to the stripped profane dump, "the the." In Stevens, the obdurate declivity between authorial subject and textual object quickens, so that Foucault's "possible room for possible subjects" begins to emerge. In

this regard, Stevens provides a prelude to Ashbery's cast of shifting pro-
nouns, where the idea of a single self, coherent and cogent, gives way to
plural subject positions, aspects of perception and response, within a char-
acteristic habit of mind.

Beginning No. 6

Perhaps in the crowded complexity of the information age, we no longer wish
or need to know the subjectivities so long affiliated with our habits of think-
ing about poetry. We can barely keep up with our significant others, relatives,
and friends, and so to be invited into yet another intimacy is more than our
individual economies can afford. Instead, television's stock figures and
celebrity exposure, "lives" we can tune in and out at will, is all we really want.
My upstairs neighbor, mother of three, lives in a chronic extremity of de-
mand that I witness from below as a kind of human storm. I do not think she
would want to read poems that posit the singular solitary investigations of
the privileged "I" of lyric poetry.

Beginning No. 7

I take my last Beginning almost wholly from Allan Janik and Stephen Toul-
min's *Wittgenstein's Vienna*, which portrays the cultural, personal, and philo-
sophical context for the great philosopher's thought. In it, the authors take
up Søren Kierkegaard's 1846 essay "The Present Age":

> Comfort, reflection, temporary apathy and equally temporary en-
> thusiasm, [Kierkegaard] asserts, characterize the present age. It
> is an age of abstract thought in which passion plays no role. In
> such an age of indolence, revolutions are inconceivable. It is thus
> an age without genuine values. "An age without passion has no
> values, and everything is transformed into representational
> ideas." In an age that cherishes abstractions, no morality is possi-
> ble; all that such an epoch is capable of producing is sham life.
> The age itself becomes an abstraction. As such, it is characterized
> throughout by a leveling process that leaves no room for individu-
> ality. In effect, the age becomes incarnated in "the public."

They quote directly from Kierkegaard's essay:

> In order that everything should be reduced to the same level, it is
> at first necessary to produce a phantom, its spirit, a monstrous
> abstraction, and all-embracing something which is nothing, a
> mirage—and that phantom is the public . . . This abstraction has
> a way of crushing the individual, by means of the further abstrac-
> tions that it produces—public opinion, good taste, and the like.
> In a deteriorating society, this public is the fiction of the press.

Against this bleak picture, Kierkegaard posits "subjective truth," which he
defines as "an objective uncertainty held fast in an appropriation of the most
passionate inwardness."

The idea of an "objective uncertainty" is, in my view, a key to postmodern
poetics. If the "I" finds its way out of the egotistical sublime and toward the
alterity implied by all imaginative acts, then it will once again initiate paths
away from self-absorbed narcissism to a recognition of the linguistic matrix
that binds us to each other and to the world. A few weeks ago, I saw another
piece of graffiti, on Eleventh Street and Fourth Avenue in Manhattan: DI-
VERSITY IS NECESSARY. How fortuitous, I thought. If American poetics is once
again to illuminate the passage from private to public discourse, it must seek
diversity of method, resource, and means. If a poem is a portrait of how a
mind works, a soul is formed, how a heart translates affective response into
language, it is also a portrait of how language forms and informs our neces-
sary diversity.

Jack went on to Yale and got his degree in architecture, then went to Hong Kong and
worked for some years. He now works for the architect Robert A. M. Stern in New York
City.

AS (IT) IS: TOWARD A POETICS OF THE WHOLE FRAGMENT

This talk was given first at a conference, "Where Lyric Meets L=A=N=G=U=A=G=E," at Barnard College, organized by Claudia Rankine and Juliana Spahr, in a slightly altered version and without the second part. The first part, under the title "On Flaws," was published electronically in Theory & Event *by the Johns Hopkins University Press in fall 1999. The whole piece was published in* American Women Poets in the 21st Century, *edited by Rankine and Spahr (Middletown, Wesleyan University Press, 2002).*

1.

It is precisely out of the flaw or excess in an equation that meaning springs.

—Barbara Johnson, "Disfiguring Poetic Language"

When you pick up a piece of old crockery in a secondhand shop, often there is a little
white tag on which the price is written, along with the phrase "as is."
"As is" indicates that
the object, say it is a cup, has a flaw: a crack or a chip or some
other anomaly testifying to
past use. If the object in question is a textile, say a slip or a sweater, "as is" indicates a
rip
or a stain. "As is" suggests the distance
from perfection which the object has traveled
through the course of time, its fall from Platonic grace or virgin purity. "As is" is a
variant

of "as if," the way in which desire ineluctably turns into fulfillment
or disappointment,
and in that turn, "something" is simultaneously lost and found. As has
    become abundantly
clear, and not to overstate the obvious, contemporary poetic practice
    negotiates this terrain and
its
recapitulating dualities—presence/absence, materiality/transparency,
    text/performance,
and so on, more insistently than any other current human activity.

The lost/found place of "as is" thus could be seen as a poetic methodology,
    through which we
might revise the modernist fragment. The poem now is rendered
as an address that
eschews totalizing concepts of origin, unity, closure, and completion, and is
    construed as
a
series of flaws or openings through which both chance and change register
    a matrix of
discontinuous distributions, where contingency itself is offered as an
    affective response to
the "is" as is. Meaning is rendered as an unstable relation to sites of
    objective and
subjective
value. The reader/listener participates in the construction of significance
    not by filling in
the gaps and elisions, but by appropriating whatever fragment is "useful" to
    her. The hope
is that the relation between epistemology and power is kept regenerative.
When Bill Clinton remarked, "It depends on what the meaning of the word
    'is' is," he
unwittingly allowed us to witness the flaw between the reified "is" of
an imaginary yet knowable present and the imperfect or furtive "is" of the
    actual as is.
Between the first and the second "is" is—however inadvertent on the
    president's part—an
acknowledgment of interpretative ambiguities which

the generation he and I share came to understand as the only possible
   negotiation with reality
and the ways in which language pictures or captures it.

For a while I have been interested in the notion of a whole fragment. This
   fragment is not
one in which one laments a lost whole, as in Stein, Eliot, and Pound, but
   which acknowledges the fact
of our *unhandsome condition,* where we suffer from having been being, and
   in that
acknowledgment foreground what is: the abraded and indefinite
accumulation of an infinite dispersal of sums. In this construction, meaning
   abides
or arises exactly at the place where "use" appears, "use" here meant both as
   pragmatic
and as wear. It is my desire or intention to construct a poetics in which
   meaning is found
within the terms of such contingency.

The consolation of a distilled or stabilized "reality" is nothing if not an
   illusion of
syntax, where syntax stands for any logic of recognition. I have a love for
   this construct of
a normalizing stability, but I recognize its habit of formulating, at the least
   impulse,
categorical imperatives that obscure and resist the actual conditions,
   possibilities, and
complexities in which we find ourselves.

The world constellates significance out of habits of congruence, continuity,
   and context.
These signifying terrains often elude or evade my own sense of being on a
   flexible and
indeterminate boundary, even one which eschews boundaries to celebrate
   inwardly mobile margins.

I think world presses on language and language on world at every point, and
   by "world" I mean material,
spiritual, political, and cultural presence,
a continuous flux of *is* recuperated as is.

2.

> It, say it, not knowing what. Perhaps I simply assented at last to
> an old thing. But I did nothing. I seem to speak, it is not I, about
> me, it is not about me. These few general remarks to begin with.
>
> —Samuel Beckett, *The Unnamable*

Ideas of perfection and wholeness can easily translate into ideas of moral
absolutes. We have, at the core of the rhetoric of
jurisprudence, the notion of "the whole truth," enjoining us to tell
   everything, to withhold
nothing, and in that inexhaustible narration to somehow fully capture what
   transpired.
But as John Ashbery told us, whether you leave it all in or out, "truth
   passes on,"
escaping through the leak, or the rip, of the ever-porous, ever-shifting
   linguistic fabric. It is at this
moment that one begins to think again about asking the question "Who is
   speaking?" and only then to further
ask, "What is she saying?" Certainly one way in which we have
shifted our understanding of works of art is to know that the *how* and the
   what are so
profoundly intertwined that there is no possibility of separating them into
   such easy
categories as forms and contents. *How* and *what* in combination make
   content, and
content, when it comes in contact with the other, the one who listens or the
   one who reads,
then informs what we hope can be construed as meaning.

Poets and other artists have been concentrating on, drawing attention to,
    the relation
between the *how* and *what* of artmaking
throughout the twentieth century.

In re/citations of Ezra Pound's injunction to "make it new," emphasis has
    invariably
fallen on the word "new," the word which most conjures the operations of
    commerce.
We have been in thrall to the new, even
as it
has worn itself through with recyclings, a kind of *déjà new,* which has
exhausted our attention and made us all victims of fashion. As Jean-
    Francoise
Lyotard says, "Hidden in the cynicism of innovation is certainly the despair
    that nothing further
will happen."
We have ignored the
other two words, "make" and "it," as if they were of no significance. But it is
    precisely in the
ordeal of the making, and in the powerful ambiguity of the "it," that we
    need to refocus
attention. For me, the "it" is the fragment of reality out of which we each
    make our poems.
I have a phrase which I use often to express my sense of a work that has
    exposed the
vitality at the core of making: *the it of it.* I think this is not
an entity, not a thing, but a force
around which everything else swirls; without *the it of it*
everything that swirls would be only an inchoate, inarticulate miasma.

We want to believe that language, as a vehicle of inclusion and closure,
can somehow contain/reflect all of the it, which of course is not possible.
    Or rather,
language can and does contain all of it; one might say that what we know
    and perhaps what we
believe is only

because of the bearing of
language, but we have learned that for every instance of this knowledge
    (of it)
there is another, with another
portion of
it about to be. Even in the seamlessness of the
Internet, in
which "everything" rides into and out of view, there are still the
determinants of scale, or relation, and emphasis, or inflection. And there
    are still the
operations of choice, although these seem increasingly obscure. At the
interstices of an environment of sameness and homogeneity (which
    purports to be variety
and vitality) there is still the possibility of an
organizing intelligence that must select one it/is over another.
These selections or choices are what finally or eventually allow us
    to participate in the
making of
meaning, however flawed, however partial it is.

THE NIGHT SKY I

In 1995 Arthur Vogelsang, one of the editors of the American Poetry Review, *asked me to contribute a bi-monthly column to that magazine; the seven "Night Sky" pieces ran in APR from 1996 to 1999. I set two formal limits: to recycle the letters and/or words from each of the internal headings, and also to "turn" them, so that the last heading of the first piece became the first of the second, and so forth.*

1. There Is No Topic Sentence

but perhaps one could be borrowed, like a pretty dress for a party that, once worn, changes the life of the one who borrows it. In New York City, it would have to be a black dress, but the closet is full of black garments and the whole reason for borrowing a dress would be a need for color. But why have a party anyway? According to the *New York Times*, many more planets are on the verge of being discovered. An astronomer in California, where party dresses are rarely black, says, "It's almost like the second coming of Marco Polo or Columbus. We're finding new worlds." What color dress does one wear for the finding of new worlds? Just now some persons are floating in the sky trying out new thermal gear. The temperature is about one hundred degrees below zero, so Captain Scott had better button up. It was expensive, the trial suit: it cost ten million dollars. Makes DKNY seem like a bargain. But this new gear would be too warm for a party here on earth. The *Times* makes no mention of the color of the ten-million-dollar space suit.

> Please come to a party to celebrate the discovery of a planet or planets as yet unnamed orbiting 47 Ursae Majoris. RSVP. Dress accordingly.

As if, in going in a borrowed dress, one were hoping to directly encounter something that would shape itself into an Event to be carried forward with little tassels of attachment and awareness which had not been there before. A few persons, or maybe many, gathered Under One Roof, curious to see each other—perhaps for the first time, perhaps not.

> As literature proceeds along its tortuous course to become absolute, it encounters satanism. The two come together in their shared passion, a sin that only the greatest theologians have thought to include among the mortal ones: curiosity. The image of the writer then becomes Milton's Satan when, 'reaching the earthly paradise, he flew immediately to the Tree of Life, the tallest tree in the garden, and perched there, like a cormorant, without trying in the least to recover his life, but rather using the tree only to see further on, *for prospect* .'[1]

A new planet coming along just in time, Webs and Nets cast out into the firmament by newfangled fishermen, prospecting in the Dark Matter.

> *Go and catch a falling star;*
> *Get with child a mandrake root;*
> *Tell me where all past years are,*
> *Or who cleft the Devil's foot;*
> *Teach me to hear mermaids singing,*
> *Or to keep off envy's stinging.*[2]

A Party with the variety of a night sky, lest everyone speak the same lines:

—Where did you get that dress?
—Great dress. Do you mind my asking how much it cost?

These are not wicked curious questions. They are questions that lead to a party with no memory trace, sending the revelers back to their rooms to await signs of life. But perhaps it would be preferable if everyone did wear the same dress after all, because then these inevitable dead questions could be skipped over. But if everyone wears the same dress there will be a great outcry, and people will immediately think that their right to Free Expression had been infringed upon, that some Authority had come along and proclaimed, "You must wear the Same Black Dress or you cannot attend the

Party!" It is O.K., of course, if by some strange consensus everyone *decides* to wear the Same Black Dress (SBD)—that would be just a coincidence, or even serendipity, which is a coincidence with a happy prospect. In New York, for example, no one *tells* you you have to wear black.

Like the night sky itself, waiting to be addressed or undressed.

Certainly if everyone were to wear the SBD[3] it would be easy to discern the physical differences among the guests: long thin, short plump, tawny hair, blond hair, and so forth. It would be almost as if the SBD were not the same at all, because it changed so much according to whom was wearing it. And then there is the whole question of *accessories*. Some persons would wear it with a simple strand of pearls, with glittering rhinestones, some with a nice paisley scarf, with dangling earrings, a bow tie, a sweater, a cravat. And there would be the one who wears it without ornamentation, not even shoes.

—You aren't wearing any shoes.

—I know.

—Aren't you cold?

—Not really. I don't like shoes.

—Why?

—Because they make my toes feel crowded and hot. When you wear shoes you cover your feet and tend to neglect them, as if they were of no importance. The skin gets dry and flaky and the toenails get too long. With bare feet, you have to take care of them.

—I saw a man on the subway last week with bare feet. He didn't seem to be taking care of them.

Turns away, miffed, bored, thinking, *Chill out, it's a party for a new planet, not a rally for the homeless,* perfectly manicured toes shining crimson on the cool polished floor. Her interlocutor wanders away thinking *dress, feet, toe, shoe.* These must be some of the "little nouns" that George Oppen liked so much.[4]

dress, v.t. & i. 1. (mil.). Correct the alignment of (company's etc. in relation to each other, or men in line), (intr.) come into correct place in line etc. (*up,* i.e. forward, *back,* or ibs.). 2. Array, clothe (*~ed in black, serge,* etc.); provide oneself with clothes (*~ well,* etc.); put on one's clothes; put on evening dress (esp. *~ for dinner*); *~ up,* attire oneself, attire (another), elaborately or in masquerade; *~ out,* attire conspicuously. 3. Deck, adorn (ships with flags, shop-window with tempting wares); provide (play) with costumes. 4. Treat (wound, wounded man) with remedies, apply dressing to. 5. Subject to

cleansing, trimming, smoothing, etc.; brush, comb, do up, (hair); curry
(horse, leather, & fig., often ~ *down*, thrash, scold). 6. Finish surface of (textile fabrics, building-stone). 7. Prepare, cook (food); prune (plant); manure.

dress, n. 1. Clothing, esp. the visible part of it, costume (*full* ~, that worn
on great occasions; *evening* ~, or ~, that worn at dinners or evening parties;
morning ~, ordinary; a ~, ladies' gown, frock). 2. External covering, outward form (*birds in their winter* ~, *French book appearing in English* ~).
3. // ~ *circle*, first gallery in theatres, in which evening- ~ was once required; ~ *coat*, swallowtailed for evening ~ ; ~ *-guard*, on bicycle, etc. to
protect ~ ; ~ *-improver*, = BUSTLE; ~ *-maker*, -king, (woman) making
women's ~*es*; ~ *rehearsal*, final one in costume; ~ *-shield*, *-preserver*, piece
of waterproof material fastened under the arms of a bodice.

2. Possible Topic Sentences or Opening Remarks at the Party[5]

1. "I have always been meaning to explain the way in which I came to
   write certain of my books . . ."

2. "It has pretty much come to this."

3. "At a banquet given by a nobleman of Thessaly named Scopas, the
   poet Simonides of Ceos chanted a lyric poem in honour of his host
   but including a passage in praise of Castor and Pollux."

4. "You put on an ornate ballgown
   You say 'someone has to do it' "

5. "not in 'Sir'
   but *companero*
   as you wd prefer it in *hispanol*"

6. "And you've been here before?"

7. "A bode where lost bodies roam each searching for its lost one."

8. "I think it was that the future had deadened for me, had become a
   soft, deadened wall."

9. "What would my potent master? Here I am."

10. "A silver Lucifer
    serves
    cocaine in cornucopia

    to some somnambulists
    of adolescent thighs"

11. "My mother's favorite image was that of the church as a great speckled bird, which she took as a simple parable."

12. "If necessary a prosthesis could be fashioned out of lime, hair, and dung."

13. "I do not know that knowledge amounts to anything more definite than a novel and grand surprise on a sudden revelation of the insufficiency of all that we had called knowledge before."

3. Strange Encounter

What pressure must come to bear, swift and obstreperous as an Annunciation slammed onto the beach, tenacious and blooming? The Heroine folds herself into a tiny nugget and is kept in an obsidian box. All day, all night, she scribbles in her confines, stitching dreams onto a tapestry under a palimpsest of cloud. Here she is temporarily safe from the great noise and its occult smoke, the origins of which cannot be diagnosed. One day, she comes out of the box and sees it is the Last Day. The Last Day, always before a conceptual punctuation to her internal gaze, now rises up as a fact, gleaming and ready.

As if, she scribbles in the pitch dark, wondering where the light switch might be, where the sun is, what time it is. Quickly she folds back into the minuscule compartment where all categories obtain, where she can sort and file and choose accordingly.

The night sky, with the rhythm of a language, urging connection to come forward out of its roomy, uncontaminated vat. Nothing in it has a price: a vast mine of futility, useless, where great gaps are witnessed as patterns of shine. She copies a file.

> Beneath the belt of Orion is an indistinct feature identified as his sword, the star iota at its southern end. To the naked eye, the area just above the star seems fuzzy. This is the great Orion nebula,

No. 42 in Messier's list. A fair telescope will show four stars at its brightest part, called the trapezium, after their arrangement. These very hot stars are believed to provide the ultraviolet energy that makes the surrounding gas glow. Dust reflects much of this glow, making a great cup-like flower. The dust obscures a very compact cluster of very young stars that may be studied through their infrared emissions, which penetrates dust clouds. What is seen as the nebula is about 1,500 light years away, yet is larger than the Moon in our sky. It is only a very small part of a huge dark cloud of dust and molecules that extends to the west nearly to the head of Cetus, the whale. In this celestial nursery, more stars are being formed.[6]

And another:

But if much poetry, music and the arts aims to "enchant"—and we must never strip that word of its aura of magical summons— much also, and of the most compelling, aims to make strangeness in certain respects stranger. It would instruct us of the inviolate enigma of the otherness in things and in animate presences. Serious painting, music, literature or sculpture make palpable to us, as do no other means of communication, the unassuaged, unhoused instability and estrangement of our condition. We are, at key instants, strangers to ourselves, errant at the gates of our own psyche. We knock blindly at the doors of turbulence, of creativity, of inhibition within the terra incognita of our own selves. What is more unsettling: we can be, in ways almost unendurable to reason, strangers to those whom we would know best, by whom we should be best known and unmasked.[7]

The flare of intimacy, like a great cerulean curtain behind the eyes, covering nothing and located nowhere, when the self briefly dissolves out of the constraints of causation and locale: this must be the original site which draws her *toward*, knowledge of which slips through the gaps, like light through a veil. So language responds to the desire to somehow seal over the lesions between this and that, while at the same time drawing attention to the difference between that *this* and this *that,* fretting distinctions. And when the real Others jog into view, what then? What signs of apprehension will be employed to subvert familiar categories of encounter: *friend* or *foe?*

Who is smiling, who weeping? And our artifacts but a jumble of jargon, abstruse as the mute history of rain.

> The informing agency is that of *tact*, of the ways in which we allow ourselves to touch or not to touch, to be touched or not to be touched by the presence of the other (the parable of doubting Thomas in the garden crystallizes the manifold mysteries of tact). The issue is that of civility (a charged word whose former strength has largely left us) towards the inward savour of things. What means have we to integrate that savour into the fabric of our own identity? We need a terminology which plainly articulates the intuition that an experience of communicated forms of meaning demands, fundamentally, a courtesy or tact of heart, a tact of sensibility and intellection which are conjoined at their several roots.[8]

The first planet that was found orbiting around another sunstar was in the constellation Pegasus.

Pegasus: The steed of the Muses, fancifully thought of as carrying his riders in periods of poetic inspiration; loosely, poetic ability, fancy, inspiration.

The new planets have been found circling around one of the stars in the Big Dipper, the huge rectangular tureen that holds, swimming in its black currents, the primordial soup of the universe. She remembers first trying to prise this image out of the myriad shining things which seemed so random; to see the Dipper in among the scattered luminosity: to impose this idea, this implement, onto the inscrutable abstract decor of space. Once perceived, the stars in that constellation would never again be solitary or autonomous; they would belong to a visual syntax. And yet each of them, each literal visible point, was really a pivot out of which might come dozens more etymologies of space-time, apparently inexhaustible elaborations of transparency and density, form and emptiness, processionals of dust, gas, orbs, disks, clusters, spirals, velocities, spectrums, dwarves, and giants.

The *little noun* "sky" holds an infinite vocabulary.

> What separates works of art from the fallible empirical world is not their higher degree of perfection but their ability to actual-

ize themselves in a brilliant and expressive appearance just like fireworks.

In every work of art something appears that does not exist.[9]

4. Haranguc Fandango

She wishes now to speak in such a way as to include others, to be able to say "we" and "our" without the filtering presumptions of authority; to move easily, as on a dance floor, without stepping on toes or taking the lead, responsive to the music that everyone could hear and yet interpret it so her body didn't freeze awkwardly, miss a beat, flail across the illumined floor. The last time she had danced she had in fact been unable to find an answering rhythm, as if the material of her being were alien to music. She had waited too long between dances, although back at home she had put on a disc and danced up a storm, alone on the linoleum floor of the kitchen, unselfconscious and giddy, moony and exuberant, transparent to the girl who had first danced in the arms of a bulky boy holding her close on a summer afternoon, singing murkily off-pitch into her ear *earth angel, earth angel.*

Could she begin a sentence *our* predicament or *our* difficulty without feeling queasy, listening to the Serbs in Sarajevo speak bitterly as they prepared to leave home, burning their houses, one by one, behind them, so that no Croat or Muslim could live in them? Every time she heard a politician proclaim "The American people want . . . ," she felt a stiffening in her spine, an antithetical resonance. Every time she hears the word "community" she is on alert for an incipient imposition of some frame or idea, although when the blizzard came into the city, persons walking in the middle of the carless streets with their dogs and children smiled at her and she at them in an assent which felt communal, as if something had been agreed to, tacitly. Communities these days are too often places with locked gates around them, like a medieval keep, to make their inhabitants feel *safe.* Communities are virtual, sites on screens in rooms at great distances from each other. It seems to her that this word, along with so many others, has been usurped and hollowed out so it drifts in an echo chamber of ventriloquism; that whole patches of language hang like so many husks. It all makes her want to twist around so she can see things from the subversive angle of a clown with the irreverent humility of, say, Chaplin's tramp, wide-eyed, ragged, and endlessly resourceful, swerving out of the way of the onrushing gang that sees in every petty infraction the incarnation of evil, and virtue where none is. She keeps thinking, *In the name of one thing, other things are happening.*

As if we should all retreat to the originary status of our beings, never expecting to change through an exposure to, or involvement with, what is *not us.*

cormorant, n. Large lustrous-black voracious sea bird; rapacious person. cf. *peasant, tyrant.*

5. She Drinks Too Much and Refuses to Go in Fear of Abstraction

Perhaps it goes without saying that our two main ways of representing ourselves and the world, telling stories and picturing, are not so much outmoded as exploded. There is no one abiding master narrative, and there is no single comprehensive image. Instead there is an unceasing stream of stories and images, versions of stories and images, contending for our attention, however fleet it might be. At every moment, we each walk around with access to a vast array of pictures and tales, in some of which we are actual participants and actors, in others passive witnesses and bystanders, in still others mere receivers of another person's vast array of pictures and stories. As Jonathan Schell writes,

> Formerly, when you awoke in the morning and saw the sun rise and prepared to face your life, you were pretty much stuck with that. Today, a hundred other sunrises, other dwellings and other lives are on call at the touch of a few buttons. Do you not like the person who stands before you? Do you not like his face? Then summon up, on some screen or another, another person with a nicer face—say, Candice Bergen. Is your apartment drab and cramped? Then live, vicariously, in more glamorous and commodious apartments. Are you lonely? Cheerful people will come and keep you company. Do you not like your life? Other lives are available to be lived, in abundance, 24 hours a day.[10]

Reality, empirically knowable, does not exist, just as the self as a static subject, empirically knowable, also does not exist. And the great deluge of facts, of information, zooming from every conceivable origin along every con-

ceivable trajectory, is not so much a *highway* as an immense unwieldy mo-
bile. How are we are to decide which to look at, which to listen to, which to
believe, to prize, to resist, to love, to include, and which to doubt, contest,
and discard? We need to question the link between what we take to be real,
as in an accurate rendition, and what we take to be true, as in worth attach-
ing a value that might allow us to fashion our choices, decisions, and judg-
ments *about* the real. We need to discriminate between technological and
imaginative innovation, just as we need to notice the differences between
law and justice, or medicine and compassion. There is a distinction between
the art of fiction and the art of lying.

A young poet friend remarks, "The divine part of humanity is its capacity
to see the interconnectedness between all things. To be that interconnected-
ness." If this is so, then the Divinity we wish to resemble is testing us in sub-
tle new ways, asking us to worship at the Temple of Information, whose
Disembodied Oracular Source (who is speaking?) is lost in a thousand thou-
sand transcripts flying through the stratosphere, like pixilated ghosts, each
with its particle of fact. To see connections in this, to find in it *the syntax of
the heart*, to invent compelling stories and stunning images: to impose on
this astounding influx *form?*

Form, after all, is chosen limit.

Limit, as a formal characteristic, is the expression of choice in the service
of the possible.

The *possible* is the indeterminate futurity of *meaning.*

Form posits the optimum conditions for meaning to occur.

> *To discover winter and know it well, to find,*
> *Not to impose, not to have reasoned at all,*
> *Out of nothing to have come on major weather,*
>
> *It is possible, possible, possible. It must*
> *Be possible. It must be that in time*
> *The real will from its crude compoundings come . . .*[11]

When limits, or choices, are displayed in the service of the possibility of
meaning, in the making of art objects, we call the result *beautiful.* That is,
we stand before a painting by Vermeer, or we read a poem by Paul Celan,
or we listen to Shostakovich's Twenty-four Preludes and Fugues for piano,
and we say *this is beautiful.* But what we are really announcing is our plea-
sure and gratitude in the fact of the *choices* the artist has made. We *recognize*

something in how one stroke of the brush brushes up against another stroke of the brush; how one note moves toward and away from the next in an astounding sequence; how one word attaches itself to another and to another to another until something that has to do with all the words separately—the history of their meanings—gathers into a nexus which allows us, which invites us, to experience something like the *meaning of meaning*. It is the nature of meaning, like the nature of reality, and the nature of truth, to be unfixed by temporal/spatial constraints, so that persons in and of any age may participate in their re/construction.

Art is not entertainment, and it is not decor. It is one of the rude fallacies of our time to want to reduce all art forms, and in particular literary arts, to their most facile and elemental role, and so deny their potential to awaken, provoke, and elicit our *glee* at being agents in the construction of meaning. As Martha Nussbaum points out, "We are accustomed by now to think of literature as optional: as great, valuable, entertaining, excellent, but something that exists off to one side of political and economic and legal thought, in another university department, ancillary rather than competitive." We have, she adds, "narrowly hedonistic theories of literary value."[12] Our world—late-twentieth-century America—is relentless in its desire to dictate to us what we desire; it wants to assign and to determine how we construct and construe meaning in our lives, it wants to tell us from where our pleasures come. It wants us to believe that only Wealth, Fame, and Power (WFP), in some combination or another, are worthwhile goals, because only WFP can confer—what?—*celebrity*.

Celebrity: the modern, secular form of martyrdom, where individuals are cast into the riotous blast of an eviscerating, obliterating light. How many personal disasters of every conceivable kind—suicide, homicide, divorce, addiction—before it is understood that celebrities are *victims*? "Their divorce was more predictable than their marriage."

6. Penance

With the insistent picturing and telling of Celebrity, it is of course not uninteresting to be a poet. John Ashbery once remarked, "To be famous and to be a famous poet are not the same thing," by which he simply wanted to point out that the world of poetry is not *included* in celebrity picturing and storytelling. Why is this? Because the *economy* of being a poet subverts the received relationship between ambition, money, and success. Poets must acknowledge this fact a priori, at the outset; must, in a sense, agree to it. Many persons in many fields have an increasingly hard time making a living, and endemic poverty caused by social oppression is not something to be lightly set aside. To be poor in this culture carries all kinds of stigmas, and invites all kinds of rhetorical evocations of the American Dream, which holds that the pursuit of happiness is *necessarily* tied to the capacity to earn a living. (What constitutes a "living wage" in a culture driven by WFP is worth a pause, as we witness the slow but certain shrinkage of the middle class and the institutions of social transformation—schools, libraries, museums, newspapers, research universities, concert halls, and so forth—in which it has traditionally invested.)

A living wage: that which allows a person sufficient freedom to feel she/he has some control over her/his destiny; an alignment of capacity to activity which leads to a sense of sufficiency.

Nonetheless, persons who wish to become poets in this culture must make a kind of promise or vow, like Saint Francis, in which they agree to economic obscurity, at least in relation to the writing of poems. The history of the embedded relation between poverty and poetry is not just a romance but is linked to the history of *spiritual resistance,* a resistance which characterized the initial founding of America, sometimes with dire consequences, and which finds its greatest secular expression in Emerson's "Self-Reliance." People are *disturbed* when poets make a decent living as professors; they think it is a sort of *bad joke* (but of course newsworthy) when Allen Ginsberg sells his archive to a major university for big bucks, as if some breach of decorum had been committed. They are not equally bemused when movie stars, baseball players, or television news commentators get millions upon millions for acting a part, playing ball, or reading aloud the news in front of a camera.

When poets make money something is askew. As if for every celebrity— say, Michael Jackson or Madonna—exploding in the firmament like a giant star, there needs to be a *shadow figure,* an obscure Other toiling away in the dimmest corner, lost in the dark matter of the universe, never to be found by the searching lenses of far-reaching cameras. Poets must *hold down* this invisible portion of the universe, the part that we never see but guess at, lest the whole thing fly apart in a final radiance of destruction, on the incendiary flames of outrageous (mis)fortune.

Off-camera and out of earshot, watching the night snow fall, noticing that *snow* contains myriad *nows.*

There must be some remnant habit of *willed obscurity,* of *volunteer poverty* for an acceptance of an inequity, a gap, between work and recompense, in which some vague need is met, a sort of *spiritual critique,* an antithetical motion, however far-off, however imperceptible, of the equation of happiness with the capacity to *buy things, many things, more things than one could ever possibly need.* As if on the Day of Judgment, poets will step forward out of the crevices—the tiny rooms, the smoky bars—by the *hundreds and thousands,* wearing dark glasses, like a great witnessing chorus, to proclaim the faith of little children, the hope of the excluded, and "the charity of the hard moments."[13]

(She catches sight of herself in the mirror. *Go in fear of hyperbole.*)

In America, we celebrate and honor poets from other cultures (and, of late, poets who "represent" minority groups here, whose Identity is their subject) who have expressed their resistance to the tyranny of their homelands; we are generous and attentive to the many writers who have come to this country to find *liberty.* These poets have, for us, great symbolic value, and much ideological hay can be, and is, made from their courage.

The *New York Times* (January 26, 1996, front page):

> Joseph Brodsky, the persecuted Russian poet who settled in the United States in the early 1970's, won the Nobel Prize for Literature in 1987 and became his adopted country's poet laureate, died yesterday at his apartment in Brooklyn Heights . . .

> The poetry of Joseph Brodsky, with its haunting images of wandering and loss and the human search for freedom, was not political, and certainly not the work of an anarchist or even an active dissident. If anything, his was a dissent of the spirit, protesting the drabness of life in the Soviet Union and its pervasive materialist dogmas.

> But in a land of poets where poetry and other literature was officially subservient to the state, where verses were marshaled like so many laborers to the quarries of Socialist Realism, it was perhaps inevitable that Mr. Brodsky's work—unpublished except in underground forums, but increasingly popular—should have run afoul of the literary police.

The exploitative layers of cultural hypocrisy in this moving account are profound. There is no mention, for example, of what Mr. Brodsky thought about the "pervasive materialist dogmas" of his adopted country, of his desire to have poetry *here* available to all, his wish that students memorize reams of stanzas, his desire to put books of poetry in every hotel room across America alongside the Gideon Bible. Brodsky, "unpublished except in underground forums, but increasingly popular"—there's the rub: there was an *audience* in Russia, a desire to read poems despite, or perhaps because of, the brutal suppressions of the State.

American cultural and educational institutions venerate Mr. Brodsky (and others of similar ilk) not so much for the power of his work, but because he could be rendered famous, an icon to display our liberal values, our tolerance.

The means of oppression in a "free country" are indirect, but effective, and they often have taken the form of "benign neglect," though of course neglect is never benign. *Ignore them, pretend they do not exist, keep them separated in their journals, their schools and academies—the academy is very adept at ignoring the living—do not include them or their works in general coverage, do not review their books, unless they keep to a format of neat little pictures and accounts from their personal lives.* American poets are shunned in the public domain of the media not for what they say (nobody knows) or for how they say it (nobody cares), but for their *spiritual dissent from the pervasive materialist dogmas of the United States.*

Poets do not think that the sole purpose of language is to convey experience as a stream of information reducible to sets of categories with subject headings. Frank O'Hara, deciding to give up music as a career, said, "In too many places I have information but no knowledge." When the *New York Times Magazine* made a "map" of American poetry and poets, they made of it a travesty, as inaccurate as it was outdated (e.g., any poet not writing within a narrow paradigm is ipso facto a L=A=N=G=U=A=G=E poet), arising from their determination to fit poets into ludicrous categories ("the richest," "the most beautiful," etc.), which, undoubtedly, they thought was amusing, but which in fact reflected both ignorance and disdain. Instead of asking why there might be disagreements and animosities, as well as affection and respect, between and among poets, informed by the relation between experience and aesthetics and the real communities that result, they debased these into petty quarrels and competitions. Simultaneously, they did their best to erect a hierarchy of petty power bases and fiefdoms organized around the most parochial (if typical) prototypes. That Bill Moyers did a series on poetry for PBS is great, but it too was driven by entrenched conventions which gave little sense of the extraordinary variety and complexity of contemporary American poetry.

Say the guy sitting next to you on the plane, or the train, or the bus, asks you what you do, and you answer, "I am a poet." There is a moment when a tiny abyss opens, a hairline fracture across the skyline, through which a meagre gnostic light shines. This is a millisecond of time, nothing really. Then, his voice slightly strained, slightly throttled, the voice of an estranged father talking to his kid about her grades, "A poet! How wonderful!"

But even as this affirmation rides into the air like a sunburst, it is followed *quickly quickly* by shadowy, anxious clouds, puffing across his mental horizon as he tries to find some reference, some contemporary sighting, anything, which shows that he knows something about living poets or their work. But no, nothing comes, not a single page or a single book, not a single title or name; instead, a set of images from . . . what? Cartoons flicker up onto his scanner. *Flick:* a disheveled creep, vaguely addicted, vaguely suicidal or homicidal in a dingy room. *Flick:* a wispy creature with stringy hair in pastel drapery, mooning over love lost. *Flick:* a shrill, hysterical maniac ranting about some kind of injustice. But, yes, he can hear Garrison Keillor's Heartland voice, on that program on NPR, the *Writer's Almanac,* intoning, "Here's a poem for today by . . ."—blank. Usually something about some guy remembering some sad tale from his childhood—a dead cat or uncle or something. Sweet dreams.

Still smiling (the smile of frozen animation), your companion sees that you do not resemble any of these images. You seem, well, normal. You are quite nicely dressed. You smell pretty good. He realizes, with a strange sort of embarrassed jolt, that he thought, well, he thought *poets were extinct.* Desperate now, as the silence between you begins to slide into the gnostic crack, he realizes that there *is* a way to proceed:

"Have you published?" he asks eagerly.

Funny, really. You are not exactly a kid, not even what could be called a young person, you are quite *mature,* and you wonder how your companion imagines that you could claim to be a poet *without* having published, unless, of course, you are, well, delusional. But of course the real purport of your poor baffled companion's question is: *I didn't know poetry actually got published these days I mean do they actually pay you for it if so how much can't be more than a few bucks so how do you make a living do you turn tricks are you married to a rich guy or what?*

You will annoy persons in the Real World. They will not like knowing that there is a discrepancy between what you are doing to earn a living and what you are doing in pursuit of happiness. They will not want to know that you are not wholeheartedly taken up by an idea of a progressive climb *up up up* to more more more: more Money, more Power, more Fame. They will find it baffling if you tell them that you spent forty-three hours, thirty-nine minutes, twenty seconds writing *one poem,* and waited seven months to hear if it was accepted at a little magazine that can pay you only by sending you two copies when it is published in another six months; that you will fly, if asked, across the United States to read for twenty minutes to fourteen students and one faculty member, a poet, at a small college for a fee of two hundred dollars plus dinner at the local trattoria. They will find it inscrutable that you wish to spend all your time puttering with the most ubiquitous, the least rare, and therefore least inherently valuable of substances, *language.*

> So, strange young man,—it is at his command, remember that I say this to you; whether I agree with it or not is neither here nor there—you have decided on the conjurer's profession. Somewhere, in the middle of a salt marsh or at the bottom of a kitchen garden or on the top of a bus, you heard imprisoned Ariel call for help, and it is now a liberator's face that congratulates you from your shaving mirror every morning. As you walk the cold streets hatless, or sit over coffee and doughnuts in the corner of a cheap restaurant, your secret has already set you apart from the howling merchants and transacting multitudes to watch with fascinated distaste the bellowing barging banging passage of the awkward profit-seeking elbow, the dazed eye of the gregarious acquisitive condition. Lying awake at night in your single bed you are conscious of a power by which you will survive the wallpaper of your boardinghouse or the expensive bourgeois horrors of your home.[14]

7. Green

The world, for many poets, is apprehended *as* language; language is the material of the world. Every object is simultaneously itself and its word. For some poets, the word has more significance than the thing itself; for others, the thing takes priority over its word, and for still others, neither word nor thing has precedence. Although this might be seen as a mere matter of shift in focus, the consequences, in terms of the poem's form, its construction, can be profound. Poets move around in the shadowy space between a word and its object, sometimes wanting to make the difference between the two appear seamless, and sometimes calling attention to the distinction between them.

Some poets stitch a kind of linguistic web between sites of picturing (description) and sites of telling (narration); some poets make clusters of sound which do neither and both at once, calling attention to the constellating properties of language, its capacity to confound temporal and spatial reality into a third thing: an event which participates in the construction of that reality. The idea that a poem can be granted the status of an *event* that shifts the course of cause and effect in a writer's or reader's life, has little to do with the idea of a poem as a bauble of verbal expressivity. Poetry, on this view, is an enterprise of making a path from a given vocabulary into a revised vocabulary. As Richard Rorty has it:

> What matters in the end are changes in the vocabulary rather than changes in belief, changes in truth-value candidates rather than assignments of truth-value . . . Those who speak the old language and have no wish to change, those who regard it as a hallmark of rationality and morality to speak just that language, will regard as altogether *ir*rational the appeal of the new metaphors— the new language game which the radicals, the youth, or the avant-garde are playing. The popularity of the new ways of speaking will be viewed as a matter of "fashion" or "the need to rebel" or "decadence" . . . Conversely, from the point of view of those who are trying to use the new language, to literalize the new metaphors, those who cling to the old language will be viewed as irrational—as victims of passion, prejudice, superstition, the dead hand of the past, and so on.[15]

Translated to aesthetics, we can see how the resistance to innovation is a resistance to the difficulty of giving up old vocabularies of value—what constitutes beauty or truth, for example—for new ones. We seem ready to herald each new fashion season with open arms, trading in last year's wardrobe at the drop of a hat, or hem, or glove, but art that attempts to alter our final vocabulary of judgment is viewed with disdain, suspicion, or outright hostility. As art critic Dave Hickey has said, "Once we acquiesce in the reification of formal values, questions of whether one manifestation is 'better' than another, derives from another, is displaced by another, or transforms itself into another, become inexplicable and irrelevant." As if to say: it is not a matter of having an experience and then writing about it; a poem is, in itself, an experience, where the idea of "experience" is not neutral, but one that changes the way we think about what came before it and what follows from it.

So that writing a poem is involved with creating a self, in which the self (and so the world) is an anthology under constant revision, to slightly revise poet Ron Silliman's remark.

Although the word "word" is a noun, words are not exactly things, and yet they are not not-things either. The fact that they can be simultaneously *sounds uttered* and *marks written* allows poets to play between aural and visual components, to draw attention not only to the relation of word to white space, but to an infinite number of minute compositional shiftings, alignments, and turns, each of which influences the way in which meanings accrue onto the reader/listener's resonating ground. To notice the facticity or materiality of words is to give them a certain autonomy, as if you could free them of their literal relation to objects (reality), and allow them to form virtual attachments to each other. The dazzling fluidity and malleability of language implies an infinite number of relations and attachments, each of which has the potential to subtly shift how, and what, we perceive of ourselves and our world.

A child learns that the leaf is green, but there is no innate physical relationship between the word "green" and the delicate elongated coolly opaque thing in his hand. Even if there were an argument, something about that long e sound that carries a sensation, an openness, which one could attribute to this color, green has hundreds, thousands, maybe tens of thousands, ways of being green; each time it appears it is in relation to myriad other conditions: shine, opacity, scent, motion, texture, not to mention the presence or proximity of other colors.

May I borrow your green dress to wear to a party?

> *And find*
> *What wind*
> *Serves to advance an honest mind.*[16]

THE NIGHT SKY II

1. Green (thought, shade)

The cicadas came and went. The blue moon came and went. Neither went the same way as it came. Across the river, the sound sheer and loud as if the air were rubbing against itself, unoiled molecules roughly scraping: *skreek skreek skreek*. The story got pieced together. At first I thought they were locusts; they swarmed hectic in the heat at the tops of trees: the river valley with its angry spirits: *a plague upon your houses:* the gothic fatal imagination. Enormous diffuse sound, without a single source. Every seventeen years. Then I thought the sound was of their eating the leaves of the trees, remembering the fat green caterpillars and the huge gypsy moths' muted putty wings. But someone said they don't eat, they copulate, and then they die. Tiny bright eyes like drops of blood when you prick your finger. Delicately transparent orange-veined wings. The floor of the porch littered with their corpses; some turned up, their thread-thin legs stiffening. In the strangeness of their ecstasy, the fabric of myth, remembering Persephone.

> The . . . reason that you might think you do not understand what I am telling you is, while I am describing to you how Nature works, you won't understand why Nature works that way. But you see, nobody understands that. I can't explain why Nature behaves in this peculiar way . . . The theory of quantum electrodynamics describes Nature as absurd from the point of view of common sense. And it agrees fully with experiment. So I hope you can accept Nature as She is—absurd.[1]

In my room, the sound of something hitting against the window, a delicate thud like a small pebble. Early in the morning, not long after dawn. The windows filthy, a blur. *Thrut, thrut.* It's a bird, beautifully subtle soft mauve reds, with a bright orange beak: a female cardinal. She has a loud voice; she chirps on a branch of the bushy tree and then plunges into the window, pecking at it. At first I thought she was crashing into it in bird madness, driven crazy by the sound of the invading cicadas, a bird version of a nervous breakdown. I look for something on the window she would want, but see only the murky residue of winter weather. I take pictures of her, long tail fanning and wildly beating wings against the window, afraid that no one will believe my story of the window-batting bird. One morning, her mate, decked out in scarlet, is on the branch with her. They seem to be conversing; they peck each other. He flies away; she continues to fly against the window.

Why should we import rags and relics into the new hour? Nature abhors the old, and old age seems the only disease; all others run into this one. We call it by many names,—fever, intemperance, insanity, stupidity and crime; they are all forms of old age; they are rest, conservatism, appropriation, inertia; not newness, not the way onward . . . This old age ought not to creep on a human mind. In nature every moment is new; the past is always swallowed and forgotten; the coming is sacred. Nothing is secure but life, transition, the energizing spirit. No love can be bound by oath or covenant to secure against a higher love. No truth so sublime but it may be trivial tomorrow in the light of new thoughts. People wish to be settled; only as far as they are unsettled is there any hope for them.[2]

What we intuit is that something needs to be solved, that an impediment needs to be absorbed and, as it is absorbed, to become manifest. The subject trying to find its way out of the long sequestered drama of suspension. If the impediment is merely formal, there is a corresponding aridity, the aridity of convention, of exhausted iconographies, vocabularies, habits of mind, a pretense of discovery. If all that is happening is a mirror reflection, or the old vocabulary recycled into new technology, the result is quickly perceived as arid and stale. You cannot experiment with only the history of experimentation as your archive. The century, mesmerized by its own inwardness, sucks back into its frames so that soon all we will have is an attic full of empty frames to pass on. A catalogue of self-conscious reiteration, a stalled inventory of choices, hall of mirrors and quotations like a family or a nation or an institution unwilling to change its self-perpetuated image. But we know from basic biology what happens when such willed enclosure occurs: a gradual weakening and perverting of the very traits that were once admired for their efficacy and beauty. "The field cannot be well seen from within the field," Emerson remarked in 1864.

In a high room, overlooking festoons of it, coming down into the cool color-stripped predark, robins on the grass hopping and stopping, the pond flashing under wavering branches, titles strewn about—*The Illusion of the End; Frame Structures; The Castle of Crossed Destinies.*

> *It was Him*
> *Power of the Clouds*
> *Judge of the Dead*
> *The sheep on his right*
> *The goats on his left*
> *And all the angels.*
>
> *But from the book*
> *backward on their knees*
> *crawled neolithic adventurers known only to themselves.*
> *They blazed with artifice*
> *no pin, or kernel, or grain too small to pick up.*
> *A baby with a broken face lay on the leaves*
> *Hannibal—a rough looking man*
> *rushed by with a bundle of sticks.*
> *"Ah, this is fortunate," cried Forebear*
> *and helped himself to me.*[3]

Let's say there is always something outside the frame, lurking or knocking or waiting, unwelcome perhaps or unnoticed—the stranger or the strangeness that refuses to come inside, or that we ignore, or deliberately keep at bay. What happens if the frame breaks and this thing, this otherness, gets inside? Doesn't everything change, the frame as well as each thing it once held apart? And doesn't the fact of our acknowledging it shift our focus, alter the syntax from one of tidy resolution to one that verges on chaos, or cacophony, or meaninglessness, as we enter this suspended irresolute space of rejection and acceptance, until this strangeness is absorbed? It is the pressure of this strangeness that might in fact produce the work of art in the first place; the desire to accommodate it, to bring it into relation with what already is; we might say that what comes to be known of a particular age or spirit has to do with this adjustment, this inclusion, which alters old habits of thought.

Now this scrupulous realism, this aspiration to render exactly all natural details, is the characteristic feature of the spirit of the expiring Middle Ages. It is the same tendency which we encountered in all the fields of the thought of the epoch, a sign of decline and not of rejuvenation.

Apart from the occasional dream of fantasy, clearly framed and controlled by a realistic context, there is no surrealism, no magic realism, no mythic subtext, no overt intertextuality, no metafictional frame-breaking, no word games, no abrupt switches of style of type of discourse, no parody, no radical deviation from well-formed syntax, no unconventional layout and typography.[4]

A pattern of dead insects on the green floor. But if

2. "there is no topic sentence"

then how to proceed? You go to a museum and you cannot look at what you are looking at without first reading the caption, tidily printed on a small white card and discreetly attached to the wall just to the right, or blown up into a narrative spooled onto the tasteful gray wall, telling you what you need to know in order to look at the picture. Of course it is useful to know that the artist was born in a place, at a time, and it is interesting to know the name of the person who loaned or gave the object to the museum, and what the materials are of which it is made, these points of orientation are undoubtedly important to understand certain things about the object you are viewing. But are there moments when you want to go into the world, even the world of the museum, and see what is there as if it were a raw fact, unmolested by these codes of telling?

When I say I believe that women have a soul and that its substance contains two carbon rings the picture in the foreground makes it difficult to find its application back where the corridors get lost in ritual sacrifice and hidden bleeding. But the four points of the compass are equal on the lawn of excluded middle where full maturity of meaning takes time the way you eat a fish, morsel by morsel, off the bone. Something that can be held in the

mouth, deeply, like darkness by someone blind or the empty
space I place at the center of each poem to allow penetration.[5]

Captions cannot provide a full context but only edited snippets, easily di-
gested, to ease your fear of ignorance, your distrust of your sense of things.
So you can leave the exhibition with the data as if it were essential; you can
substitute information for your response. But this very data acts as a kind of
leak into which the energy of the work is siphoned; the work becomes an il-
lustration of its caption, and the caption proliferates into the weedy morass
of captions in which we live. Before you can say "postmodernism" you are
mouthing received notions of value or significance, and you have no way to
truly know either context or example.

> Miracle, the suspension of normal laws of nature, is to be seen less
> as an example of "irrationality" or credulity than as an instance of
> the symbolic interface of human and divine: it functions as a rhe-
> torical device to express what is otherwise inexpressible. In much
> the same way, parable (currently a major topic of study from the
> rhetorical standpoint) surprises by suspending normal expectation.
> It operates by telling—not through argument, but by revelation,
> through hidden meanings. The texts rely on these devices; indeed,
> they lay some stress on their importance and on the difficulty of
> understanding them, as when Jesus says to his disciples, "unto you
> is given to know the mystery of the kingdom of God, but unto
> them that are without, all these things are done in parables." It is
> this feature, in particular, of early Christian discourse that de-
> serves much more attention than it has received except through
> specialists, for it raises exactly those issues of language and repre-
> sentation that are now for us again problematic.[6]

The inexplicable is inexhaustible. Without it we live in a barren literal
landscape, in which every action and event is rendered into its simplest,
most reductive, equation: this is this. In language, the birth of the new is
often created by juxtaposition and analogy, wherein one thing is related to
another to produce a third term. The system of unlikeness relies on an essen-
tially dichotomous paradigm, in which the world is carved out in bald oppo-
sitions: this/not this, yes/no, good/evil, day/night, love/hate, subject/object,
us/them, and on and on. These are necessary couplings, but they have pro-

liferated so deeply into our way of perceiving that we less and less tolerate the murky spaces between extremities in which we actually exit, and through which we come to make our choices, decisions, and judgments. Someone loves his wife and another person. A man who has killed two people is acquitted because the event itself is so profoundly entangled with historical and social parameters that it is impossible to decide on his, on whose, culpability. Time is not the opposite of space. Male is not the opposite of female. Democracy was never the antithesis of communism. The habit of oppositions is as old as or older than the image of the Tree of the Knowledge of Good and Evil, the seminal site of instruction when curious, courageous Eve risks uncertainties of Difference and enters the moral, mortal universe.

> For Danforth, in short, errand has the ambiguity of the figura. It unites allegory and chronicle in the framework of the work of redemption. And in so doing, it redefines the meaning not only of errand but of every term in New England's Errand into the Wilderness . . . The newness of New England becomes both literal and eschatological, and (in which was surely the most far-reaching of these rhetorical effects) the American wilderness takes on the double significance of secular and sacred place. If for the individual believer it remained part of the wilderness of the world, for God's "peculiar people" it was a territory endowed with special symbolic import, like the wilderness through which the Israelites passed to the promised land . . . the American Puritan jeremiad went much further [than the European]. It made anxiety its end as well as its means. Crisis was the social norm it sought to inculcate. The very concept of errand, after all, implied a state of unfulfillment. The future, though divinely assured, was never quite there, and New England's Jeremiahs set out to provide the sense of insecurity that would ensure the outcome. Denouncing or affirming, their vision fed on the distance between promise and fact.[7]

An abyss opens up between the idea of a promise (futurity) and the idea of a fact (reality). Promises are one way the present conceives of the future; promises transport the vagaries of hope into concrete examples; they help us to align our desires to our actions, our intention to our will; they help us to braid the true into the facticity of the real. A promise imagines a condition, a conclusion; it propels a syntax—the sentence comes to an end on the trajectory of its promise. The "mise" part is from *mittere*, send, which of course is related to "mission"—errand in the wilderness. Futurity is inscribed on the arc of a promise, across the temporal space that opens and closes between intention and action. But one might imagine that the promise is not of something known, concrete, tangible, but merely a *disposition toward,* a willingness to put at risk that which is already at hand. The fulfillment of a promise produces another, unknown promise. What if the pattern of language which knows beforehand what its conclusion is were subverted? Syntax and grammar might break apart, causing anxiety and terror, as if there were a shaky bridge over a cavern through which waters sluice dangerous currents, and the other side is only sunset itself and the odd noise of unknown insects. A poetics which explores such risks is one that might be seen as responsive to the inertia of contemporary political and aesthetic discourse; the sense of betrayal when promises are emptied into a dump of false news, voyeurism, sanctimoniousness, waste sites of a debased and vacuous time.

> But lest I should mislead any when I have my own head and obey my whims, let me remind the reader that I am only an experimenter. Do not set the least value on what I do, or the least discredit on what I do not, as if I pretended to settle any thing as true or false. I unsettle all things. No facts are to me sacred; none are profane; I simply experiment, an endless seeker with no Past at my back.[8]

Or put it this way: reality appears to have outwitted us, has run off, out to the horizon and beyond into the sparkling *not yet not here.* And we, a band of disputatious kids, whining and exhausted, having come so far but not far enough, want to turn back and find ourselves in the safety of our old haunts and retreats, under the trustful eye of our goodly god or guide. We are glad for reason, and for the secular, but yet feel cheated, as if in our hurry to get to the future we had dropped our most precious belongings along the way, and now they are tangled in the overgrown path. It was thought, wasn't it, that love of beauty (art) would replace faith in god (religion)? It was hoped, wasn't it, that the beautiful would be understood as a sign of the good, the true, and so we could align ourselves with it without the invocation of a greater authority to keep us civil? We could not have seen how easily the discourse (the discord) of desire would ingest all spiritual, social, and moral resistance, strip beauty of its alignment with the difficulty of finding or knowing the true, and fold the moral imagination down until it was a mere blip on an academic syllabus or co-opted by those who wish to impose their values on others. The model of science, which has held our faith in reason, and by which the real is aligned to the true through test and experiment, has not so far shaped our moral imaginations or informed our spiritual quests. "If we possess the *why* of life we can put up with almost any *how*," Nietzsche remarks.

"We have been a little insane about the truth. We have had an obsession," Stevens remarks.

When they find out—tomorrow, next week, next year—what happened aboard Flight 800 that made it disintegrate into a thousand thousand particles over the roiling sea—it will not answer the questions of the grief-stricken. They will not be consoled to know if it was a terrorist bomb or a mechanical error. The vulgar insistences of the media demand that private incomprehension become public display, and that a microphone be shoved at the mouth of the weeping widow to ask her *how she feels*.

3. Let Pics Enter Arks That Reap Art

The Platonic and Kantian idea of rationality centers around the idea that we need to bring particular actions under general principles if we are to be moral. Freud suggests that we need to return to the particular—to see particular present situations and options as similar to or different from particular past actions or events. He thinks that only if we catch hold of some crucial idiosyncratic contingencies in our past shall we be able to make something worthwhile of ourselves, to create present selves whom we can respect. He taught us to interpret what we are doing, or thinking of doing, in terms of, for example, our past reaction to particular authority-figures, or in terms of constellations of behavior which were forced upon us in infancy. He suggested that we praise ourselves by weaving idiosyncratic narratives— case histories, as it were—of our success in self-creation, our ability to break free from an idiosyncratic past. He suggests that we condemn ourselves for failure to break free of that past rather than for failure to live up to universal standards.[9]

Go figure. I had a really bad dream this morning. It seems I was to be a bridesmaid in someone's wedding while simultaneously I was supposed to be in a play; I had thought I could somehow be in two places at the same time. The dream turned and turned on the problem of my two outfits—a yellow dress for the wedding and a black dress for the play. I also needed new shoes, or thought I could solve the problem by having a new pair of shoes, but the bride could not direct me to a shoe store. I was in a predicament between two promises, in both of which others were dependent on my actions.

I was raised in a household which seemed always to be in danger, always precariously tilted toward cataclysm. This possibility was conditioned by the fact that my father was often overseas, in a war (writing about a war), and then not long after the war was over, he died and my mother, at home, was increasingly inclined to places of degradation most children do not get to witness. Often drunk, she did not get out of bed from one day to the next except to walk in her slip down the long corridor of the apartment to the bathroom. She was intelligent, beautiful, and well educated, and there were moments, sometimes whole sequences of moments, when she was radiant and articulate and sweet-smelling. She had lovers, most of whom were unkind and usurious, and all of whom had, as far as I could tell, little interest in her three children. She was beaten by some sailors and came home bloody and wretched, a fragment of her pearl necklace clutched in her hand. One of her lovers, Arthur, a huge, powerful, handsome man, half Indian and half African-American, had epileptic fits; my brother and I held him down and put a spoon in his mouth to try to keep him from choking on his tongue. For breakfast my mother often wanted a glass of tomato juice with a raw egg and some bitters in it. She smoked. She listened late into the night to Billie Holiday.

I never wanted to write directly, explicitly, about my childhood. I did not want to make poems in which I would appear either as victim, telling her story, or as heroine, telling her story. I wanted to stroll away from this first place and make my way, without its melodrama dragging me to the mirror of doubt and self-pity, on the one hand, or dreams of transformation and nobility, on the other. If I wanted attention, I did not want it for things over which I had no control, or, for which, responsibility; I did not want to be the object of the petty terrorism of fate or the seductions of pious concern. I wanted to escape on the most ephemeral and yet most sturdy of human paths, word by word, line by line, poem by poem, book by book. This ambition was at first merely a hunch, a plume. It was born, I think, of an acute wish for order, for things to recover, magically, ineluctably, and forever. This order was not the order of system but one that could *make use* of these same raw materials, the stench and fear and precariousness. In my mind's eye I invented phantom realities to displace or replace the actual, but the materials for this revision were made from those of the actual, had their source in its graphic, mundane terrain. As in a fairy tale, the world I was in would be converted, translated, into one of harmony and possibility; it was a primitive intuition, common in childhood, that there must be a way to redemption and freedom. My own fantasies formed around visions of decorum in which calamity and turmoil were miraculously rendered into a habitude of clarity, a serene setting in whose sanctuary there would be room for attention and receptivity.

The point is this: I needed to find figures or tropes to house these eventful figures and their consequences, by which to free myself from their grip. I needed to revise a claustrophobic and anomalous reality into one in which I had some choice, into which I could peer without suffering from its contagious degradation. Many years passed before I understood that the figure of my mother had slowly transformed into an idea: alluring, frightening, unkempt, neglected, uncivil, primal, transgressive, dangerous, and endangered, she took up residence in my work as an idea: *wild*. I recall seeing a figure walking along the horizon in a slip—was it a dream? I don't know—and I knew it was the outer perimeter, the limit, extremity, which would always escape the logic of syntax and the syntax of logic. The figure was the site of the unknown and unknowable, a conundrum of futility and fertility: *the night sky*. My father became the whole lexicon of absence and desire, of longing and delay, of beginnings, and endings, which realize themselves with each enactment of the writing process. He was the fable of escape from acute inwardness and separation to ideas of inclusion and community, configured as "audience" or "world": *the new morning's day*. This transformation of personal private experience into a poetics which might be congruent with other historical, epistemological frames offered a possible way out of an intractable subjectivity.

4. Strange Encounter

"Depression," I once observed, "is the better part of squalor." The easiest, quickest, and most ubiquitous of all escapes is the lit screen, where a constant rattle of voices and images obliterates the litany of lists that render inner life a tag sale of tasks: calls, bills, things to fix, to mend, to wash, to write, to ask, to read, to respond. Press the little button and here comes—*The Wizard of Oz!*—slightly fuzzy on the aging machine, but nevertheless there they are: Dorothy and her affecting cohorts just at the moment of disillusion, when they discover the Wizard behind the curtain with his deceitful contraption: a good man, he ruefully admits, but not a very good wizard. In dismay, the Tin Man and the Cowardly Lion and the Scarecrow each lament, and each is presented with what he most wants: the Tin Man, a heart; the Lion, a badge of courage; the Scarecrow, a brain. And Dorothy, eventually, gets to go home.

This luminous tale illustrates how a literary imagination sets up play between figural and literal reality, making a seamless narrative which gives birth to the difference between them (there is no *real* Wizard) as well as the dependence of one on the other. Dorothy insists, when she wakes at home, that she has been somewhere, and she is right: she has moved from Kansas to Oz to Kansas again, and in that perilous journey has become the author of her own destiny, having lost not so much her innocence as her credulity, not so much her will to believe as her dependence on others. I once asked my class of students in World Humanities where they would look to find examples of a "moral imagination." They stared blankly at me, wondering to what I was referring. I coached them along. Finally they answered: "a lawyer," "a doctor," "a priest," "my parents." Not one of them suggested a novel, a memoir, a poem, a painting, a film. Understand: I was not asking about places in which a moral code or view is prescribed or proscribed, but one in which the world is presented as one in which there are questions, irresolutions, quandaries, predicaments that allow the reader/viewer to negotiate his or her responses, responses which might quicken tolerance while enlivening inquiry. The moral imagination does not simplify, but wavers and blurs, complicates and elaborates, distinctions. Traditionally, the moral imagination is housed in literary structures where an imagination braids the sites of reality and truth by engaging our capacity to interpret, which, in turn, helps us toward moral clarity and ethical choice.

lit·er·al, a. & n. 1. Of, in, expressed by, letter(s) of alphabet (~ *error,* also ~ as n., misprint). 2. Following the letter, text, or exact or original words (~ *translation, transcript,* etc.) whence ~ISM(4) n. 3. Taking words in their usual or primary sense & applying the ordinary rules of grammar, without mysticism or allegory or metaphor (~ *interpretation; I hear nothing in the ~ sense of the word,* with the ears as opp. other means of getting news), whence ~ISM(3), ~IST (2), nn.; (of persons) prosaic, matter-of-fact. 4. So called without exaggeration (~ *decimation;* often incorrectly used, as a ~ *flood of pamphlets*).

lit·er·al, adj. (OF. [F. *litteral*], fr. LL. *litteralis, literalis,* fr. L. *littera, litera,* a letter. See LETTER; cf. LITERATURE.) 1. According to the "letter," or the natural or usual construction and implication of a writing or expression; following the ordinary and apparent sense of the words; not allegorical or metaphorical; as, the *literal* meaning of a passage; the *literal* execution of a command. 2. Hence: a Literally so termed; so called without inaccuracy; as, the *literal* destruction of an army. b True to the fact, not exaggerated or embellished; as a *literal* description. c Giving a strict or literal construction; unimaginative; matter-of-fact;—applied to persons.

5. Rag

> The space now is such that a horned roiled (figure) has no origin, is entirely the foreground, floating on a flesh-hued cloud. The background is here, the horned roil does not arise from it. The demon floating has no origin, spatially. Spatially is emotionally here. I want to subject emotion to space; and also to subject observation to it.[10]

As if Atlantis could haul the past up into the sky, the weightless void of a there that has no here, and dump it, disassociated and infinite, bursts of event, lost loves, revolutions, *matter matter, murmur murmur,* all the hoodlum detritus of our hopes, dreams, triumphs, and defeats, construed into the frozen region. The screen's flatness, the world's flatness. Loss of depth of field, of vision, of the tactile variety of hair, skin, limb, the *disembodied* wilderness in which we now live; metaphor of the cycle expunged, surface lifted up so as to exclude periphery and vanishing point, whatever illusions of inclusion we had invented along the way. A bar. Television on, sound on, music on, talk, eye contact, orders, moneys exchanging hands, things on a wall, scents. How much is enough? All on the same plane, on the horizontal field that is not horizontal at all but flat, upright and flat. This is the space on which the literal basks.

> But the Object of your thought is really its entire content or deliverance, neither more nor less. It is a vicious use of speech to take out a substantive kernel from its content and call that its object; and it is an equally vicious use of speech to add a substantive kernel not particularly included in its content, and call that its object . . .[11]

At City College of New York, where I taught, the English department was in a state of protracted demoralization that verged on despair. I will not enumerate all the reasons why, assuming you know something about the situation of public education and the general low priority it has in political will and public discourse. But I will say that students came to the college without the ability to read or write at more than the most rudimentary levels. Faced with the syllabus of a World Humanities, which included the *Odyssey* and *Macbeth,* the *Metamorphoses,* the *Sundiata,* and even some English Romantic poems, many students were simply unable to comprehend figurative writing.

> A reading is strong . . . to the extent that it encounters and propagates the surprise of otherness. The impossible but necessary task of the reader is to set herself up to be surprised.[12]

The racism and classism hidden in the current pedagogical approach to the teaching of writing and reading is not something that is being discussed. Many if not most of the students at City College are first- or second-generation immigrants—Chinese, Spanish, French, Arabic, Korean, Japanese—and the view is they need to learn to read and write English as a special skill to help them get jobs; the young black woman who taught Composition called this "cash English."

> "That American conditions have produced the opposite of Dickensian high-definition personality has to do with the uncrowded social space into which each new person has to insert himself or herself and with the subtraction of differences from diverse immigrant groups that is the first stage of personal self-characterization in American life. Cultivation, even manufacture of difference played the part in the nineteenth century European city culture of Baudelaire, Dickens and Dostoevsky that subtraction of difference played in the United States. This Whitman catches in his wonderful phrase "the loose drift of character." The "Making of Americans" as Gertrude Stein called it occurred first of all by those thousands of negations by which the children of Italian-Americans, German-Americans, and Chinese-Americans erased letter by letter the accent, style of laughter, customs of family life, dress, and idiom of the old country so as to be, at last,

simply American. In every American personality there exists a past history of erasure.[13]

Among my graduate writing students there was a noticeable deficit of references to sources, literary or otherwise, outside their immediate foreground; among African-American students, I found a tendency to write from the perspective of racial identity that demanded a public stance toward the self, as if the self were a stereotypical example whose voice must uphold, and reflect, the most unnuanced and prolific negative assumptions about black life in America. *Individuality* was conflated with *identity;* approbation seeming to come from the litany of cathartic self-expositions and exhibitions, the fast food of our social constructions. These students were reluctant to depart from stereotype, from set expectations, lest they be perceived as traitors to their community. They did not see that such loyalty also constitutes a form of betrayal, that the self-images they promulgate are largely those propagated by white racist America. This is a paradox, of course, where on the one hand you have an institutionalized approach to writing as self-expression, and on the other you have a numbing reiteration of status quo assumptions about identity, in which an individuated experience is forsworn.

The literal can be dressed up in figurative language, and this is often mistaken for poetry: banal situations and ideas gussied up (as my mother would have put it) in fancy, poetic, language. But powerful figural language is based on the risky business of undoing the stale promises which threaten to undermine the real opportunities our particular ethos might hold. This idea of promise is not literal, not the usual junk jargon of opportunistic commerce, but is constituted by a vision that puts the past in the service of, at risk to, the future. American democracy, after all, rests on a few declarations that animate the distance between intangible promise and manifest fact. This distance is essentially linguistic; it embodies a literary paradigm.

6. She Thinks Too Much and Refuses to Go. In Fear of Abstraction,

she sidles up to a Particular. "Hey there, you with the stars in your eyes," she whispers, "love never made a fool of you, I bet."

"Can't say as it has. I like to stick to things as they are."

"Like?"

"Well, you know: breakfast, lunch, dinner. Early to bed, early to rise. Two heads are better than one. A stitch in time saves nine. I like, in particular, numbers."

"But numbers are more abstract than anything else! Remember our credo: No Ideas but in Things!"

"Quite frankly, I never understood what the good doctor meant by that. I suppose he must have meant that ideas are formed through or by the relationship between things, on which so much depends. But things, if he meant objects, do not have ideas, only persons do, at least as far as we know. It must have had something to do with a desire for a poetics based on the objective real world rather than on subjective perceptions, so-called, of that world, feelings about it. It is the empiricist modernist monkey on the back of the solitary weeper. Of course Stevens tries to subvert this intolerable duality by bringing imagination in as a major figure, ready to make love to reality. Wittgenstein gets it right when he talks about color and pain."

Or look at this:

LETTER 3

Our errors at zero: milk for mist, grin
for limbs, mouths for names—or else hours

of barks, stammers and vanishings, nods
along a path of dissolving ice. The sign

we make for "same as"
before whatever steps and walls,

shutters flapping in the lighted body
called null or called vocative. I'd wanted to ask

about dews, habits of poplar, carousel,
dreamless wealth, nets, embers

and folds, the sailing ship "desire"
with its racks and bars

just now setting out. This
question to spell itself. And the waves of us

following what follows,
retelling ourselves

what we say we've said
in this tongue which will pass[14]

7. Penance/penance

Gentle Reader:

I had not meant to complain, but to celebrate, as the urban might be said to celebrate the peripheral and autonomous, gathering in and giving out in untold narratives, creating an infinite pattern of possible coherences. The fact that the millions who live there are for the most part indifferent about the enterprise of poetry is often liberating, almost giddy in its implied freedom. When the bus loops up out of the tunnel, and the city comes into view like an enormous postcard of itself, the sense of this vast animated map of human will, thwarted or not, is one which suggests that there is no centrality, no apex, no order other than the one each of us singles out, like a constellation in the beaded veil of the night sky. I get to bead my own constellation and then to fling it up, an image traced on the dark for all, or for none, to see.

Or you may leave it   forever   and never return to it   ,
          for we pos-sess nothing   .   Our poetry now
            is the reali-zation   that we possess   nothing
      .   *Anything   therefore   is a delight*
(since we do not   pos-sess it)   and thus   need not fear its loss
      .   *We need not destroy the   past: it is gone;*
at any moment,   it might reappear and   seem to be   and be the present
      .   *Would it be a   repetition?   Only if we thought we*
owned it,   but since we don't,   it is free   and so are we
      .   *Most anyone knows a-bout the future*
        and how un-certain it is   .[15]

THE NIGHT SKY III

1. Peace

on earth, good will toward all. Surprised to find *peace* lurking within *penance*,
along with the enclosing, confining *pen* and its liberating twin, my favorite, a
dark

2. green

one, lost now. It was sent to me from Paris by a French poet. Now I have the
option of telling you a long anecdote about how it came to pass that this per-
son sent me a beautiful Waterman green pen. I could then also tell you how
I lost it (not at the movies). You know how it is: you find yourself divulging or
relating something, an incident, to a person or persons, you have their atten-
tion, they appear to be listening, and you suddenly pause and ask yourself,
"Is this at all interesting to anyone but me?"

> "But when I imagine something, something certainly happens!"
> Well, something happens—and then I make a noise. What for?
> Presumably in order to tell what happens.—But how is *telling*
> done? When are we said to *tell* anything?—What is the language-
> game of telling?[1]

The undeniable privilege of an empty space proffered, even if it exists
merely to give support to adjacent sales pitches, which are not in the margins
except by visual convention.
The text *penned in*.
The as yet unforeclosed.
The "open" invitation, the "blank" before "blanket."
(The bank before banquet.)

The tablet erased of residue, the mind's field without inhibition, not a fence in sight. But watch where you step or you might set off an event:

"hitting and killing the driver"
"in hope of maintaining calm"
"one crew member was killed"
"weather conditions were good"
"assigned to the carrier *Enterprise*"
"engineers investigating five cases of . . ."
"if an airbag should expand"
"if there was a defect"
"the Dow Jones is up more than . . ."
"and skies are sunny"

You have a sense that the mindscreen is violent, an obstruction, possibly a violent obstruction. Not so much filter as hindrance, letting too little through. Mallarmé claimed to have seen, to have been, Nothingness. This absence he vowed to make into presence, an Absolute stripped of its Figuration. Michel Leiris (in an essay on painter Joan Miró) writes:

> Today it certainly seems that before writing, painting, sculpting, or composing anything worthwhile, one has to have accustomed oneself to an exercise analogous to that performed by certain Tibetan ascetics for the purpose of acquiring what they call, more or less (I say "more or less" because the language of the West, which presents everything in a dramatic form, must very probably turn out to be inadequate), the *understanding of emptiness*.[2]

The stories I could tell, if only this were another century and we were writing to each other over distances to tell ourselves this or that anecdote, this or that notion, not yet polished to certitude. Exchanging mere hunches; nothing like testimony or even so much as intention's attention, just a murmuring up from the other side—a butterfly flits from flower to flower, anointing each with its secrets—

(The cursor pulses, pumped by an artificial heart.)

In the morning, I stare. Otherwise, the day is a rattled cage.

With a glance I shall gather up the virginal absence scattered through this solitude and steal away with it; just as, in memory of

a special site, we pick one of those magical, still unopened wa-
terlilies which suddenly spring up there and enclose, in their
deep white, a nameless nothingness made of unbroken reveries,
of happiness never to be—made of my breathing, now, as it stops
for fear that she may show herself. Steal silently away, rowing bit
by bit, so that the illusion may not be shattered by the stroke of
oars, nor the plashing of the visible foam, unwinding behind me
as I flee, reach the feet of any chance walker on the bank, nor
bring with it the transparent resemblance of the theft I made of
the flower of my mind.[3]

There are times, this being one, late November, everything, from air to
hair, turning gray, when a person wants to withdraw into a steady-state of re-
ception, to become as mutely supple as a telescope scanning the night sky.
Time darkens and opens simultaneously as if it were a large inhaling mouth
whose throat is a tunnel into which all the tidings of life incessantly spill. In
this mode or mood, writing seems antithetical, an outgoing against an in-
coming tide. *Murmur murmur,* references ebbing, tears of the saints staining
a chipped cup, the night's dream pulled away on morning's pale scarf. Lifting
the voice up over vacancy, wondering at the naked eaves. The cud, the smol-
dering detritus. I bought a new television yesterday. I lugged it home, a heavy
box, black object within, ugly, inert. Once turned on, an upheaval—cars, so
many cars, and bright smiling women, and persons talking about stories in
Genesis, about Jacob wrestling with the Angel, and these stories *underwrit-
ten.* Fund upon fund. The Corporation for Public Broadcasting. Outside of
the frame, a silence. Inside the frame, the churning organs of America.
Remote control.
Another morning with a pall cast over it, sky lowered with cloud, radiance
concealed. Weather tells the day's time, unfurling aimless plots that mime
our goings on. *And then, and then.* What was it like when the day opened
with only one plot cast up instead of the braids we now confront—multiplic-
ities of facts and instances which accompany our own narrow course? Writ-
ing is a way of steadying this? Of ferreting one strand from so many? There is
no way the linearity of language can possibly accommodate this—the radio,
on now, Steve Post on WNYC reading this morning's news: "As a civil rights
leader, he apparently offered information . . ." "The state reimburses the
state for each inmate . . ." "New York City Hall was a place for protests
yesterday . . . the high cost of AIDS drugs . . ." "Campaign war chest totaled
six point two million dollars . . ." Writing into or against these renditions of

the day demands a kind of tenacious hubris, as if to claim that what you have to say can compete with those others, that those of you who may be reading this now (weeks or even years later, an infinite number of stories later) have chosen to do so, thinking that I might tell you, tell you what?

What is the language-game of telling?

What do I want to be telling you—"you" in the plural, that is? How to span the infinite gap between the personal and the public, if you in fact constitute the *public*. This could be the subject, this could be the

topic sentence

we, I mean I, have been searching for. If I were to isolate a single perplexity for "us," poets as well as presidents, it would address this disturbed sphere where the distinction between the private (personal) and public (political) has all but vanished, and in its vanishing our language-games of telling have become hopelessly tangled. If our current technologies have now made communications between and among each other virtually instantaneous, they have also all but eliminated our sense of *physical* presence; even our voices are mediated by screens and machines. Disembodied, we float on a sea of words and images. We have endless exposure to every conceivable visual and verbal permutation of human emotion—passions of love and hate, crimes of head and heart, images of the sick, the dying, the dead, the grief-stricken—but they all take place in a place which *displaces* response—compassion or empathy or disgust or praise or blame (although representations of these are ceaselessly, grimly available). In cities, we move through the streets clinging to cell phones, talking aloud, so one walks along eavesdropping on half a conversation in dead-eyed anonymity; the only persons who ever speak now to others are either homeless or tourists.

> To appropriate the historic transformations of human nature that capitalism wants to limit to the spectacle, to link together image and body in a space where they can no longer be separated, and thus to forge the whatever body, whose *physis* is resemblance— this is the good that humanity must learn how to wrest from commodities in their decline. Advertising and pornography, which escort the commodity to the grave like hired mourners, are the unknowning midwives of this new body of humanity.[4]

The relation of poetry to the human body to the body politic. Can a poetics based on personal commentary and description compete with the disembodied idealizations and logos infesting (investing) the world? What difference is there between the voice recorded and the actual person standing before you, live, reciting or reading her or his work? What are the poetic structures that might wrest from these isolations a sense of presence, and is it important or necessary to do so? Are the text, the page, the book, vestiges of corporeal presence, talismanic remnants of a specific intimacy, a nearness, which involves each reader in physical sensation—touching, turning, receiving, establishing a rhythm of contact with an other through the most complexly attuned of our organs, the eye?

> The reader's position has been specified as that of the stranger. To write to him is to acknowledge that he is outside the words, at a bent arm's length, and alone with the book; that his presence to these words is perfectly contingent, and the choice to stay with them continuously his own; that they are his points of departure and origin. The conditions of meeting upon the word are that we—writer and reader—learn how to depart from them, leave them where they are; and then return to them, find ourselves there again. We have to learn to admit the successiveness of words, their occurrence one after the other, and their permanence in the face of our successions.[5]

Is one of our *jobs* to try to span, or notice, or illuminate, or articulate, the gap between private and public discourse and the activities associated with each? What is the nature of this gap? Where does it exist? In time? in space? Is it a gap at all, or is it rather a sequence of interleaving and overlapping contingencies? Is there a sense that, in the onrush, we find ourselves feeling increasingly both confined *and* outside, invaded *and* remote, active *and* static, isolated *and* surrounded? So close, and yet so far away. What can we (you and I) prevent from happening? What can we (you and I) cause to happen? For what or for whom are we responsible?[6]

> Ideology is a specious way of relating to the world. It offers human beings the illusion of an identity, of dignity, and of morality while making it easier for them to part with them. As the repository of something suprapersonal and objective, it enables people to deceive their conscience and conceal their true position and their inglorious *modus vivendi*, both from the world and from themselves. It is a very pragmatic but, at the same time, an ap-

parently dignified way of legitimizing what is above, below, and on either side. It is directed toward people and toward God. It is a veil behind which human beings can hide their own fallen existence, their trivialization, and their adaptation to the status quo.[7]

*

To engage in an imaginative project of rethinking our selves involves a particular way of understanding some of the connections that might be made between space and the practice of being free and the expressions of their various relationships in aesthetics and ethics. It involves as well a willingness to lose a kind of certainty associated with the solidity of one's own habitation of voice, one's ownership, if you will, of the language through which one enunciates one's self, presenting one's self to the world in the effort to be free. It also entails an element of old-fashioned liberal tolerance, made fresh through an admission of the instabilities of the truths one might admit or reject from serious consideration.[8]

3. Not Here

I don't really understand corporations, unless fear is a form of understanding. Then again I don't understand many things. But there is a sense that the world is steadily and increasingly glued together by or through them, their strategies and lingo, their mergers and downsizings and profits. *Top down, bottom line.* An invisible ubiquitous *they* has haunted the whole twentieth century, coiling around places of decision and power, colliding or colluding authority with autonomy, pulling action and consequence further and further apart into an aporia of unimaginable size. I do not mean to imply that corporations are the new enemy, like the military-industrial complex, or terrorism, abstract entities evoked to threaten and instill insecurity and fear. Nonetheless, one does have a sense of growing monster enterprises wielding immense influence over our institutions: universities, publishing houses, magazines, museums, libraries, cinemas, film, radio and television stations, each more and more dependent on, beholden to, and "managed" by corporations whose purposes and goals are severed from those of the institutions they own and their individual employees.

On the radio yesterday, a commentator used the phrase "the chaotic garden of private enterprise." The old word "wild" is replaced by the new word "chaos," thus creating an oxymoronic object, a chaotic garden, that calls up the ungardened, urban, multiplex landscape in which we actually live, the "garden" wholly metaphoric, invoking no rural images; we have no mental pictures to accommodate ideas of chaos with ideas of gardens. A cultivated chaos.

> *I placed a jar in Tennessee,*
> *And round it was, upon a hill.*
> *It made the slovenly wilderness*
> *Surround that hill.*
>
> *The wilderness rose up to it,*
> *And sprawled around, no longer wild,*
> *The jar was round upon the ground*
> *And tall and of a port in air.*
>
> *It took dominion everywhere.*
> *The jar was gray and bare.*
> *It did not give of bird or bush,*
> *Like nothing else in Tennessee.*[9]

Corporation. *Core, coeur, corps, cop, co-opt, poor.*

There was a time when institutions had distinct personalities, recognizable ways of behaving that reflected their interests; sometimes the personality was a reflection of the person who founded them. For example, Time Inc., now Time Warner. I worked for Time Inc. a long time ago, when it was essentially still part of Henry Luce's empire, adding a new publication from time to time, slowly branching out into books and television. I worked for *Sports Illustrated* magazine. The best thing that happened to me there was meeting Cassius Clay, aka Muhammad Ali. I was delivering mail from the mail room to the various editors' offices and suddenly there he was in a pale yellow angora sweater. As it happens, I was wearing a pale yellow sleeveless cotton dress (this was before the hegemony of the black dress) and so Cassius/Muhammad and I briefly bonded over the coincidence. I believe there was some banter about which of us looked prettier (he did). At that moment in time (are there moments not in time?) Cassius Clay was as famous as Michael Jordan is now, not only for his extraordinary grace and prowess as a boxer, but for his brilliant linguistic antics (which he used not only to amuse but to persuade). At that time, high-profile athletes did not sign huge contracts with corporations to promote their wares, at least as far as I know. At that time, there were only a few brands of white shoes, called sneakers or, maybe, tennis shoes.

What is the language-game of telling?

Time Inc. had a personality. Those who worked for it were quickly acquainted with this. It modeled itself on the Patriarchal Family and, in fact, often hired persons whose immediate family had worked there, so as to carry on the tradition. Women were never editors, rarely writers. They did research, worked in the photo library and the newsroom, handmaidens to male writers and editors.

> To say "This combination of words makes no sense" excludes it from the sphere of language and thereby bounds the domain of language. But when one draws a boundary it may be for various kinds of reason. If I surround an area with a fence or a line or otherwise, the purpose may be to prevent someone from getting in or out; but it may also be part of a game and the players be supposed, say, to jump over the boundary; or it may show where the property of one man ends and that of another begins, and so on. So if I draw a boundary line that is not yet to say what I am drawing it for.[10]

Divisible day, what vocabulary?

4. tenses

I have been asking myself about the nature of memory again. Rememory. It has occurred to me that when we are writing we are remembering not the past or an event in the past, not a thing or a person or a flower, a place or a meal, a painting or a song, but first and foremost we are remembering *words*. This is the primal quarry that sits under whatever specific sites we elaborate into what we write (about). When we write we are trying to remember the right word. But what constitutes "right"? Accuracy? The word that will carry most clearly the sense, or senses, we intend? In a poem, if the words remembered are the same words that have always been used to carry that sense, the result is a cliché, isn't it, that is, a phrase which places us in an all too familiar space so that it fails to bring the reader into his present? But let's say that the problem for the poet is not essentially one of vocabulary.

The problem is how to take the old vocabulary and put it in new settings, new structures, which revivify it. So the function of memory is not simple: one needs to know the words and what they mean, but one needs to forget the settings in which they are habitually found.

On his little book on Proust, Samuel Beckett comments, "Proust had a bad memory—because he had an inefficient habit. The man with a good memory does not remember anything because he does not forget anything. His memory is uniform, a creature of routine, at once a condition and function of his impeccable habit, an instrument of reference instead of an instrument of discovery."

To imagine a language is to imagine a form of life.[11]

Joan Retallack writes:

> It may seem that our uses of language have always been overwhelmingly occupied with memory, with telling ourselves more and more stories, gathering more and more factoids for our collective consciousness—of late, culturally mutated into microchip archive. So much so that we may forget the zero-sum fact that knowing is itself a kind of forgetting. Forgetting the other sides of structures, for instance, forgetting to surprise ourselves into entertaining the currently inconceivable; forgetting to pass from one world to the next, not as sci-fi adventure but in order to envision things better than what we have resigned and habituated ourselves to. This is enormously difficult. It sometimes takes what at first glance may seem to be cruel and unusual artifice.[12]

There are a number of contemporary poets, Retallack among them, for whom the act of writing poems, the taking up of the social role "poet," is specifically linked to a desire to reconstruct, or reimagine, contemporary ways of (thinking about) life, what Retallack herself has called a "poethics." This reimagining is understood, I think, as a rigorous re-evaluation of the various ways in which language constructs both who and how we are (in) the world.

The attention of these poets is to linguistic *structures*. The old word "form" has been replaced by the new word "structure," to foreground the architectonic nature of language, the ways in which language-acts construct our understanding of the world. What constitutes the "real world" is a kind of momentary consensus of different subjective responses; history is the archive of such responses, and as such is open to endless renovation as different subjectivities come to animate their versions. To tolerate these different visions and versions might mean a renovation of what we mean by individual (the one) and what we mean by community (the many).

The poet Kathleen Fraser, in a marvelous talk she gave at a (1996) translation conference at Barnard College,[13] spoke persuasively about the many contemporary women poets who have extended Charles Olson's poetics, articulated in his seminal essay "Projective Verse" as well as in many of his essays, letters, and poems. Olson brought a new emphasis to the poem's physical, visual presence, its location in the world not as "the lyrical interference of the individual as ego, of the 'subject' and his soul," suggesting that the poem, like the poet, is "an object among objects."[14] Olson's notion of *composition by field*, most fully realized in the later *Maximus* poems, frees the poem's body from the left margin, the spine of the book, and relocates it in the field of the page, *foregrounding* its spatial/material/visual aspects. This visual deployment of the poem shifts the reader's attention away from temporality and narrativity toward a metonymic mapping, an embodiment. Fraser shows how many women poets, including Susan Howe, Barbara Guest, Myung Mi Kim, Laura Moriarty, Hannah Weiner, Norma Cole, Rachel Blau du Plessis, and herself (among others) have variously explored the visual/physical properties of language, the physical relation of word to word and word to page, as a way to, as Fraser has it, "em/body space and its terrerae of human utterance."

Here we find a radical development of the long tradition of women writing through a sense of limitation and boundary, both within their bodies and within their dwellings, out into the uncertain shifting planes/plains of multi-perspective, layered inclusions, which characterize and reflect their (feminine/feminist) perceptions. The text, embodied, becomes a *matrix* for gestating/generating a new poetic topos, free from dominant modes of narrating which pen the poet and the poem in a single alignment of self/language/world. You might say that the work of these poets is partly recuperative, a desire to retrieve the lost space of the body, an effort to bring us, by analogy, into a relation to physical contingencies of human contact.

Michel Foucault, pressed in an interview to explain his apparent inattention to the various tropes for space in his own writing, commented, "A critique could be carried out of this devaluation of space that has prevailed for generations. Did it start with Bergson, or before? Space was treated as dead, fixed, the undialectical, the immobile. Time, on the contrary, was richness, fecundity, life, dialectic."

In America, you might want to assert the opposite: that *space* is the prevailing animating trope, that our narratives have been drawn from it, from a constant "dialogue" with boundaries, locales, maps, crossings, discoveries, movements (and their realization in ownership, land use, and so forth) in which the perceiving *eye* is privileged over the receiving *ear*. So Olson, writing about Herman Melville, comments:

> Congruence was spatial intuition to Kant, and if I am right that Melville did possess its powers, he had them by his birth, from his time of the world, locally America. As it developed in his century, congruence, which had been the measure of the space a solid fills in two of its positions, became a point-by-point mapping power of such flexibility that anything which stays the same, no matter where it goes and into whatever varying conditions (it can suffer deformation), it can be followed, and, if it is art, led, including, what is so important to prose, such physical quantities as velocity, force and field strength.[15]

Olson, I think, wanted to claim for poetry a terrain, a mental geography, that would collapse the separation between, and privileging of, sight over sound, giving each equal status on the linguistic field of the poem. And, like the contemporaneous Abstract Expressionist painters, he was interested in the relationship between the discrete (the one, the particular, the gesture) and the continuous (many, the abstract, ground); and, like them, he understood that a unique American aesthetic vocabulary came from relation, scale, and measure, rather than through narrativity or substitution (metaphor, analogy, symbol). The structures that would come from such a vocabulary would move laterally, horizontally, rather than vertically, suggesting American ideals of democratic mobility.

5. Returns

The day after Charles Olson died, I gave my first poetry reading, in Plymouth, England. I read with an English poet named John Keyes, who, in a state of anguish over Olson's death, read Olson, drunkenly, to the assembled ladies of Plymouth. It may seem strange, but in certain literary circles in London (where I then lived), the poets and artists around Black Mountain were viewed as avatars. The reasons for this are too numerous and complex to go into here. There were, however, a number of persons then in London who

had direct contact with these figures, including the cultural critic Suzi Gab-
lik (who had been at Black Mountain) and the expatriate American painter
RB Kitaj, who was a great reader of poetry (I met Robert Duncan at his
house). Eric Mottram, a teacher, poet, critic, and editor, was an astute and
enthusiastic supporter of American poetic departures from classic Anglo tra-
ditions. *In Cold Hell, in Thicket*: My copy, now dog-eared and discolored,
easily flips open to the title poem—

> *In cold hell, in thicket, how*
> *abstract (as high mind, as not lust, as love is) how*
> *strong (as strut or wing, as polytope, as things are*
> *constellated) how*
> *strung, how cold*
> *can a man stay (can men) confronted*
> *thus?*

> *All things are made bitter, words even*
> *are made to taste like paper, wars get tossed up*
> *like lead soldiers used to be*
> *(in a child's attic) lined up*
> *to be knocked down, as I am,*
> *by firings from a spit-hardened fort, fronted*
> *as we are, here, from where we must go*

> *God, that man, as his acts must, as there is always*
> *a thing he can do, can raise himself, he raises*
> *on a reed he raises his*

> *Or, if it is me, what*
> *he has to say*[16]

For cadence alone it is spellbinding; the turns from line to line demonstrate
Olson's use of the left margin to at once animate and anchor the semantic
field of the poem. I remember feeling that the subject of the poem was over-
whelmingly *masculine*, that I had almost no point of direct identification
with it, but that the peculiar uneven shaping and interleaving, pauses,
breathings—all those parentheses!—seemed a possibility for a poetics free
from the singularity of tone/voice which was so prized as proof of a poet's
validity.

When I lived in London, I worked for a time at the Institute of Contemporary Arts, where I wangled myself into a position in which I could plan poetry readings. I planned a series, called Poetry In/formation, on contemporary Eastern European, French, and American poetry. We raised enough money from various sources to invite one American poet. The poet was John Ashbery, who was not yet well known on either side of the Atlantic (the year was 1971). Ashbery's presence in London had the effect of a mild tornado. He read his poems on more than one occasion, poems as if written on the air itself, filling the atmosphere with a peculiar, vital vocal wind that seemed to catch everything up in its wake. One of the poems from that period that astonished me is a short lyric, "A Blessing in Disguise," which stages a dazzling spatial-temporal slippage, a vertiginous cinematic fluidity within the confines of its seven quatrains, showing, as Ashbery so often has, how so-called traditional forms can liberate semantic boundaries. Here are the last four stanzas:

> *I cannot ever think of me, I desire you*
> *For a room in which the chairs ever*
> *Have their backs turned to the light*
> *Inflicted on the stone and paths, the real trees*
>
> *That seem to shine at me through a lattice toward you.*
> *If the wild light of this January day is true*
> *I pledge me to be truthful unto you*
> *Whom I cannot ever stop remembering.*
>
> *Remembering to forgive. Remember to pass beyond you into the day*
> *On the wings of the secret you will never know.*
> *Taking me from myself, in the path*
> *Which the pastel girth of the day has assigned to me.*
>
> *I prefer "you" in the plural, I want "you,"*
> *You must come to me, all golden and pale*
> *Like the dew and the air.*
> *And then I start getting this feeling of exaltation.*[17]

6. "And

then I start" . . . A poem that ends with the beginning of an exaltation, caused by the subsuming of the individual "you" (the beloved) into the plural "you" (audience). The space of the poem breaks open, the confines of its own stanzas (Italian *stanza*: standing, stopping-place, dwelling, room, strophe) are transgressed. The "room" we are in is not quite indoors and not quite out; it is neither a domestic sitting room, a church, nor a public auditorium. This transforming agility is achieved by the poem's syntax, which blurs directionality and perspective in order to create rooms (stanzas) without walls, what Giorgio Agamben has called a *"topos outopos* (placeless place, no-place place) in which our experience of being-in-the-world is situated."[18] Closer here to Dickinson than to Whitman, Ashbery gracefully configures an intimate, personal voicing onto a public ground, the ground that is "plural" in its potential expansion among the individual *yous* that make *us*.

7. Abstraction

I saw the film *The English Patient* the same afternoon as I saw a Jasper Johns exhibition at the Museum of Modern Art. Some of the delicacy and nuance of the Michael Ondaatje novel found its way onto the screen, his brilliant threading of a thematics of boundaries, between cultures and persons, between personal (love) and historical (war), violence and obsession. Jasper Johns also found an iconography to attach an inward, almost hermetic sensibility to "public" images—the flag, the map, so forth. In each case, our attention is drawn away from conventional modes of telling and showing (the novel's plot; the picture's subject) to the material itself. In each case, the result is not an arid game, but an elucidation of the continuum between private vision and public (common) knowledge. The consequences of this knowledge are experienced as aesthetic pleasure.

Lateral, permuting, reiterating surfaces are evident, differently, in the work of Gertrude Stein and John Cage, in the paintings of Jackson Pollock and Andy Warhol and, to some degree, of Willem de Kooning, in the works of more contemporary artists such as Agnes Martin, Robert Ryman, Carl Andre, Brice Marden, Donald Judd, and, more recently still, Ann Hamilton (although she has radically reimagined the idea of repetition through her interest in language); in composers such as Steve Reich, John Adams, and Terry Riley. In each case the distinction between figure and ground is muted; the "figure" is extended over an entire field in a sequence of unique but similar marks/gestures or placements: a rhythm of contingency; or else is rearranged to emphasize scale and relation, as in the work of Philip Guston and Elizabeth Murray. The relation of part to part, rather than part to whole, the internal syntax, is the point of interest; the construction of the work revealed, on its surface, is, in some sense, the content of the work. There is perhaps in our initial iconography a contracting conjugation *space/place/locale/local,* a peculiar span from abstract to particular ("radiant details") which privileges neither. This system of relations is spatial rather than temporal—it resists the implied narrativity of figure/ground and promotes instead an uninflected parameter in which incidents (proximities) occur. Both Walt Whitman and Emily Dickinson, in entirely different ways, announce a poetics of (American) space: Whitman by his insistence on a Self as Representative and Inclusive (a specific instance or example, an incident, one among many, leaf among leaves), and Dickinson by releasing narrative into prismatic structures, so her poems do not so much move forward in time (tell stories) as turn in space: they are aspectual, perspectival: mobiles, constellations.[19]

Space in many of these works is neither secular nor sacred, the landscape neither urban nor rural, domestic nor wild. It is the space in which a body might be found telling. Perhaps the language-game of telling is a game played on a board, a field. What are the rules? Who makes them? Who moves first? Monopoly? Baseball? Chess, anyone?

THE NIGHT SKY IV

Inheritance is never a *given*, it is always a task.

—Jacques Derrida

1. Action

Victory and Doubt dance at a masked ball; together they form a single figure, a gorgeous Thing, its many petals floating in perfumed air, the spectral filmy effluence of costume: Vienna's charade. Their embrace moves across the boundary-less floor, a fluid duet in which there is no dominant gesture, only permutation and extension. In the ballroom, all mirrors have been removed and with them the dissonance between real and fictive, ideal and true, vanished. Neither male nor female, neither soul nor body, these distinctions also have been erased by the equivocations and valences of the spectral conversation.

Under this music
flags of memory

logged
streaming

unquelled at the root of news
its signature ode

house rescaled above the river
road altered

and such details as if hinges
particular war, particular lie

bodies concealed in the mattress
indented there

seals and sayings
the theater's opaque window

beautiful arms
the boys' desiring

familiar actors
speaking their durations

A room with a window, a room without a window, a windowless room. So that the light must be from another, artificial, source. Here, we had been in bed, the bed took up most of the room; it was where all the dreams were stored. Then the bed was removed, but the place of the dreams remained and so the room became darkly crowded. This dark crowd shifted in its shadows, shadows without objects, like the layered shadows of buildings on a late afternoon listing out into and through the tunnels between them. There was a sense of collapse, of density, as if portions of the air had settled in strata from which temporal shifts had been excluded. It could be called a reliquary or an homage.

The days.

The unanalyzed partition, the event undisclosed.

Slippage and delay, the outbound current.

Another month begins. It comes with a thaw: sodden clumps drop and there are intermittent dribblings and thuds, a sense that something, or perhaps everything, is leaking. The second month, the infant year. It was during this month that my sister died and now I have lingered on, each year modulating distance and nearness as I travel away from her death and toward my own. With each crossing of the same, each incursion, I try to make

2. Peace

with her death as I witness the odd sense of temporal cessation: the threshold cannot be crossed.

Finally, the third type of aporia, the impossible, the antinomy, or
the contradiction, is a nonpassage because its elementary milieu
does not allow for something that could be called passage, step,
walk, gait, displacement, or replacement, a kinesis in general.
There is no more path (*odos, methodos, Weg,* or *Holzweg*). The im-
passe itself would be impossible.The coming of the event would
have no relation to the passage of what happens or comes to pass.
In this case, there would be an aporia because there is not even
any space for an aporia determined as experience of the step of
the edge, crossing or not of some line, relation to some spatial fig-
ure of the limit. No more movement or trajectory, no more *trans-*
(transport, transposition, transgression, translation, and even
transcendence).[1]

These anniversaries are peculiar, they make their own discrete shape, infin-
ity's circle eight, during which the event summons itself again, its authority,
its mark. I am thinking this as this month begins with its thaw. I am thinking
about how the Voice gets lost, wanders out of earshot, and of how the poem
wants to resist this lost Voice, recuperate it, bring it back into earshot. The
poem seems to want to do this but it too seems to be at an impasse. We have
now many acknowledgments of this, we speak about exiles and margins and
nomads and we go so far as to make of this condition a sort of privilege: the
freedom of the wanderer, the exhilaration of the unaffiliated and unattached;
perhaps, even, the ancient jittery wisdom of the fool. We join the diaspora
willingly (is that an oxymoron?), the ragtag outpost oppositional insurgency,
gathering up shards as they fall on the path that leads to no place and comes
from no place. But this fable of *excursus* outside the confines of the con-
textual map, each of us still tattooed with the emblems of our separate and
several contingencies, has as its counter, its underside, the obliterating con-
dition of *banishment,* of a deliberate, conscious Will that expunges from the
conversation at table (the inscription on the tablet) these very options and
privileges.

Anne Hutchinson to John Winthrop: "I wish to know wherefore I am
banished."

Anxious about all the heresies of our moment: heresies of identity, of be-
longing, as well as those of the passing millennium, we are contracted and
caged in historical moment(um) and accumulation, and at the same time
rudderless, at liberty, infinitely free. We do not know what scale we are in,

which language does not help us to ascertain. (As I wrote that last sentence, something crashed across the open window: meteor? bullet? stone? ice? big bird pecking?) The question *Who is speaking?* is answered only by another, *Who is listening?* The two questions pivot and surround each other like antagonists in a ring. Certainly some poets go happily along making their poems, and do not ask or need to ask about who is speaking/writing (I am!) or who is listening/hearing/reading (you are!), nor about where they come from (New Jersey!) nor where they are going (well, we thought we might go to Greece and visit the ruins!). But for some, there is a sense that the poem itself cannot step up to the first line without quavering like a soldier at his first glimpse of real war.

A militaristic vocabulary seeps in, like blood into a porous text/ile. Poor us, to be thus stained.

3. Green

> The next morning it was time to join the battalion in the field. They were way down south, near DiAn, where it still hadn't stopped raining. The other guys and I went down on that afternoon RON ship, another big Chinook, along with needed supplies. Once again, the lift-off toward the unknown, which would never get better with time. Once again, the anticipation of something unfathomable. Everyone in Quan Loi had spoken in lowered tones about the relentless fighting and heavy casualties the battalion was facing. I was in over my head, and would soon be exposed, ridiculed and then killed. I should have listened to my father, instead of seducing myself with war games. The gray murk outside and below was like the miasma of death itself. There was plenty of time to think about all of that before the ship finally began to rear and settle. I could see the battalion position slowly materialize below. It was a circle of tan-colored water with bits of green stuff floating in it, and it had all the appeal of dog vomit. As we hovered lower I could see that the green stuff was people. They were angrily waving their fists at us because our rotor blast was blowing their makeshift shelters away. As soon as the helicopter settled, I jumped out into the muddy water. Splat. Welcome to the end of the pipeline.[2]

*

But to place Grenier's latest work unproblematically in literary history also distorts it since it seems to manifest a desire to escape all literary historical grids and to make direct contact with the world via pen and paper. His writing has become intensely personal and does not seem constructed to represent anything other than itself. But though his allegiance to a group identity such as language writing is now decidedly tepid, I find a conflict in his work that occurs to some extent in the work of other language writers. At a basic level, this conflict is between the autonomous activity of writing and the structures of meaning—letters, words, lines, sentences, genres—that cannot begin to exist without becoming entangled in the widest literary mediations . . . The singularity of each new word is simultaneously involved with its own compositional context and with the tactical battles of literary history: the future is up for grabs (and in some cases the past as well). Unsecured area is being fought over: reviewers, critics, students, professors, publishers, owners of book stores, not to mention the writer's own practice.[3]

Struggles, conflicts, tactical battles, unsecured territories: poetry wars. Who is the enemy? Another poem, lurking in the bushes, camouflaged, speaking in an unknown tongue? No, the enemy is annihilation, absolute silence, corpse. The poem wants to make apparent this most furtive and unknown of temporal realities, the slight hinge between *being here now* and *not being here now.* It wants to utter this space in its displaced eventness, to inscribe the Here with the Now, and the Now with the Here. It wants to be *figure and landscape, soldier and field, girl and meadow, babe and maternal embrace.* A poem gives forth this *configuration,* an object in the temporal unfurling of space (a book on a shelf) which houses the inert, innate traces of having been being. All this sounds like a bad rerun of Heideggerian lingo, but still one presses on.

It is true, Ulysses was really sailing, and one day, at a certain date, he encountered the enigmatic song. And so can say: now—this is happening now. But what happened now? The presence of a song which is still to be sung. And what did he touch in the presence? Not the occurrence of an encounter which had become present, but the overture of the infinite movement which is the encounter

itself, always at a distance from the place where it asserts itself
and the moment when it asserts itself, because it is this very dis-
tance, this imaginary distance, in which absence is realized, and
only at the end of this distance does the event begin to take
place, at a point where the proper truth of the encounter comes
into being and where, in any case, the words which speak it
would originate . . .[4]

As if you could see time and arrest it, portray it, catch up its obliterating
smile. Or hear time and record it, play that song again! and the trinkets call
from their shelves to be fondled: *this, this, this,* pointing at the igniting fur-
nace, glass twirled on its long stick like candy cane, molten, changing to hard
cold: a vase to hold spring flowers.

To stand on the threshold, to be always between.

The room where the heaped dreams are kept yellowing like letters in soft
boxes. The one who died dies again as the woman moves from room to room,
placing one thing next to another, making a still life. She pulls a long silver
spoon from its plastic wrappings. The dining room had a large table and long
dark sideboards. Behind the old woman the light fell against the window and
the stiff icily clad rhododendron leaves.

Upstairs, a long mirror in a dark movable frame.

4. re: Topic Sentence

If our sense of public space and public discourse is eclipsed, then so also is
our sense of individuality, the two are in fact interdependent: as one begins
to erode, the other goes with it, like opposite ends of the same scarf, fraying.
The question ghostly Heidegger asked comes like a searchlight on a foggy
shore: *What are poets for in a destitute time?* We seem to live within the para-
meters of a jaded and cowardly pragmatism, whose use-value equations have
stripped our capacity to recognize persons not driven exclusively by market
goals and their attendant signs of success. Poets are a special case within this
generalization, since there still attaches to the *idea* of the poet a belief that
poetry should be, is, exempt from market forces, from brute commerce and
commodification. And yet, into this abstract, distilled sanctity, the protected
solitude of Rilke's Beloved, comes the Angel of History with his Anthology
under his Wing.

It was then a matter of thinking another historicity—not a new history or still less a "new historicism," but another opening of event-ness as historicity that permitted one not to renounce, but on the contrary to open up access to an affirmative thinking of the messianic and emancipatory promise as promise: as *promise* and not as onto-theological or teleo-eschatological program or design. Not only must one not renounce the emancipatory desire, it is necessary to insist on it more than ever, it seems, and insist on it, moreover, as the very indestructibility of the "it is necessary." This is the condition of a re-politization, perhaps of another concept of the political. *But at a certain point promise and decision, which is to say responsibility, owe their possibility to the ordeal of undecidability which will always remain their condition* [italics mine].[5]

This instant, on the radio, someone asks, *What is extra time?*

My kitchen clock has stopped at twenty minutes to nine. I still walk past it dozens of times a day and glance at it to see what time it is.

What Henry James wrote cannot be transcribed into visual images propped up by a script, without denuding the entire work; the subject remains, the story remains, but the true content drifts away in the haze of the director's willed visualization. James wrote in the interstices of action, in the pulse between desire and intentionality, promise and consequence; at the core of his writing is an astonishment that human beings can communicate at all, given our divergent subjectivities, our cultural and social affiliations—gender, class, nationality, and so on. For James, only the most nuanced and hesitant of linguistic structures could possibly convey the actuality of any individual, and only the most animated invasion, such as love, could alter the set of a person's characteristic habits of being. The result was an indrawn *suspended* prose in which action and reaction are set on an intricate field of possibilities that erupt, sometimes violently, as human connection. (This is especially the case in his late novels, *The Wings of the Dove* and *The Golden Bowl*.) For James, only the dense textures of a nearly opaque prose, which worked not so much to delineate a plot as to map the variousness of a constant flow between subjective and objective states, could capture the irreducible complexity of individual natures: the unique self on one hand, and the web of cultural and social contexts that in/form that self, on the other. His brother William also championed the intricate elaborations and elaborate intricacies of the individual self, believing that the self was the only inviolable *property* we own.[6]

Not long ago I went to a talk by the writer Michael Brenson on the legendary French photographer Henri Cartier-Bresson. The talk was remarkable for its unstinting admiration for its subject as well as for its pronounced lack of critical/theoretical jargon. In it, Brenson spoke about the nature of perception. Perception, he said, is neither an observation nor a response, but a concentrated event or act in the world in which such binaries as intelligence and desire, reason and passion, are fused. He said also that the world in which we now live has not much use for perception as he understands it, but instead values "analysis, strategy, and instrumental thinking." He spoke of Cartier-Bresson's "discretion," which allowed his viewers to contemplate the nature of such affective dispositions as kindness, respect, and generosity.

According to Brenson, Cartier-Bresson had stopped taking photographs, and had turned to making drawings of his friends and of landscapes. This rejection of the camera interests me, since it implies that for some reason the camera had ceased to capture Cartier-Bresson's perceptions. One might hazard the guess that it was not the camera per se that failed, nor the eye of the great photographer, but rather a culture that has appropriated the world as image in the service of a reified iconicity that delivers a false sense of nearness, intimacy, and knowledge, and so short-circuits modes of vital relation and patience which these perceptions need in order to be.

Perhaps the tangled Web site called Radical Privileges: Avant-garde Poetics, Politics & Practice needs to be elucidated, especially in relation to the post-1970s turn to Continental theory, and the relation of that turn to the academy, and the relation of the academy to the creation of reputations or careers within the far-flung community of poets.[7] Indeed, we need to question the notion that we can talk with any clarity about the academy when there are so many institutions that now invest in contemporary writing, each of which has a different perspective on, and alignment to, poetic lineage and practice. These perspectives are often directly attributable to the specific poetics of poet/teachers within a given program. We need to look at the relation between publications, prizes, and critical response, although the latter is now all but nonexistent. Even if there were such critics, they would be hard-pressed to find outlets for their judgments, since there is now a virtual blackout on poetry in all major media, as if somewhere it had been decided unanimously that poetry has nothing of interest to say to, to do with, the public. We need to ask whether and in what ways this virtual consensus of noninterest is a direct outgrowth of an addiction to, dependence on, and exploitation of popular culture. We need to ask about the extraordinary proliferation of small presses (including university presses) that publish hundreds of volumes of poetry each year (of every aesthetic stripe) *despite* the view that there is an almost nonexistent nonspecialized audience/readership. Do poets write only for other poets and students of poetry? Does this audience constitute a *public*?

In most bookstores, the Poetry section is segregated from the one called Literature.

We need to think about how so-called "schools" come into being, through what agencies they disseminate and become part of an historical narrative. I am thinking, for instance, of the poets in and around Black Mountain, the New York School, the Beats, the San Francisco Renaissance, the Harlem Renaissance, and L=A=N=G=U=A=G=E, each of which represents a particular extension and hybridization of a recognizable poetics. At what point does a group of poets with a loose configuration of affinities and concerns become a school or movement, and at what point does this named entity become the property of literary history, a commodity?

The current relation between poetry and the academy needs demystification. It needs to be pointed out, for example, that certain writing programs work both to attract good students and to graduate them into successful careers by introducing their work to editors, publishers, and even, on occasion, agents. Some writing programs have elaborate structures for grants and awards, since, again, these signify, in the eyes of the academy at any rate, achievement. (Granting institutions have a habit of looking at previous grants, to historicize the prize as it were, just as publishers have a habit of looking at previous publications. This collection and dissemination of judgment eventually becomes a consensus.) These forms of success have now replaced old ones that relied more heavily on reviews and their influence on the market. Certain writing programs mimic commercial marketing strategies by solicitation and advertising, hoping to turn their investments (i.e., students) into successes which, in turn, reflect back on their institutions.

This strategy of grooming and graduating persons who will carry on the tradition of a particular institution has no more vivid example than Harvard. Harvard, with its historical status as The Best, confers on its students not only a Sterling Education but, more importantly, a conviction, a Certificate of Certitude, that translates into the ineffable but consequential relation between *confidence* and *power* (mediated, as it were, by knowledge). The direct connection between poets in the canon, particularly the "avant-garde" canon, and Harvard is formidable (Wallace Stevens, T. S. Eliot, Gertrude Stein, John Ashbery, Robert Creeley, Frank O'Hara, Charles Bernstein, Michael Palmer, the list goes on and on). Furthermore, the relation between a figure like Helen Vendler, who teaches at Harvard, and other influential institutions, such as Columbia University, the New Yorker, the New York Times, the Iowa Writers' Workshop, the Guggenheim Foundation (I will not name publishers, but of course they are the Grail at the end of the rope), and so forth, is not happenstance, but a signifying chain of considerable consequence. I do not mean to suggest something untoward or unseemly here, but only that, in the absence of an ongoing open dialogue with the public (marketplace), certain individuals and institutions have perhaps more influence than they might otherwise.

All this brings up the paradoxical relationship between the "avant-garde" (e.g., permission and desire to experiment with, resist, change, traditional forms and accepted ideas) and privilege. The American version of class, as we know, is determined not by bloodlines (ideas of innate superiority) as in some Western European cultures, but by a perceived relation between being and doing: you are what you do. Our myth says that anyone can shift class identity, anyone can pursue, and capture, the citadel of success/happiness. What I want to suggest is a relationship between socioeconomic privilege and a resistance to normative paradigms, and, in turn, to relate this to our concept of elitism. Our code wants heroes to be "working-class" heroes: nothing makes us sappier or happier than tales of rags to riches, humble origins to presidential powers, orphan exiles to skating stars. A nation of immigrants, we align with the underdog; we admire tenacity and ambition, luck and pluck pitted against fate. Persons who succeed against the odds are the classic heroes and heroines of the American dream; their stories pour forth, as from a churning, regurgitating, unappeasable, and insatiable Charybdis. Witness, as two examples, the recent success of two literary memoirs, one by a poet, Mary Karr, The Liars' Club, the other, Frank McCourt's Angela's Ashes. These stories and countless others attest to the democratic ethos of social mobility and fluidity, heavily inflected by the Romantic ethos of "rugged individualism" and, however reductivist, Emersonian "self-reliance." But we are less sanguine, by far, with persons who come from privilege, those who already have material and social security (Emerson an important case in point), who then go on to question received forms, be they social, political, or aesthetic (or combinations thereof). These persons we view as members of an elite.

There still exists a phantom paradigmatic ur-poem, childlike in its candor, its ability to speak directly, to express feeling, as if it were an extension of nature by other means, which in its full maturity gives forth a morally accessible parable, a lesson, the Wise Fruit of Experience. (The master of this model is Robert Frost.) Given this entrenched site of poetic value, one can see how the introduction of *theory* as part of the poetic process itself might be construed as a wholesale attack on our appetite for representative selves telling instructive, illuminating, identity constructing stories. Moreover, we do not know how to address the apparent contradiction between progressive/transgressive ideas and so-called middle-class "lifestyles." The legacy of 1960s activism, whose players included sons and daughters of a white middle and upper-middle class (educated, comfortable, often urban), has affected directly and indirectly the shape of some contemporary poetic practices. Now well into midlife, we would turn our attention to language itself as the most problematic (because least examined) site of cultural production. This new awareness of language as both product and construct of cultural ideology (as opposed to a transparent "given," the emanation of individual sensibility) is one way to explain the turn to theory. To put it another way: this generation understood that personal agency is mediated not through persuasive rhetorics based on individual claims, but by examining those claims at the level of historical and cultural bias; an attention, that is, to signifying frames outside of the knowledge/control of the individual writer. This understanding was both a *perception* generated by the willful suspension of truth on the part of our government during Vietnam and Watergate, and an engaged reading of primarily Continental, post-Hegelian, post-Marxist, post-Freudian thinkers.

Two critical linguistic/poetic habits (as in location) came under intense scrutiny: the self (in the guise of the shifty signifier "I") as assumed site of authenticity and/or authority, and conventional, normative, discursive narration as a way to connect selves to historical (linear) structures, causes to effects. Within this dual resistance, the lyric as a form was particularly suspect. Lyric became synonymous with a very loose notion of "confessional," a one-to-one relation between a given poet's life and his poem's subject matter, particularly when invested in affective display and catharsis. The displacements of irony became one way for a poet to be personal, especially if the irony was directed toward the poem itself. Jack Spicer and Frank O'Hara, both intensely personal poets, were exempt mainly because of an ironic stance toward both the persona in the poem and the poem itself (see O'Hara's *Personism*; see Spicer's *Thing Language* poems). Replacing the transparency between the poet and his or her *narrating I* would be a formalist investment, calling attention both to the *materiality of language*, its *thingness,* and, perhaps more importantly, to its existence, so to speak, outside of the particular psychic house of the writer—its ubiquity, fluidity, indeterminacy. Much of the talk about postmodern undecidability arises from a new awareness of the reader/listener as the site where meaning is made, since each reader comes to the poem/art object with her "set" in play, and she cannot find her way all the way over to the (subjective) space of the writer. All writing is a construction. "I" is a construction. Questions which then (now) arose around affect (emotion, feeling), traditonal domain of the lyric, have had at least in part to do with this new apprehension of the crisis of the subject, in relation to its historical, sociopolitical, context.

The art critic Hal Foster, in his introduction to *The Return of the Real,* writes:

> Since the middle 1970s critical theory has served as a secret continuation of modernism by other means: after the decline of high-modernist painting and sculpture, it occupied the position of high art, at least to the extent that it retained such values as difficulty and distinction after they had receded from artistic form. So, too, critical theory have served as a secret continuation of the avant-garde by other means: after the climax of the 1968 revolts, it also occupied the position of cultural politics, at least to the extent that radical rhetoric compensated a little for lost activism (in this respect critical theory is a neo-avant garde in its own right). This double secret service—as high-art surrogate and an avant-garde substitute—has attracted many different followers.[8]

5. The Possible (Party)

in memory: Allen Ginsberg

All the poets in America

old, young

unpublished, published

*of every ethnic derivation, gender orientation, class identification, aesthetic
    and political persuasion, famous and unknown, student and teacher*

those who shout and those who whisper, who live on farms, in small towns and
    in cities, skeptics and believers, bar-keeps and brokers, pragmatists and
    preachers

who understand what Emily Dickinson meant when she wrote "I dwell in
    Possibility / a fairer house than Prose,"

what Walt Whitman meant when he wrote "Words follow character—nativity,
    independence, individuality"

what Rimbaud meant when he wrote Je est un autre

each of whom is compelled to discover a relation between how language is used
    and what it is saying

vocabularies and structures
and the consequences thereof—

Pantheon of Singularities, Anthology of Strangers,

gather and read their poems, one by one,

The Million Poet March!

6. re: Strange Encounter

A Sunday, so drab as to be itself a ghost. Deep in its gloom, a foghorn's
mournful call, a warning that sounds as much like a plea, a conjuring, as if in
the mists one could find one's way out of this world into another, the passage
itself marked by a watery dissolution of the real. Fog elucidates the journey
from fact to fiction, a natural veil that mimics the one out of which our "com-
poundings" come (Stevens). When I was young, this same sound haunted
the nights, and gave curious comfort. It represented the limits of the known
world, beyond which the unknown took up its pleasure and mischief. Since
my nights were spent always listening for this boundary, an attempt to locate
its exact position in space, where the familiar dissolved into the unfamiliar,
the boundary into the unfathomable, the sound of the foghorn acted as
sentinel.

It was one of the only reminders that we lived on an island.

What does it mean, now, to "waste time" or to "waste space"? What is the difference between the crowd and the implied non-utility of these invaluable abstractions, or between the crowd (when is a crowd a public?) and waste itself, the excess that is more than, but not useful, not operative, that falls away from pragmatic necessities? Mother says, "Stop wasting time!" For those of us who know the deliriums of procrastination, who live in a morass of a relentless *wait* that refuses to realize itself in action, so that the actions themselves gang up and gather into a mound or heap of *pending,* a *depending,* this question has a strange ring to it, like a summons which is also an alarm, an invitation to exile.

Julia Kristeva, writing on Beckett:

> Banishment: above/beyond a life of love. A life always off to one side, at an impassable distance, mourning a love. A fragile, uncertain life, where, without spending the saved-up, paternal capital in one's pockets, he discovers the price of warmth (of a hothouse, or a room, of a turd) and the boredom of those who provide it—but who waste it, too. It is a life apart from the paternal country where nonetheless lies the obsessed self's unshakable quiet, frozen forever, bored but solid . . . *To love* is to survive paternal meaning. It demands that one travel far to discover the futile but exciting presence of a waste-object: a man or woman, fallen off the father, taking the place of this protection, and yet, the always trivial ersatz of this disincarnate wisdom that no object (of love, necessarily) could ever totalize. Against the modifying *whole* of the father's Death, one chooses banishment toward the *part* constituting a fallen object of an object *of* love (*of* being possessive and genitive partitive). How trivial, this object of love— transposition of love for the Other. And yet, without banishment, there is no possible release from the grip of paternal Death. This act of loving and its incumbent writing spring from the Death of the Father—from the Death of the third person (as *Not I* shows).[9]

How does one write against knowing? How does one get under the skin, away from presence which is an absolute absence, the literal hereness that invades at every point and whose energy insists that the conversation turn on a litany of trades, incidents, details, opinions, from which the energies of in-dividuated thought have been stripped? So that one is in a kind of waste site, a dump, a spill.

Topics of conversation:

1. Film and TV
2. Sports events
3. Weather
4. He said she said

And I was like blah blah blah. Young woman in a loud voice on the subway late one night. She was describing to her friend an episode with an un-wanted suitor who refused to leave her room after they had sex.

A little overheard strip of language with virtually no content except the content of no content, of waste.

Henry James, January 22, 1879:

> Imagine a door—either walled-up, or that has been long locked—at which there is an occasional knocking—a knocking which—as the other side of the door is inaccessible—can only be ghostly. The occupant of the house or room, containing the door, has long been familiar with the sound; and regarding it as ghostly, has ceased to heed it particularly—as the ghostly presence re-mains on the other side of the door, and never reveals itself in other ways. But this person may be imagined to have some great and constant trouble; and it may be observed by another person, relating the story, that the knocking increases with each fresh manifestation of the trouble. He breaks open the door and the trouble ceases—as if the spirit had desired to be admitted, that it might interpose, redeem and protect.[10]

interpose, redeem, protect

At some point after the death of my father I invented a ghost. The Ghost, which I called a Dragon, and which I conjured ostensibly to "interpose, re-deem, protect" my younger brother, David, would knock on the wall beside my bed. I would feign not to hear this knocking, until my brother, whose bed was across the room from mine, would whisper loudly and insistently:

Yataw is calling!

We called the Dragon/Ghost "Yataw." I have no idea why or how this name came into being; I did not know then that the God of the Old Testament was called Yahweh.

I pretended to be asleep.

Yataw lived in the Night Sky, a vast emporium or constellation spread across the entire curve of the dome, shared only by Orion, whose belt and sword we, my brother and I, knew on sight (by heart). In my fable, Yataw was a kind of Mansion, a celestial Jonah's Whale, whose vast mouth opened to allow access to a capacious interior, in which various meetings were held. I was often called to these meetings to Discuss Something, and had to leave David behind alone in his bed. This of course terrified and fascinated him, and he would ask how I got to the sky in the first place, and I would fabricate a methodology of escape and flight.

> But with Descartes and the birth of modern science, the function of phantasy is assumed by the new subject of knowledge: the *ego cogito* (observe that in the technical vocabulary of medieval philosophy, *cogitare* referred rather to the discourse of the imagination than to the act of intelligence). Between the new *ego* and the corporeal world, between *res cogitans* and *res extensa,* there is no need for any mediation. The resulting expropriation of the imagination is made evident in the new way of characterizing its nature: while in the past it was not a "subjective" thing, but was rather the coincidence of subjective and objective, of internal and external, of the sensible and the intelligible, now it is its combinatory and hallucinatory character, to which Antiquity gave secondary importance, that is given primary. From having been the subject of experience the phantasm becomes the subject of mental alienation, visions and magical phenomona—in other words, everything that is excluded by real experience.[11]

7. Hard Rag Ague

Wold—

> Perhaps the reason that poetry is mostly ignored in our time has to do with its assertion of combinatory and coincidental experience, its desire to refute the various ways in which modernity has contrived to

separate us from the authority of our existence, real and imagined,
separately and together, to make the dark glass darker as the screen is
more and more illuminated—

at ground level

looking out

not at   piecemeal

the sky in its rectangle

the snow-footed trees

                  perch

                       where the turtle and the echo

resilience unsighted

                 habitat

screen: a movable device, as a panel, designed to divide, conceal, or protect.

The ghost's lair.

(Into what is apparent memory-things drift through.)

Quotidian scribble at the edge of a pink shelter, banal rhapsody and twinge
repeated as outside. Against the crimson visitor and the faded enemy,
betrayal (silence).

Pat pay care father bib church deed pet be fife gag hat

Railings and covetous lingering perceptions. As when twilight drinks the day.

Have I, have you

to soothe the screen of its incipience, ghastly or ghostly, to tire it out? Are these paths, known or unknown, our daily allowance? And the Site of Instruction, is it a mime, a dance, a conversation, a romance, a parade, a story, a desire to begin again despite the spoils of war, the hidden agendas: *have you heard? did you listen? did you see?* Late at night, she watches as the animals are led into the cathedral, beautiful mute beasts, to honor Saint Francis, and then a few days later, reads:

"She was a happy little girl," Mr. Maeder said. "She grew up loving animals and nature."

And at least at one point, she thought that material things were worth pursuing. In her high school yearbook, she wrote that her ambition was "to be rich and famous."

She also wrote she liked red satin sheets on a water bed, cats, irises, hugs, Chinese food, horror movies, The Far Side and black clothes.

When she killed herself last week, Miss Maeder wore black.[12]

paw noise out took boot

brew fib fiber.

New is what cannot be experienced, because it lies "in the depths of the unknown": the Kantian thing-in-itself, the inexperiencible as such. Thus, in Baudelaire (and this is the measure of his lucidity) this search takes the paradoxical form of aspiring to the creation of a "lieu commun"—a common place ("créer un poncif c'est le genie"—to create a commonplace is genius; think of Baudelarian poetic rhythms, with their sudden footholds in banality that so struck Proust). By this was meant what could be created only from a century's accumulation of experience, not invented by one individual. But in a state where man has been expropriated of experience, the creation of such a "lieu commun" is possible only through a destruction of experience which, in the very moment of its counterfeit authority, suddenly discloses that this destruction is really man's new abode. Estrangement, which removes from the most commonplace objects their power to be experienced, thus becomes the exemplary procedure of a poetic project which aims to make of the Inexperiencible the new "lieu commun," humanity's new experience. In this sense the *Fleurs du Mal* are proverbs of the inexperiencible.[13]

An arc lifts from the shadow's range

and tilts, coming up to away: a limit.

And the one said

is it folded or is it extended

out of any and all sighting?

I have awakened in a crowd of mourners.

A vase, a lamp, a curtain, a door.

va la ta do

sings the echo

its restive partial connection

frayed.

The origin of language must necessarily be located at a break with the continual opposition of diachronic and synchronic, historical and structural, in which it is possible to grasp as some kind of Ur-event, or Ur-faktum, the unity-difference of invention and gift, human and non-human, speech and infancy.[14]

shadow pillars

rope & America.

We demonstrate ourselves.

THE NIGHT SKY V

Attempts to dominate or monopolize the character of what is meaningful constitutes a profoundly political project, perhaps the most important project of the late modern era, when the struggle over material goods has extended most explicitly to the domains of language and communication, and when the spectacular casts a large shadow over small and quotidian matters.

—Thomas Dumm, *A Politics of the Ordinary*

*

Furthermore, there are an infinite number of worlds both like and unlike this world of ours. For the atoms being infinite in number, as was proved already, are borne on far out into space. For those atoms, which are of such nature that a world could be created out of them or made by them, have not been used up either on one world on on a limited number of worlds, nor again on the worlds that are alike, or on this which are different from these. So that there nowhere exists an obstacle to the infinite number of worlds.

—Epicurus

*

Artifacts are congealed ideology.

—Iain A. Boal, "A Flow of Monsters"

1. Ragged

Perhaps I should begin to make amends for the zigzag and apparently arbitrary inclusions in these, the foregoing, writings. Trusting to intuition's links, and my own game with the subject, the *topic*, probably has gone too far, or maybe not far enough. Attention deficit disorder, a tendency to digress; perhaps just a desire to experience things as an endless set of beginnings, with the implied promise and permission; a sequence of dawns, of first kisses, a constellation without the picture-making lines drawn.

Against the sense of belatedness comes the desire for earliness, to be a creature born into birdsong and sun breaking over the far ridge, to feel the turn of the earth.

The romance of the turn, whether it is *toward* or *away*. My turn, your turn.

Paul Celan's turn:

> The poem holds its ground . . . the poem holds its ground on its own margin. In order to endure, it constantly calls and pulls itself back from an "already-no-more" into a "still-here."
>
> This "still-here" can only mean speaking. Not language as such, but responding and—not just verbally—"corresponding" to something.
>
> In other words: language actualized, set free under the sign of a radical individuation which, however, remains as aware of the limits drawn by language as of the possibilities it opens.
>
> This "still-here" of the poem can only be found in the work of poets who do not forget what they speak from an angle of reflection which is their own existence, their own physical nature.
>
> This shows the poem yet more clearly as one person's language becomes shape and, essentially, a presence in the present.[1]

Celan's "still-here" implies a spatio-temporal presence, the "still" evoking the temporal stasis of duration, and the "here" fixing that stasis in place. The poem on this reading might be what most fundamentally stands for, or stands in for, the fact of someone's existence. The someone here is not necessarily the author—that is, the poem need not be in a literal sense "about" the author—but a re-enactment of the poet's self-witnessing in, or as, language. It is as if the poet were composing her or his own ghost and sending it out to the place where it vanishes, leaving behind the herald of its having been. (Jean-Luc Nancy: "Present is that which occupies a place. The place is *place*—site, situation, disposition—in the coming into space of a time, in a spacing that allows that something *come* into presence, in a unique time that engenders itself in this point in space, as its spacing.")

The poem is a temporal-spatial alignment of a given self with language, and this alignment is such that the poem exactly configures that self's transformation or inscription into linguistic experience. Here *aura* and *excess* spill from the text, questioning whether an idea of exact alignment is sufficient, as if a poem were an object that casts no shadow, or a shadow from which the object had been withdrawn, a residual presence whose materiality is a kind of illusion. Somewhere is the desire to separate the poem from the poet, while still allowing for a poetics of identity that does not inhibit, conceal, or overdetermine the poem's meaning.

Celan continues:

> The poem is lonely. It is lonely and *en route*. Its author stays with it.

> Does this very fact not place the poem already here, at its inception, in the encounter, *in the mystery of encounter*?

> The poem intends another, needs this other, needs an opposite. It goes toward it, bespeaks it.

> For the poem, everything and everybody is a figure of this other toward which it is heading.

> The attention which the poem pays to all that it encounters, its more acute sense of detail, outline, structure, color, but also of the "tremors and hints"—all this is not, I think, achieved by an eye competing (or concurring) with ever more precise instruments, but, rather, by a kind of concentration mindful of all our dates.

> "Attention," if you allow me a quote from Malebranche via Walter Benjamin's essay on Kafka, "'attention is the natural prayer of the soul."

> The poem becomes—under what conditions—the poem of a person who still perceives, still turns towards phenomena, address-

ing and questioning them. The poem becomes conversation—often desperate conversation.

Only the space of this conversation can establish what is addressed, can gather it into a "you" around the naming and speaking I. But this "you," come about by dint of being named and addressed, brings an otherness into the present. Even in the here and now of the poem—and the poem has only this one, unique, momentary present—even in this immediacy and nearness, the otherness gives voice to what is most its own: its time.

Whenever we speak of things in this way we also dwell on the question of their where-from and where-to, an "open" question "without resolution," a question which points towards open, empty, free spaces—we have ventured far out.

The poem also searches for this place.

A musical alliance, the residual trace of what was once experience and may be, who knows, soon again, now that we are saturated with information and might want to dig our heels, our hands, into the loam we have created: the great Compost Heap. See here, I have found one half of a corn cob, and a shard from a Hellenic amphora, and some strange seeds, and that thing blinking on the horizon: a kite made of *what*? beach debris, condoms knit with seaweed.

I stepped on a wasp.

But every time the sun makes a gold scrim across the trees, which is any morning without cloud, there is simple amazement, a desire to hold it in place, but it goes, and comes again, and goes, and so forth, so one is, finally, glad for the repetition which erases the fear of only once, once only.

Your turn, as if you could invite the morrow to save today.

2. re: Act

Tuesday morning, July:

I am back in the same room where the female cardinal batted against the window; this time there are no cicadas and no sign of her, although her mate has been flitting about, assiduously avoiding the glass. A woman across the rough ground has come out of her house with her dog, an Irish setter on a leash, to her red car, and urged the dog to get into the backseat, but the dog balked. She said, "Make up your mind," and then "O.K., back to the house," and pulled the dog to where I could not see it. Then she reappeared and, once again, offered the dog a choice between the backseat of the car or the house. The dog looked morose, even from this distance, his head and tail hung low. Finally she gave up and attached the dog to a long tether which slides along a sort of clothesline running between the garage and the house, so the tether can move. Now she has gone off to work and the dog is lying on the grass.

While watching this scene I have also been reading essays by the artist Robert Smithson (1938–73). His writings perch between his own particular set of interests and concerns and the world's somewhat arbitrary—that is, uncontrollable—events: examples, scenes, artifacts, linguistic as well as concrete, from which he draws. There is a mobile pleasure in this writing, in reading this writing, borne along by confident exploration, which seems now rare, cauterized in our mediated, indirect age.

The sense of the life of the mind, its rootedness in experience.

Smithson's freedom arises from a combination of intense focus, Celan's *attention,* linked to the *is*-ness of the world, the world as a full place, a place full of so much stuff all you have to do is choose one thing over another until you build a sculpture or a poem or a house or a plane or a garden. Your being here gathers around you the way weather gathers around a day. Here is Smithson describing the site of his most revered work, the Spiral Jetty in Great Salt Lake, Utah:

> About one mile north of the oil seeps I selected my site. Irregular beds of limestone dip gently eastward, massive deposits of black basalt are broken over the peninsula, giving the region a shattered appearance. It is one of the few places on the lake where the water comes right up to the mainland. Under shallow pinkish water is a network of mud cracks supporting the jig-saw puzzle that composes the salt flats. As I looked at the site, it reverberated out to the horizons only to suggest an immobile cyclone while flickering light made the entire landscape appear to quake. A dormant earthquake spread into the fluttering stillness, into a spinning sensation without movement. This site was a rotary that enclosed itself in an immense roundness. From that gyrating space emerged the possibility of the Spiral Jetty. No ideas, no concepts,

no systems, no structures, no abstractions could hold themselves together in the actuality of that evidence. My dialectics of site and nonsite whirled onto an indeterminate state, where solid and liquid lost themselves in each other. It was as if the mainland oscillated with waves and pulsations, and the lake remained rock still. The shore of the lake became the edge of the sun, a boiling curve, an explosion rising into a fiery prominence. Matter collapsing into the lake mirrored in the shape of a spiral. No sense wondering about classifications and categories, there were none.

I aspire to such fulsome engagement with the world, through or by which all things solid are absorbed into attention. It is an enviable economy, one that does not register deficit, but converts, by the concentration of focus, a Circean call that draws forth from the vagrant and diverse only what it wants, only what is of use. Smithson was not interested in the art object as such, but in the process of creation, in the synthesis of divergent realms of knowledge into the specifics of response. His work was inseparable from its spatio-temporal context.

The scale of the Spiral Jetty tends to fluctuate depending on where the viewer happens to be. Size determines an object, but scale determines art. A crack in the wall if viewed in terms of scale, not size, could be called the Grand Canyon. A room could be made to take on the immensity of the solar system. Scale depends on one's capacity to be conscious of the actualities of perception. When one refuses to release scale from size, one is left with an object or language that *appears* to be certain. For me scale operates by uncertainty.[2]

The Spiral Jetty remains an icon, the talismanic emblem of an artist who achieved a harmonic and haunting relation between specific site and individual perception. Like Marcel Duchamp's before him, Smithson's legacy rests as much in the *turn of his mind* (now most clearly available in his writings) as in manifestations and embodiments of physical objects. Smithson (who did not particularly admire Duchamp) resisted a Cartesian worldview, setting in motion a constant dialectic of engagement (*site and nonsite*), fed by as many sources as were necessary.

America Online: twenty-one channels to choose from, one of which is called Learning and Culture.

3. Penance

I took a trip. I went to Istanbul (once Constantinople, once Byzantium) and then flew to Izmir, and thence to Bodrum, where I (and others) boarded a ship, *Orfeus* (sic), and sailed down the southwest coast of Turkey. This is a part of the world about which I knew next to nothing. What initially drew me to this journey was a desire to stand inside of the Hagia Sofia, the astonishing cathedral in which currents of the Islamic East and Christian West converge.

> It is always good to know something of a city's history. It helps us to understand many of the things we see, and we are better able to cast our minds back hundreds of years and to imagine what things were like in olden days. In the case of Constantinople it enables us to see a city which, in early Greek times, was called "the Dwelling of the Gods"; then to become, under Constantine the Great and those emperors who followed him, the Queen City of Christendom and, until recent times, the heart of the most powerful Muslim country the world has known.[3]

—*minaret, mosque, the Golden Horn, the Hippodrome, obelisk, sultan, the Grand Bazaar, seraglio, harem, Bosporus, muezzin, Mecca, Topkapi, Ottoman, caliph, Persia*—

I had seen slides of the Hagia Sofia when I was in college, and it had stayed in my mind as a central vision: mysterious, monumental, a place where a spiritual history, however dark, must be palpable. Dedicated in 537 by Justinian, it was the Church of Divine Wisdom for a thousand years; in 1453 it became a mosque, minarets were added. Under Ataturk, the leader of the modern Turkish Republic, it was made into a museum in 1935.

Most of the Christian mosaics have been eradicated, leaving desolate stretches on the vast walls; those that remain stare from their niches like the last creatures of a nearly extinguished species. The central nave is filled with scaffolding; and high above, huge discs, inscribed in a beautiful curvilinear Arabic with prayers to Allah, like shields against the infidels, stare down. I began to think about how we in the West derive so much of our self-knowledge from the relationship between image and story, icon and text, figure and landscape. It is a geometry of space, figure, and horizon (the image of a cross); Islam is all curvilinear, inscription, dome, a legacy of prophecy without icons, a call to prayer.

> Historically, the various modes of communication have competed with one another. The replacement of the older narration by information, of information by sensation, reflects the increasing atrophy of experience. In turn, there is a contrast between all these forms and the story, which is one of the oldest forms of communication. It is not the object of the story to convey a happening *per se,* which is the purpose of information; rather, it embeds it in the life of the storyteller in order to pass it on as experience to those listening. It thus bears the marks of the storyteller much as the earthen vessel bears the marks of the potter's hand.[4]

The role of storyteller on our trip was taken first by Cornell Fleischer, an American historian of the Middle East, who speaks impeccable Turkish and knows the intricate lines of the region's narratives as if he had woven them himself. His familiarity helped to ease the embarrassment of our ignorance.

Walking barefoot in the Blue Mosque, the cool sensuality of material; *prayer rug, magic carpet.*

Once we were at sea, our navigator was a Welsh archaeologist named David Price-Williams, who led our expeditions over rough rocky ruins, up steep hills, across torrid empty agoras. Everywhere, he would piece together a story of an ancient Dorian village, the site of a Byzantine religious pilgrimage, a Roman fortress, a Hellenic temple. Gemili, a high island promontory overlooking a narrow anchorage, gave rise to an incredible narrative, spanning three centuries (the fourth through the seventh A.D.). The ruins were like a broken syntax, and as we climbed up to the highest point overlooking the bay, we found ourselves in the grips of a story unfurling through the brilliantly illuminated open arches of a processional way. Here, according to Price-Williams, was probably the site of the death of Saint Nicholas, whose relics were carried down the mountainous terrain from the tiny high church to a lower church. He told the story as if it were a detective novel, animating the ruins with anticipatory intrigue, in which he asked over and over: *Why would they have put this stone, this column, this wall, this ambulatory, here? What is this for?* At each juncture, one could sense a physical relationship between particulars of place and the narration of histories. But without this continuous contextualization, the constant transformation of information into knowledge, we would have climbed as if through so much mute rubble. Even reading the brief descriptive texts we were given, there is simply no way to apprehend the profound drama elicited from the actual site and Price-Williams's telling, so that one could hear, descending the treacherous, luminous path, the chanting of monks bearing sacred relics.

A woman knelt at the site and burned incense.

And there was yet another storyteller, Richard Steffy, a nautical archaeologist, whose work on classical and medieval shipwrecks has made him a legend in the field. There is the story of the stones and the rocks and then there is the story of the underworld, the seabeds, strewn with relics, wrecks, cargoes of ancient glass, amphorae, arms, hulls, masts, caskets: "The death of a lady," he said. "She came apart in fits and starts and gently settled to the bottom of the sea."

Later, sailing on the flat disc of sea, I wrote in a little journal:

> Rocks along the coastline look folded, like elephant skin, with deep crevices, and you can imagine the faces and forms of creatures. The landscape emerges as a series of low horizontal but curvaceous outcroppings, one behind another behind another, so it has the effect of a veiled sequential layering. The forms of the rocks also resemble the piling up of wet clay; there are bright

4. green

> patches and low bushes and small trees, like punctuation marks. As has happened before, I am aware of how a given landscape might give rise to the central myths of a culture.

I say to students: Write from the known into the unknown, as if on a journey. This is not a matter of forgetting everything so much as a coming upon the place where all belongings and habits and familiar surroundings are suspended, and you begin to move on, out, away, and what propels this movement, this *trajectory*, is a desire to find out what you do not yet know. As if language were a sea, buoyant, which will hold you up as you go along.

I say: Notice when the words you choose seem to come from the same word bag, and so to have the same weight or value, the same specific gravity, as if you had taken along only T-shirts, all the same color. This is poetic *scale*.

You want your poem to have variety; no word is intrinsically poetic; there is no vocabulary that belongs only to poetry.

I say: Create enjambment between the rhythm of meaning and the meaning of rhythm.

I say: What I value most in a writer is candor.

The morning as crisp and bright as any idea of pure vision, glittering little nodules of dew making their tinsellated drama of passage. Staring is good for the soul, what passes for the soul.

5. Optics

The world of information and communication on line, much hailed as a technological advance, is also a social retreat accompanying a loss of the public and social space of the cities, the aesthetic, sensual and nonhuman space of the country, a privatization of physical space and a disembodiment of daily life. A central appeal cited for the new technologies is that their users will no longer have to leave home, and paeans accumulate to the convenience of being able to access libraries and entertainments via personal computers that become less tools of engenderment than channels of consumption. This vision of disembodied anchorites connected to the world only by information and entertainment mediated by the entities that control its flow seems more nightmarish than idyllic. Postulated as a solution to gridlock, crime on the streets, the chronic sense of time's scarcity, it seems indeed a means to avoid addressing such problems, a form of acquiescence.[5]

Literacy is not about books read, not just about bibliographies; it is not synonymous with "literary." A literate culture is one in which distinctions are drawn in order that choices can be made, not just choices between the red and the black dress, but between Bill Clinton, say, and someone less intimidated by what he cannot be facile and ingratiating toward, in a lip service that passes for his word: the National Endowment for the Arts, for example. Literacy is a tool, an empowering weapon against ordinations of what constitutes a good and happy life. Literacy is one of our most subtle webbings between personal vision and public will, between personal will and public vision. Literacy is necessarily dialectical; it instills a habit of question and answer, proposal and counter, supposition and elaboration, it breaches the gap between domestic intimacies and shared enthusiasms, between past histories and current journeys; it nurtures and supports habits of independence; most importantly, it does not shirk from the complexities of the multifaceted syntax of our reality. One might imagine a conversation that does not pivot around the computer's stark duality: yes/no, on/off. When aesthetics are reduced to marketplace agendas, then artists of every stripe begin to lose their connection to the rigors of controversy and settle instead for the easily consummated and reiterated surfaces of the unending sequels to the "new."

We need to explore the archives of our attention and attachment; we need to become archaeologists, dig around in the fertile soil of the past and redress, readdress, the lost contexts of our diverse cultural enterprise.

I feel an enjambment between these polemics and actual intervention. It's not that I want persons to agree with me—few would argue against literacy—I want to make a space for myself and others that would allow us to write without feelings of futility. Perhaps this is vanity, and in vain, to want to insist on a world where our extraordinary privileges give rise to an increased interest in the love of things that don't necessarily feed our acquisitive natures and blind ambitions.

Don't get me wrong: I love the things of the world as much as the next girl; nothing comes easier to me than spending money. Just this morning I wrote out a check for fifty-eight dollars for more plants for my garden, a garden that is never the Garden I have in my mind's eye. My garden is a constant reminder of my faults and failings: extravagance and its handmaiden, impatience; learning the hard way, by trial and error (mostly error), so that I am always undoing as much as I am doing. *If you had done it the right way in the first place,* says the meanspirited scold of my inner voice, *then there wouldn't be such a constant losing battle against the stone-encrusted soil, the weeds, the bugs.* This same voice denounces my poems. Still, when I began to make a garden, many years ago, there was only a heap of old mattresses and rusting bedsteads, broken bottles and debris, and now at least there are moments of radiance when a shaped stillness holds sway in the late-summer sun.

Fact is, this little tract of earth captures my attention for hours and hours at a go. I obsess over it as I have over a lover's call, over a poem in progress. I have made it in the form of a circle, with stone paths within, so that I walk around it incessantly, viewing it from every perspective. There are two chairs in its center, but I rarely sit in either of them. When I do, I stare out at the pond, but before long I am up, pulling a piece of grass, a weed, clipping off a spent bloom. I wonder sometimes where my desire for a garden originated; after all, I am a city girl, born and reared in the dense verticality of New York's reflecting architecture. My grandmother, who lived in the country, had gardens, and I remember seeing her crouched down among her iris beds; I remember also a sense of the secrecy of place, where stone steps dipped down into a magic as colorful, varied, and animated as a circus, only without the crowds.

But there was another garden.

I think it was the summer after my father died, which we spent near Hanover, New Hampshire, when we visited the poet Archibald MacLeish, whom I believe had taught my father at Dartmouth. In any case, I remember walking through their gardens, and I remember, dimly, that I made a connection between being a poet and having a garden, as if the garden were a sort of language with a syntax of its own; it had to do with making a place receptive to human conversation, a setting, a provision, an entrance.

Indeed, what I notice about the garden *is* a visual syntax, a structure by which each individual plant is offset or augmented not only by its neighboring plants, but by the rhythms within the whole—variations in leaf shape, color, height; it works the way any language works, by contingency, so that meaning takes shape (takes its shape, is shaped) only through the accumulations of the proximities of each individual choice and decision. If I move a plant, I change the whole garden; if I change a word, I change, however slightly, the meaning of the paragraph or stanza. Over the years, I have lost more plants than I care to name (I rarely remember names of the plants, but that is another matter), so that the garden also imitates real life, where early associations disappear, and new affiliations come into being; the garden as palimpsest, an evolving record of its own mutated past. The garden has rhymes and half-rhymes, small internal rhythms and closures.

The little pale-yellow potentilla bush my aunt Priscilla gave me ten years ago is now five feet across. This summer I planted another, a white one, as small as the original was when I first planted it.

Sometimes I am amazed at how ruthless I can be, how roughly I will tear something out, how easily allow something to die; this makes me think I am not as kind as I imagine myself to be.

Sometimes I am also ruthless with my poems.

6. The Possible (Art)

I am rereading George Trow's prescient and powerful 1980 book *Within the Context of No Context*, a harrowing, eloquent indictment of the Age of Television, which has been reissued. It has made me think more about the liberal orthodoxy of my upbringing, not entirely dissimilar from his. Trow describes the false intimacy proffered by television; he speaks about "the cold child," his haunting image of the bleak landscape of the televised:

> Television is dangerous because it operates according to an attention span that is childish but is cold. It simulates the warmth of a childish response but is cold . . . What is a cold child? A sadist. What is childish behavior that is cold? It is sadism. After generations of cold childhood, cold childhood upon cold childhood, one piling on the other, moving, *at their best*, into frenzied adolescence, certain ugly blemishes have surfaced. An overt interest in sadism, for instance, and an interest in unnatural children. Americans, unrooted, blow with the wind, but they feel the truth when it touches them. An interest in sadism is an interest in truth in that it exposes the processes of false affection. A horror of children is the natural result of the spread, across the grid, of a cold childhood.[6]

I grew up believing that the artifacts of human imagination—Woody Guthrie's, Pete Seeger's songs; the music in *Guys and Dolls* and *South Pacific*, of Billie Holiday and Burl Ives and Paul Robeson; the paintings of Matisse, Miró, of Philip Guston and Jackson Pollock and Franz Kline; the Brahms Double Concerto, Bach's Goldberg Variations, Mozart's Twenty-third Piano Concerto, the Beethoven Violin Concerto; Elvis's "Love Me Tender," Ray Charles's "What'd I Say"; Marilyn's walk across a bridge (*Niagara*), Audrey Hepburn wearing Givenchy, Richard Widmark in *Kiss of Death*; Salinger's *The Catcher in the Rye*, Carroll's "The Jabberwocky," the poems of Robert Louis Stevenson, Alcott's *Little Women*; Charlie Chaplin's cunning comedy, the grace of Fred Astaire, Beckett's plays, *The Wizard of Oz*, Yeats's "Sailing to Byzantium"—art, high and low, popular and arcane, was *necessary*.
  Necessary to whom, for what?
  There was, I suppose, an ideology: idealistic, progressive, pragmatic. The

idealism was faith in the innate goodness, good will and good sense, of every individual; the progressivism was an ethics of community, understanding, and tolerance; the pragmatics was a commitment to action over reflection, doing over saying, and a correlative notion that the best way to learn about something was by doing, or at least by bearing witness, to it. Within this framework, art had a fundamental and essential role. It was the social element, the link, that might allow individual insight to be exposed to the strangeness of the other and then, through familiarity, to bring that strangeness into the communal. We learned national anthems in their native languages, and when Pete Seeger taught us songs, we were given lessons in local history. We learned countless dances from different countries; we visited, in the sixth grade, a Mennonite village in Pennsylvania and stayed on a family farm. Culture was not an elitist enterprise; it was what nourished and united the world by acknowledging difference, individuals and groups of individuals, and then providing a space (a public space) for persons of different persuasions (age, class, race, religion) with a common sense of the possible. This belief was fundamental to my sense of personal survival, it allowed me to resist certain temptations and to give in to others, and to discover for myself a terrain. It did not come along like the scent of a rose, it was inculcated, part of a deliberate, conscious, strategy on the part of parents and teachers. Things went awry. Things do. But a fundamental notion was instilled: imagination makes form, and form is the exploration and cultivation of the limits of freedom; form is the fruition of choice as an expression of limit. The relation between the freedom to chose and the limits of choice was a relation of judgment, the basis of a morality anchored in ethics; it was, so we were taught, essential to democracy.

What interests me now about this vision is, apart from its obvious lack of cynicism toward human nature and the nature of human history, its sober, unironic earnestness, its optimism, is that the portrait of the artist that emerged was neither that of an individual isolated genius, romantic recluse, separate and insular, nor that of the celebrity icon. Artistic value was inseparable from, locked into, the ongoing need for social transformation; there was not a separate, privileged vocabulary for art. Art provided gladness and hope and exuberance while simultaneously naming our darkest sorrows, struggles, and oppressions. We were encouraged to be iconoclastic, to resist homogenization as the sole means of integrating differences. The point was to encourage difference, to nourish individuation, while at the same time cultivating an ethos of response, of reciprocity and responsibility, by which to thwart pure self-centeredness. But if art were to be a vehicle for social change, then it would have to be of and in its time, and individual artists would need to be aware not only of the history of a chosen genre, but of other significant intellectual and political events. Art was the result of many contexts.

The role of art was to be both a means of nonviolent protest, resistance, critique, and a source of spiritual consolation, historical compensation. This dual aspect continues to interest me, as it implies a relationship between form and content that is often overlooked. Artists had a job to do: to intercede and subvert, on the one hand, and to maintain and augment, on the other. The former aspect would be a vigilance against received notions of the Right, the Fair, and the Good, especially when used for advancement (for power), political, social, economic, or aesthetic; the latter had to do with respecting and caring for lines of legacy, to keep fresh earlier artistic expressions and their historical bearings. The context of an art object gives it cultural meaning; once it has been cut away (a flower in a vase), it quickly devolves into a commodity, lending itself to consumer ambitions, institutional as well as individual. Artists are persons who resist facile assimilation and false prophecies, truncated versions and quick-fix solutions; persons who, in fact, delight in the messy, warm refulgence and inexhaustible reformations from which their particular will to order arises. On this view, new forms are inevitable.

Perhaps it is not that modernism failed, but that we have failed modernism.

What I have said here makes me feel dated, perhaps a little embarrassed. (I mean, we *begged* our mother to allow us to have a television set, and she finally relented, and we were *glued* to it.) My list of Early Artifacts is an attempt to say something about personal context, not about influence, to name some specific passages that have stayed with me as recoverable experience. For each, I could narrate how I came to know it, who first read it to me, when it was and where I was when I heard or saw it, found myself mystified, alerted, enchanted. The list in itself is nothing; it is in a sense a *public* list; everyone has her or his list. But loving the songs of Woody Guthrie somehow made it possible for me to be around when a scruffy kid named Bob Dylan wandered through Madison, Wisconsin, when I was an undergraduate there, and then hanging out on a roof one night, with others, him playing his tunes as we sang along. And who knows what precursor made it possible for me to awaken one afternoon after a nap to hear the Berlioz Requiem and think, really believe, I had died and was somewhere near Heaven, because, I thought, nothing this sublime can be *human*.

7. Encounter

find, v.t. (*found*, from Latin, *fundare, fundus,* bottom) 1. Come across, fall in with, light upon (*was found dead; we ~ St John saying; administer the law as you ·· it; found a treasure*); obtain, receive (·- *favour, mercy*, one's account in; ~ one's *feet*, get the use of them, develop one's powers); recognize as present, acknowledge or discover to be so & so (*I ~ no sense in it, ~ the terms reasonable; how do you ~ yourself?; must take us as you ~ us*, put up with us was we are); discover by trial to be or do or (*that*) or *to* (*has been found wanting; ~s rest agreeable; is found to pay; I ~ it pays* or *that it pays, pay,* or *to pay,* or *that it pays; ~ it impossible, necessary, to ~*); discover by search; discover (game), discover game, in hunting; ~ oneself, discover one's vocation, & see below; succeed in obtaining (money, bail, sureties; *can't ~ time to read; found courage to —; could ~ it in my heart to —*, am inclined; ~ *expression, place, vent*); come home to, reach the conscience of; ascertain by study or calculation or inquiry (~ one's *way to,* contrive to reach, arrive at); (Law) determine & declare (*it,* i.e. the offense, *murder:* person *guilty* etc.; *that; true* BILL) whence 'ING (2) n.; supply, provide, furnish (*they found him in clothes; hotel does not ~ tea; all found,* with all necessaries provided; of servants' wages; ~ *oneself,* provide for one's needs & see above); ~ *out,* discover, devise, solve, detect in offence; hence ~ABLE a. 2.n. ~ing a fox; discovery of treasure, minerals, etc; *sure ~,* place where something is sure to be found.[7]

"Where do we find ourselves?" Emerson wearily and warily asks as he begins his essay "Experience." His answer is a digressive list which, in turn, opens into a meditation. As he writes, the answer slowly accrues; writing leads him through thickets of negativity and an imploded grief (for the loss of his young son) so frozen he cannot acknowledge it as such, to a rhapsodic affirmation which comes to him through the transformed agency of the trope of an excited child:

> But every insight from this realm of thought is felt as initial, and promises a sequel. I do not make it; I arrive there, and behold what was there already. I make! O no! I clap my hands in infantile joy and amazement before the first opening to me of this august magnificence, old with the love and homage of innumerable ages,

young with the life of life, the sunbright Mecca of the desert. And what a future opens! I feel a new heart beating with love of the new beauty. I am ready to die out of nature and be born again into this new yet unapproachable America I have found in the West:

> Since neither now nor yesterday began
> These thoughts, which have ever been, nor yet can
> A man be found who their first entrance knew.[8]

Emerson seems to me an American writer who deeply felt the relevance of individual experience, how a self is formed by the world into which he or she comes and then *in turn* forms that world. This relationship is what Whitman, in particular, thematized:

> I celebrate myself, and sing myself,
> And what I assume you shall assume

In each case, the assumption was that an individual could be representative; that the narrating "I" could move easily from first person to the third person, gathering you up on the way, as if each dialogue could open up into a town meeting, as if the I, the Other, and the Us were coextensive. Both Emerson and Whitman imagined "genius" as a vision of practical possibility; words and actions were not severed from each other. For them, the visionary intellect had efficacy as a principal animus; both had the desire to arouse in others a sense of the joy of being through the agency of doing, and writing itself as a prime example of this activity. This is how the essay ends:

> We dress our garden, eat our dinner, discuss the household with our wives, and these things make no impression, are forgotten next week; but in the solitude to which every man is always returning, he has a sanity and revelations, which in his passage into new worlds he will carry with him. Never mind the ridicule, never mind the defeat; up again, old heart!—it seems to say,— there is victory yet for all justice; and the true romance which the world exists to realize will be the transformation of genius into practical power.[9]

THE NIGHT SKY VI

Jesus often raised questions from a literal to a metaphorical level. His sayings and parables were customarily metaphorical and without explicit application. Because his parables were told in figurative language, because the figures could not be taken literally, because the application of the sayings was left ambiguous, what he said was difficult to understand, and the disciples often did not know what he was saying. (Mark made the disciples out to be stupid, this was one of his particular biases, and it is he who has Jesus say such things to his disciples as: "Are you as dimwitted as the rest?") But Jesus did not explain. Instead, he gave them more questions, more stories with unclear references. The answer shifted the decision back onto his listeners. Jesus' style was to refuse to give straightforward answers.

—Lydia Davis, "Paring Off the Amphibiologisms"[1]

*

Above all, Ovid was interested in passion. Or rather, in what passion feels like to the one possessed by it. Not just ordinary passion either, but human passion in extremis—passion where it combusts, or levitates, or mutates into an experience of the supernatural. The act of metamorphosis, which at some point touches each of the tales, operates as the symbolic guarantee that the passion has become mythic, has achieved the unendurable intensity that lifts the whole episode onto the supernatural or divine plane. Sometimes this happens because mortals tangle with gods, sometimes because mortal passion makes the breakthrough by sheer excess, without divine intervention—as in the tale of Tereus and Philomela. But in every case, to a greater or lesser degree, Ovid locates and captures the particular frisson of that event, where the all-too-human victim stumbles out into the mythic arena and is transformed.

—Ted Hughes, *Tales from Ovid*

*

I'm sick of love
And I'm in the thick of it.

—Bob Dylan, "Love Sick"

1. On

the flight back from London to New York I read the new Ted Hughes book, *Birthday Letters*, a series of poems addressed to Sylvia Plath, his dead wife, recounting their relationship, although "recounting" doesn't quite do it. News of the book had hit the front page of the London *Times* while I was there—REVEALED: THE MOST TRAGIC LITERARY LOVE STORY OF OUR TIME, read the banner headline—poems were quoted and editorials written, there were pictures of the two young poets, and recitations of the story of their life together, the "literary romance of the century."

The other big literary news in London was the publication of Don DeLillo's *Underworld*, the vast novel which folds into itself the complex trajectory of Cold War America, threaded together on the fate of a single baseball—our romance with possibility, with fortune's fate—and the huge accumulation of detritus, both material and spiritual, which threatens to wipe all serendipity—of love, or art, or fame—from our lives. DeLillo has written a book that argues for the essential necessity of a fictive imagination by which to rekindle and reconstrue the facts, a book which perceives that the world under the world is our responsibility and the Fiction of the Possible moves parallel to the path of Fate, with her blunt logistics, her gargoyle's delight in brute reality, her desire to eradicate Eros and to perpetuate forever the grim threat of annihilation which animated and still animates—if that is the word, which it isn't—the world's psyche.

DeLillo read from his book to a huge audience in the center of London one Tuesday evening.

> "There's a word in Italian. Dietrologia. It means the science of what is behind something. A suspicious event. The science of what is behind an event."

"They need this science. I don't need it."

"I don't need it either. I'm just telling you."

"I'm an American. I go to ball games," he said.

"The science of dark forces. Evidently they feel this science is legitimate enough to require a name."

"People who need this science, I would make an effort to tell them we have real sciences, hard sciences, we don't need imaginary ones."

"I'm just telling you the word. I agree with you, Sims. But the word exists."

"There is always a word. There's probably a museum too. The Museum of Dark Forces. They have ten thousand blurry photographs. Or did the Mafia blow it up?"[2]

As the year turned, I decided to take whim to heart and, on the cool breeze from Time's revolving door, to go on a quick journey, to surprise myself into spontaneity; I wanted to run away from home. I wanted to take transition seriously, to create a literal threshold, wander on into and with the new year, right alongside the new year. I have not yet recovered from the giddy shock of finding myself elsewhere, in another country, another history, another language.

negative content
person/body/body politic/public/publicity
connective tissue/loyalty
boundary

I prefer winter. It has real boundaries, not just flimsy lids and thin folds, mesh and vagrant shade, but wide avenues to separate one from another, one *one* from another *one*. Cold sharpens the shape of things, outlines; the short winter day plummets to sapphire before expiring into the hibernating long dark night. And the sun, in winter, is an estranged event, almost strident, as it comes slanting in across the bedsheets, through the pale green potted leaves of the paperwhites or narcissi, offering transparency's brief gift, not constant companion, not a summer tent's voluminous bower, its ineffectual effort to contain the uncontainable. Summer is motion, ease, grace, aptitude, teen love, a season for muscular indentation, cascades of things that get entwined, that slip through, in; the season of agility and flight. Summer is halcyon days for the Ad Campaign. Summer, everything wants to lose distinction, to merge, relent, give in. *O blur!* Buoyant with excess, it appears to give more than it takes, even as it readies to forget, to vacate. Slow news. Summer has not much need for language, for the effort to make things clear; summer wants dance and sails, not the differentials between a body sitting, a mind sorting, hands, fingers, feelings, all kept apart by the sometimes appalling intercession between being and meaning.

I prefer winter. The internal, the mental, the dream, the book, the obscure, the difficult, the private, the brief, the brilliant, the episode, the event, the quick kiss in frosty air. It has about it the mood of an assignation, the stark rendezvous of Chance with Fate. Winter is urban. The body wears protective garb. Only the face is exposed, eyes alert, mouth pursed, skin dry and thin, parchment frail. You might glimpse a person's soul.

You might stop in your tracks.

To go somewhere in winter is hard. It feels against the grain, against nature. Nature says stay in, tend to the near at hand, do not risk the boundary. All is sharp, nothing is soft, be careful, be slow. The ice sleek but thin. Do not rush.

> *There's a certain Slant of light,*
> *Winter Afternoons—*
> *That oppresses, like the Heft*
> *Of Cathedral Tunes—*
>
> *Heavenly Hurt, it gives us—*
> *We can find no scar,*
> *But internal difference,*
> *Where the Meanings, are—*
>
> *None may teach it—Any—*
> *'Tis the Seal Despair—*
> *An imperial affliction*
> *Sent us of the Air—*
>
> *When it comes, the Landscape listens—*
> *Shadows—hold their breath—*
> *When it goes, 'tis like the Distance*
> *On the look of Death—*[3]

2. Gag

What to do in a world strewn with *infidels*, every mouth agape, secrets spit out like so many pits, seeds, from the grapevine. Good to know that the American public is less hypocritical than its ambassadors, who clamber up on their High Horse of (Far) Right/eous Indignation and Gallop (Poll) away with Bill's head tucked into their communal saddle bag. Ho heigh! If every celeb in and out of Hollywood's chambers of deceit, if the Departed Princess and the Anointed Heir, can parade ceaselessly before said public their wanton ways, then, pray tell, who is to pass judgment on our own Sixties Boytoy Prez? Our moral codes are in disarray. Perhaps it is time to reconstitute them so that they are more or less aligned, so we can begin to find our way to a life that is not bent out of shape with remorse, guilt, sham secrets, and informant's malice.

> Casual and fleeting associations have become central to our careers, displacing the deeper and longer-term relations of old. (Such strong ties—and the paradigmatic strong tie is loyalty—require a degree of personal commitment to which contemporary life gives little support.) Prominent management gurus urge us to avoid "entanglement" in institutional loyalty, and instead cultivate a have-vita-will-travel attitude of versatility: you attain power not by putting down roots but by "networking" . . . In an age of weak ties, of free agency triumphant, the virtues of adhesion can be as fragile as the ozone layer. Awash in authenticity, we shall be true to ourselves until, perhaps, we come to realize that we have no selves worth being true to.[4]

I was talking at lunch with a friend, Tom Dumm, who teaches political science at Amherst College; we were trying to come to grips with some nub or pith. Tom suggested that we have isolated two poles of human experience, the Child and the Father, the figure of Potential and the figure of Authority. Child as sentimental vehicle for recuperation, for beginning again, for the new, and Father as resident lawgiver, judge, holder of power. Both these figures are stripped of experience—wisdom of the heart, delight of the senses, delicate web of hope, expectation, and disappointment that informs how it goes on; they are moved almost entirely by codes of permissions and punishments. Power/Powerlessness is the twirling candy-cane pole, the blinking light at the corner, around which our culture turns.

Authority denuded of Experience; Ignorance deprived of Innocence.
Result: Dads who refuse to grow up; kids who shoot other kids with real guns.

> The recurrent triumph of the primitive and mediocre over the civilized serves to point up the idea that qualities like integrity, breeding, decency, sophistication and confidence are redundant in the face of emergent social barbarism. In Amis's books, the thugs tend to win, and not only in the social sphere. Physical decay, the fact of mortality, the inexorability of the coming of death: these are the deep-structural certainties that underpin the various forms of cultural breakdown he documents with such relish and wit.[5]

At the contagious heart of iteration is a search, not for pattern, not for source, not for a little house at the end of a path wreathed in vine; the search, the picking among the stones for crumbs, is for direction, for purpose, for a reason to go on to the next step, around the next bend, beyond that shadow looming out over the road in the shape of a crow. The track is one of constant erasure, so that, turning back, one cannot see one's footprints, cannot remember the signs along the way. The track is unmarked because it is so heavily marked. The search is to get from here to there, simply, without reiteration, without rehashing, echoing, mouthing the stale blather of what we know to be the case. It is this *already known* which keeps proposing itself as *news*, so that we are worn down with the familiar repetitions of this or that response to this or that so-called event. Repetition is a form of hell, isn't it? A torture, a pornography, especially if it masks itself as something fresh, vital, replete? On this map of recitation our perceptions dull. We begin to feel that we live in a world made of *negative content*, where all that we care for is turned inside out, emptied, and we are left holding the bag, the empty bag, like an enormous shadow. One sees that the only way through is to attempt to resist the habits by which we proceed, to try to invent a new game, a new procedure, by which we can look back and see all the incredible *unused excess* that has fallen at the wayside, nuggets and seeds, buttons and ashes, clippings, threads, morsels. We have to step over and step lightly and step into the fact of our loss. We are at a loss. We do not know what is missing, we do not know why, stuffed, we feel hungry; drunk, we feel sober.

If things were really different: for of course a different history is at stake and one that will make us reread our entire history. No longer the directional and signifying history of a sense that unfolds and redeems itself, but an intermittent history, conjectural and reticulated, traversed by pulsations rather than by flux. No longer the sense of history, but a history of sense—and yet, at the same time, the recasting of an infinite liberation. And this history, our history, our *coming* of sense, is not coming to conclude a development or extend it further, but, rather, to repeat, to replay the multiple chances of what the other history, occidental history, at once set into motion and dissimulated: a permanent excess or absenting of sense. Metaphysics and ontotheology, whatever their surface effects may have been, have never truly attempted to fill up this excessive absence. Rather, they have acknowledged it—in every case, and against their wills, or, rather, against their discursive bodies—to be the transcendental/factual absolute of the world and of existence.[6]

sense, n. & v.t. 1. Any of the special bodily faculties by which sensation is roused (*the five ~s*, sight, hearing, smell, taste, & touch; *sixth* or *muscular ~*, producing sensation of muscular effort; *has quick, keen, ~s, a dull ~ of smell*); (pl.) person's sanity or ordinary state of mind regarded as secured by possession of these (*have you taken leave of, are you out of, your ~s?*, are you mad?; *he will soon come, we must bring him to his ~s*, out of mad folly; *frightened out of his ~s*, into loss of his faculties; *in one's ~s*, sane). 2. Ability to perceive or feel or to be conscious of the presence or properties of things, sensitiveness of all or any of the ~s (*~ perception; errors of ~*, mistakes in perception; *the pleasures of ~*, those depending on sensation; *has a plant ~?*). 3. Consciousness *of* (*a* or *the ~ of pleasure, pain, gratification, having done well, one's own importance, shame, responsibility; labouring under a ~ of wrong*, feeling wronged). 4. Quick or accurate appreciation *of*, instinct regarding or insight into specified matter or habit of squaring conduct of such instinct (*~ of locality, distance, the ridiculous, humour, duty, beauty, gratitude, a keen ~ of honour; the religious, moral, aesthetic, ~*). 5. Practical wisdom, judgement, common ~, conformity to these (*sound, good*, COMMON, *~ a man of ~*, sagacious; *had not the ~ to* do; *has plenty of ~; what is the ~ of talking like that?; has more ~ than to* do; *now you are talking ~*). 6. Meaning, way in which word etc. is to be understood, intelligibility or coherence or possession of a meaning (*in what* *exact ~ we shall rise again is doubtful; the ~ of the word is clear; does not make ~,* is unintelligible: *~ in the strict, limited, literal, figurative, moral, metaphorical, legal,* PICKWICKIAN, *proper, full ~; in a vague, in every, in a ~,* provided the statement is taken in a particular way, under limitations as *what you say is true in a ~ ; make ~ out of nonsense).* 7. Prevailing sentiment among a number of people (*take the ~ of a meeting;* ascertain this by putting question etc.). 8. ~body, -capsule, -cavity, -cell, -center, -organ, parts of animals concerned in producing sensation; hence ~less (-sl-) a. (esp. = foolish; *knock ~less,* stun), ~lessly adv. ~lessness n. 9. v.t. Perceive by ~, (esp.) be vaguely aware of. [ME, f. OF *sens* or L *sensus* (*sentire sense*—feel)][7]

3. Are

You can see how the body would become a locus for discourse, as if it were a curiosity: its needs, hungers, violences; its tenderness, pain, loneliness; its pleasures, desires, gestures. The body as the site of heat within the context of an indeterminate but pervasive cold. You can see how there would be a constant effort to enthrone (disown) it, to distill it, to rip it from its contingency and hold it: a doll, an effigy, a *machine* not in relation to other bodies, but to *other machines.* Just do it! Do what?

The subject of a recent issue of *Critical Inquiry: Intimacy.*

The absence of contexts for transformation is the defining condition of social existence—nationally and personally—as our politicians so effectively mirror back to us, with intimacy ideologies organizing habituation to low-level discontent so effectively that to chance transformation of any sort will seem patently ridiculous: a guaranteed laugh on a domestic sitcom or a guaranteed cover story in the *Star.* If adultery dares to stake out a small preserve for *wanting* something—even temporarily—it manages to do so largely through the always available idiom of sex. But renunciation still rules, the cornerstone of the administered psyche. Citizens are split subjects, maritally and nationally, and like spouses who know each other's vulnerabilities all too well, our national institutions—politics, the media—reproduce themselves efficiently by playing the split for all its worth. With renunciation the reaction

formation to thwarted desire, the unfortunate sequel to the enter-
tainment of national scandal is the unctuous strutting of public
virtue. Renunciation is supposed to be a cure-all for the dangerous
experimentation of a utopian imagination, an organ even politi-
cians apparently find themselves supplied with.[8]

The media, as ur-station of the real world, apparently self-appointed, self-
regulating, self-regarding, bearers of a lesser fame, feeding off the bottom
like fish, not quite celebrities but addicted to celebrity, addicted to power,
the Authority Dad and the Ignorant Kid; the media, *horde* or *army* of re-
porters (guns also report, it is a kind of *fart*), somehow annoyed or tired or
bored, after the Model Princess had finally really died only to come back as
a Doll, an Icon, a Place to Visit on your holidays; the media, that Chorus, got
really excited, maybe even a little frenzied, at the sniff of a Big Story, some-
thing to pep up the doldrums of the post-holidays, in a time of relative peace,
relative prosperity, white sales, a few murders, Winter Olympics on their
way, but nothing really worthy of a headline, a three-incher, something to
cross the boundaries of the mere column, to soar out over, to take up the
whole unfolded page of the op-eds, to consume the appetite, to focus the at-
tention, to vie with the Super Bowl, to let the pundits enunciate their opin-
ions, something to get the juices rolling, maybe even to bring down another
presidency—yes!—which would lead to a lot more films and novels and
there he is, Mr. Bob Guccione himself, offering a cool two million to Monica
for a few semi-nude shots and her story, and there's Ms. Tripp, the one who
would have been a perfect character on that old long-run series—you know,
the one with J.R., about the venal eighties—she who actually encouraged
Monica to get tapes made, and who called this literary agent—excuse me,
just how unsavory and unseemly can it get over there at the hallowed *New
York Times*?—the media, crawling with folks probably a little cynical, a little
jealous, wishing there could be something as world-changing, mood-altering
as Watergate, or O.J.'s trial, something to have all of us buying more than one
paper every day, clicking from channel to channel to find the most up-to-
date, most savvy commentary, not really ready for yet another confrontation
with Saddam Hussein since the first one was such a *bust* as wars go, and
maybe even a little tired of same old same old Bill, he of the big hug and big
smile and big hands, whose character had already been pretty well pilloried
within an inch of its life and who still managed to bounce back, still smiling,
still glad-handing, Mr. Nice Guy married to a Smart Dame—too smart for

her own good, not up to the role, not good enough in the legs department to be an icon, not like, say, Jackie or Diana, our true heroines, glamorous moms married to really powerful men—

—to Bill Clinton, who represents to many the *worst characteristics* of the 1960s counterculture: self-indulgent, undisciplined, feckless, irresponsible, disloyal, ambivalent about the trappings of authority, arrogant and facile about change, morally a little shaky, perhaps even mendacious—sex (not!), drugs (not!), rock 'n' roll—

—the media, just by the way, disdains poetry, unless, of course, it has to do with *sex, infidelity, suicide,* or sanctimonious pronouncements by the sententious caretakers of our national soul—

So here: on the op-ed page of the *New York Times*, Tuesday, January 27, 1998, side by side, one piece titled "Poetic Justice for Sylvia Plath" by Diane Wood Middlebrook, and another, by Thomas Friedman, under the column "Foreign Affairs," titled "Character Suicide."

Column A:

> The poems in *Birthday Letters* show that Hughes, too, has been obsessed by the calamity of his failed marriage. They offer a peculiar affirmation of the power of Plath's art, for they record his own slow awakening to the inner life of a woman as talented as himself. No longer does he resist the role written for him by her work, the role of Fatal Husband. He indicates that the conventional, 1950's style domesticity that he and Plath both idealized was tragic for her. She succeeded in meeting her own expectations only in her extreme emotional and physical isolation from him. Ted Hughes now endows Plath's literary achievement with the laurel of prestigious understanding. It is a big concession. If he has written the last lines in this drama, she remains its author. The formality and awe of his tribute seem exactly right.

Column B:

> I understand, and detest, all the putrid smoke surrounding this story. But what I don't understand is the spark of fire that ignited it. I don't understand how someone entrusted with the opportunity to lead this country at such a great time, how someone

whose political agenda was so substantively appealing—on issues from abortion to education to the global economy—could risk it all on a dalliance with a White House intern . . . We overlooked Mr. Clinton's past indiscretions—he was hardly the first politician with testosterone overload—on the condition that he postpone his next dalliance until after he left the White House. But he broke the bargain. I knew he was a charming rogue with an appealing agenda, but I didn't think he was a reckless idiot with an appealing agenda.

4. Pen

Make no mistake, Sylvia Plath wanted to be *famous,* a *diva.* She wanted to be seen, heard, acknowledged as great, a great poet. This was an absolute, an idée fixe, not to be modulated or modified by experience, not to be made contingent, that is to say, dependent on context, except insofar as experience might feed, nurture, expand. But she grew up in America, in the fifties, and she went to Smith College, where, without doubt, there still obtained the notion that the best way, perhaps the only way, to gain access to power was to *marry it marry it marry it.* So when she arrived at Cambridge, England, on her Fulbright, she had a keen eye out for a likely consort, someone to hitch her wagon to and help her fulfill her destiny.

I am in the shadow of this, at the far edges of the shadow of it.

When I was an undergraduate, Sylvia Plath was in her first season of fame. After Eliot and Frost, and along with a few other poets—Theodore Roethke, e. e. cummings—the American poets of note in Middle America were the "confessional poets": Robert Lowell, John Berryman, Randall Jarrell, and Sylvia Plath. Sinners confessing their sins to an absent God, but to a new audience of voyeurs. When I was in college, I was aware of Sylvia Plath, her person as well as her work: I noticed she had graduated from Smith College (from which my sister, mother, and grandmother had graduated); I noticed that her father had died at the same time in her life as my father had died. Sylvia Plath stuck her head in an oven in February 1963, the same year that John F. Kennedy was assassinated. It was my junior year at the University of Wisconsin.

I was rejected from Smith. My SATs were too low, I was too bohemian, too troubled. (By the time I was getting ready to apply to college, my mother had fled, my sister was safely ensconced at college, and I was living alone in New York with my younger brother. But that is another story.) To be rejected from Smith in my family was tantamount to a not-so-subtle form of failure, a misstep across the threshold into life.

In my own personal economy it meant simply that I would not be empowered to become a poet.

For reasons, in part, of discretion, the following forfeits the narrating "I" for a fictive "she," but the real reason is that all that transpired was *already a fiction.*

1970, London

A crowd had assembled, almost, one might say, a throng. Women in short skirts and high boots, men in flowered ties. There was a hushed milling about in the great hall outside the auditorium; the whole place seemed to have a rapid heartbeat, a rush, anticipation and expectation were colliding in their chest cavities, causing little eruptions, pulse alterations, breathlessness.

That morning, she had awakened feeling a little scared. She lived in a big room in the basement of a house facing Belsize Square. Across the street, a stone church, nestled down for the duration. The room was dank, the cement floor smooth and cold under her bare feet. Outside her room there was a hall; down the hall was a door to the bathroom and another door into another room which faced out into the garden at the back of the house. Only it wasn't a garden; it was just a space where a garden might be. There were French doors out onto this ragged plot. She had awakened feeling tense, in that way you do, into the suddenness of the world, its desire to put before you something you do not know how to do. The world greets you with a test.

Lying in bed, she thought she heard something. It sounded like someone sweeping nearby, or something being dragged along the cement floor just beyond her door. It came and went in awkward spasms, this whispery dry sound, almost a kind of dry weeping. She opened the door onto the hall and the sound became nearer but not louder; she was sure someone was just outside, doing something. She moved along the hall in the dim light, listening. The sound now seemed to come from behind the door leading into the empty back room. She stood listening, her heart jamming up into her throat, trying to get out through her open mouth. She opened the door a crack. The shuffling stopped.

The room had cartons and other stuff in it; a broken chair, some stacks of magazines; the things that sit waiting in limbo, between use and waste, the heaven and hell of the material world. The room was in limbo; the people who owned the house did not want to rent it out.

The morning tossed its cool white light into the air outside. She stood in the doorway staring into the room's uncertainty. Something moved. She jumped, maybe even a sound escaped from her contracted throat.

On the floor, the thing moved again.

Its wings spread on the floor, a pale-dusty-colored bird, a little larger than a jay. Sensing her, it flailed on the cement. She entered the room. The bird was still. She did not know what to do; she went to it and stared down into its tiny hard eye. She could see its body pulsating with terror; the bird was terror; no little part of it was telling it to calm down. She tried to tell it not to worry, but the bird did not understand. She opened the door; cold morning air rushed in, but the bird did not fly out. At last, she took an empty carton and lifted the bird gently into it.

Memory also has a muse.

5. Green

When she first saw him, in a large formal room with long windows and pale furniture, a room above a gracefully turning staircase, she felt herself arrested, stopped in her tracks, as if he were a kind of magnetized impediment. Always afterwards she described this by saying that he was like a kind of huge tree, its leafless branches bowed upwards, a basket of arms, under which she wanted to go; she wanted to stand near to the immense gnarled trunk, she wanted to go there.

When Sylvia Plath first met Ted Hughes she bit him on the neck so that he bled.

He had been hidden away, only a few people had caught sight of him. Now he had written a book of poems with a bird, a crow, as protagonist.

He read into the hushed dark auditorium from Crow.

I think I came out on stage after the reading and said, "The rest is silence." I felt way out of my depth.

In the aftermath, he was surrounded, accosted by eager persons, many of them women, wanting to say, to ask, be near. One woman, in a white shiny miniskirt and high white shiny boots (Courrèges was the rage) announced that she was writing a thesis on Sylvia Plath, and could she possibly write to him with some questions? He was gentle, agreeable with these inquisitions, these curiosities. She watched from a distance: tangents of desire, flirtations, passes around his figure, as if it were an ancient rite in which someone was about to be entrapped or entranced, aided by—whom?—Hermes, the Trickster, god of boundaries, uncertainties?

Trickster is a boundary crosser. Every group has its edge, its sense of in and out, and trickster is always there, at the gates of the city and the gates of life, making sure there is commerce. He also attends the internal boundaries by which groups articulate their social life. We constantly distinguish—right and wrong, sacred and profane, clean and dirty, male and female, young and old, living and dead—and in every case trickster will cross the line and confuse the distinction. Trickster is the creative idiot, therefore, the wise fool, the gray-haired baby, the cross-dresser, the speaker of profanities. When someone's sense of honorable behavior has left him unable to act, trickster will appear to suggest an amoral action, something right/wrong that will get life going again. Trickster is the mythic embodiment of ambiguity and ambivalence, doubleness and duplicity, contradiction and paradox.[9]

*

I mean *Negative Capability*, that is when man is capable of being in uncertainties, mysteries, doubts, without any irritable reaching after fact and reason—[10]

She was asked if she would like to accompany them to his sister Olwyn's house, for a drink, for a cup of tea, not far from her basement flat in North London. A writer, Marvin Cohen, almost deaf, came along in the car. She sat in the backseat; Marvin shouted. They came to the sister's house, a dark place, the sister a large woman with a gothic wildness in her face. They sat in the parlor; the sister and the poet wanted to do her horoscope; to read her palm. They pored over her outstretched upturned hand, whispering, consulting. There was a sense of some mystical, Celtic shenanigans, as though Yeats and Madame Blavatsky had left some version, some portent in their wake.

She has no memory of what they said. Perhaps it was noted in a journal.

Eventually, he offered to drive her home. She sat in the front seat, next to him; when they got to her place they paused, the motor idling. He asked her something about herself; she blurted out that she wanted to be a poet. He said he would be pleased to see something of hers, that she could send some poems to him. She held on to the car door handle, leaning away from the huge wind that pushed her toward him.

Then she remembered the captured bird.

"There's a bird, it was on the floor this morning, it seemed unhurt but unable to fly away."

Something like that.

"How big?"

"Larger than a jay, putty colored, with wide wings."

"It's a swift," he said. "They need leverage for their wingspan to lift. If you take it outside and toss it upwards it will fly away."

She sent the poet some poems, typed on her portable Olivetti 22. Maybe eight or ten poems. Time passed, one, two weeks, she can't remember. Then he phoned her where she worked, where they had met, and said he would like to meet with her to talk about her poems. He was coming up to London. They met in a pub, on Haverstock Hill, not far from her flat. They talked. She cannot remember the talk, she only remembers feeling surprised to be sitting in a pub in North London with this figure, this poet, the husband of the other, dead, American poet. She asked him questions; he told her something T. S. Eliot had told him about being a poet and she remembers feeling that something important, maybe sacred, was being passed to her. He walked her home, it was quite late. She doesn't recall what season it was, maybe early summer. It must have been early summer, or perhaps late summer, because the next morning she went into the little group of shops in Belsize Village and bought some strawberries and cream for their breakfast.

She doesn't think they ever mentioned the dead American poet by name. She tried to understand what had happened between this man, who seemed now to be sad, and private, and lonely, and kind, and the young American poet, now famous for dying, for writing amazing poems right at the edge of death. The poet, Sylvia Plath, had wanted Ted Hughes, the great treelike figure, to protect her, to keep her from her destructive urges, to stand between her and her romance with her other suitor, Death.

And now she thought he came to her to hide, to escape, that he wanted, above all, to be protected.

She thought about her own ferocity, the narrative of her life, how she felt invaded by her absent parents, in particular by her own dead father, who seemed to have stolen some essential thing from her, and put her directly in contact with obliteration, with the expectation of sudden catastrophe, what her friend Peter Straub had called a "fatal imagination," a sense of continuous urgency and fear that there was not, there would never be, enough time because somehow her

father had gone off with Time Itself and left her holding something like longing,
a longing for someone magical to come along and give it back. It was as if time
and death and her father were all part of the same indivisible configuration,
merged into a current of lost and found. And she knew, also, that the idea of a
normal life which went from this to this to this in a natural course, a logical se-
quence, was not likely. Life would be a series of beginnings and endings without
middles.

   She knew that it was in the middle that the habit of trust resided.

6. Tops

Sylvia Plath made for herself a sort of cauldron that did not allow one thing
to come after another; her final poems were not written so much to or about
the betraying husband, as to death itself, her real Paramour, who had captured
her father and had thus tethered her. Plath's real dialogue was not with the
awful English winter or the two small children or the missing husband, but
was with this other First Script, which Ted Hughes could not possibly rewrite.

   Plath's letters to her mother, Aurelia, are often fevered and hyperbolic, as
if the actual world had to be continuously buttressed, augmented. There is a
rampant voraciousness, an exaggerated breathlessness, that consumes her
prose.

> "The Pursuit" is more in my old style, but larger, influenced a bit
> by Blake I think (tiger, tiger), and more powerful than any of my
> other "metaphysical" poems; read aloud also. It is, of course, a
> symbol of the terrible beauty of death, *and the paradox that the*
> *more intensely one lives, the more one burns and consumes oneself;*
> *death, here, includes the concept of love, and is larger and richer*
> *than mere love, which is part of it* [italics mine].

> Dearest Mother,
>   I have not heard from you in several days and wish with all my
> heart that these times are not trying beyond endurance. . . .
>   I shall tell you now about something most miraculous and
> thundering and terrifying and wish you to think on it and share
> some of it. It is this man, this poet, this Ted Hughes. I have never

known anything like it. For the first time in my life I can use *all* my knowing and laughing and force and writing to the hilt all the time, everything, and you should see him, hear him! . . .

He has a health and hugeness . . . the more he writes poems, the more he writes poems. He knows all about the habits of animals and takes me amid cows and coots. I am writing poems, and they are better than anything I have ever done; here is a small one about one night we went into the moonlight to find owls:

METAMORPHOSIS

Haunched like a faun, he hooed
from grove of moon-glint and fen-frost
until all owls in the twigged forest
flapped black to look and brood
on the call this man made.

No sound but a drunken coot
lurching home along river bank;
stars hung water-sunk, so a rank
of double star-eyes lit
boughs where those owls sat.

An arena of yellow eyes
watched the changing shape he cut,
saw hoof harden from foot, saw sprout
goat horns; heard how god rose
and galloped woodward in that guise.

Daily I am full of poems; my joy whirls in tongues of words. . . . I feel a growing strength. I do not merely idolize, I see right into the core of him . . . I know myself, in vigor and prime and growing, and know I am strong enough to keep myself whole, no matter what. . . .

His humor is the salt of the earth; I've never laughed as hard and long in my life. He tells me fairy stories, and stories of kings and green knights, and has made up a marvelous fable of his own

about a little wizard named Snatchcrafington, who looks like a
stalk of rhubarb. He tells me dreams, marvelous colored dreams,
about certain red foxes. . . .[11]

The dead American poet had wanted poetry to intervene, mediate, be-
tween the desire to live in the normal daily real of a bitter winter in a foreign
country with two small children and an absent husband, and her desire to
live in another, permanent, fixed space, the reified space of immortality.
Death was a mere passage, a necessary door, into this firmament. The final
poems of *Ariel* wage a battle between the living force of language and the
transfiguring force of death.

One time I returned to my flat to find a scrap of paper. On it was written,
"Plenty of warmth but no Anni. A sitting Crow stares." I have it still, tucked
inside his book *Wodwo*, the triangle of white paper torn from an envelope.

Perhaps Ted Hughes understood, wanted to understand, nature, crea-
tures, forces, better than he understood persons.

> *Only there is a doorway in the wall—*
> *A black doorway:*
> *The eye's pupil.*
>
> *Through that doorway came Crow.*
>
> *Flying from sun to sun, he found his home.*[12]

Writers and their identifications: Ted Hughes with his protagonist Crow;
Sylvia Plath with an immortality that she would have to cross the threshold,
go though Crow's door, to enter; I with all of it, starstruck like a teen groupie. I
was astonished—excited and flattered and scared—to find myself, however
tentatively, swept into the eddies of their self-perpetrated myth. Sylvia Plath
was not the only young woman to suffer from the collision and collusion of
phantom and real; I was not the only young woman, who, wishing something
for herself, was seduced by the allure of an intimacy with power, the aura of
literary fate. As I look back from the stripped edifice of postmodernism, I feel
lucky to have escaped these saturated delusions. And yet, a slight rueful
pause. For what? Not for the hapless romance, but for an almost indefinable
relation between the potency of desire, the complexities of choice, the sim-
mering modalities of personal and historical event, the singularity of fact and
the manifold truths of fiction. The eye of the Crow on the cutting-room floor.

7. Possible

I came` to see that if I wanted to live my own life, if I wanted to own my life, I would have to learn to let go, to give something up, in particular the melodramatic narcissism that had determined my sense of personal fate. I would need to begin to unwrite, unravel, revise the initial script. When, many years later, I did attempt to take my own life, it was because the part of me that was wedded to this first script and its annihilations became *indifferent* to the parts that loved, forgave, grieved, believed. The will, I saw, is amoral, it has no use for compassion, failure, for the ifs ands and buts of life's transitive affective grammars. The will pinioned, blinking; on/yes, off/no. The will, as Plath understood so well, a Nazi.

> What Foucault felt more and more, after the first volume of *The History of Sexuality*, was that he was getting locked in power relations. And it was all very well to invoke points of resistance as "counterpoints" of foci of power, but where was such resistance to come from? Foucault wonders how he can cross the line, go beyond the play of forces in its turn. Or are we condemned to conversing with Power, irrespective of whether we're wielding it or being subjected to it? . . . Crossing the line of force, going beyond power, involves as it were bending force, making it impinge on itself rather than on other forces: a "fold," in Foucault's terms, force playing on itself. It's a question of "doubling" the play of forces, of a self-relation that allows us to resist, to elude power, to turn life or death against power. This, according to Foucault, is something the Greeks invented. It's no longer a matter of determinate forms, as with knowledge, or of constraining rules, as with power: it's a matter of *optional rules* that make existence a work of art, rules at once ethical and aesthetic that constitute ways of existing or styles of life (including even suicide). It's what Nietzsche discovered as the will to power operating artistically, inventing new "possibilities of life."[13]

It surprises me that many feminists blamed Ted Hughes for the suicide of Sylvia Plath, that they so readily agreed to the drama of the failed marriage turned into tragic fable of the cruel betraying husband poet and the innocent victim wife poet. It seems to me that, given the post-sixties turn in consciousness—*our bodies, ourselves; the personal is political*—there would have been a less romanticized, more culturally contextualized, psychologically nuanced, reading of the forces that doomed her. A woman of such high intensity, ambition, talent, would not have been much appreciated in London; the English are not particularly fond of women who take themselves or their work—especially their work—too seriously. Work should reflect other, more contained social ambitions—good deeds, cultural amusements, horticulture, dogs. Gratification in one's own work is somehow a little *vulgar*.

There was, as well, the culpability of 1950s American culture, which sent out continuous conflicting images for women, and for what might constitute a woman's happiness or success.

> The youth movement that never quite emerged in the United States before 1940 has, I believe, now come. It is not national in its scope, but it is national in its implications. Although there was precedence for it in the adult world, it was initiated by youth. There are members of the adult community who command the respect of the young in the movement, but less as individuals than as embodiments of an ideal. The commitment of the participants is to an ideal, not to an organization or an individual, and yet the tactics and strategy of the movement demonstrate a pragmatic grasp of political and social realities.[14]

Sylvia Plath would have benefited immeasurably from the social changes that emerged out of the 1960s; had she been born ten years later, there might have been sufficient support among her peers and the multiple forms of resistance to have given her better mooring. Plath was prey to what the psychoanalyst Karen Horney called "the overvaluation of love"; she could not meet the idealized, internalized demands for perfection in both domestic and public realms. Such women, Horney thought, were caught in a bind between images of domestic compliance (dependency) and self-sufficiency (ambition), a conflict between what Horney called the "real self" and an internalized idealization.

> The conflict begins to inform all areas of life: compliance, vindictiveness, helplessness, rage, seductiveness, envy, suffering, ambition, and self-effacement all compete and interact. The result is psychic confusion. "Patients inclined toward this kind of defense

often resemble those characters in fairy tales who when pursued turn into fish; if not safe in this guise, they turn into deer; if the hunter catches up with them they fly away as birds."[15]

As *birds*. Dinosaurs, I leaned recently, were not "horrible lizards," but birds. And poets are not extinct either. *Birds fly over the rainbow / Why then, oh why can't I?*

THE NIGHT SKY VII

Events, actions arise, that must be sung, that will sing themselves. Who can doubt, that poetry will revive and lead in a new age, as the star in the constellation Harp, which now flames in our zenith, astronomers announce, shall one day be the pole-star for a thousand years?

—Emerson, "The American Scholar"

1. There Is No Topic Sentence

as fear accumulates, everything getting more intense, more intensely difficult to manage, just at the level of output-input, so one feels one might in that old sense "lose it."

What is the "it"?

Here's Ed Hirsch talking about Federico García Lorca on National Public Radio: *Only the mysterious makes it possible for us to survive.*

careful, careful, careful
vigilance, sleeplessness, responsibility

Waking into a turning diaspora, the cat stinking of rabbit shit, she murderess, I with a pain in the pit of my stomach, some thing of the body, stone in the body, locating the missing, obdurate and singular—

Lorca murdered—

almost eternal on its stem, it looked for something else

In the pool, thinking I could just start writing and go on through to the end, as if I had that much to say about anything, that much stamina. I never write straight out, I have stopped believing that it might be possible. Turning, at night, from possible to impossible, the rumpled space there, past and future cut off, no place to go, no place from which to come, memory revoked, hope suspended like a canopy over the present, up there, the summer light filtering through, moonlight trapped in a parking lot, the erasure of what is actually the case, the hour, the actual hour. And it could be a list, turn the whole thing into a list, *this this this,* designate the place where desire harbors its value, its cost: the cost of this desire will be 1, 2, 3, minting a new price. Then say you translate desire into a desire for the knowledge of an elsewhere. What was it Joseph Brodsky wrote? Something about the trajectory of a song.

Turn, again, to Emerson:

> The world,—this shadow of the soul, or other me, lies wide around. Its attractions are the keys which unlock my thoughts and make me acquainted with myself. I run eagerly into this resounding tumult. I grasp the hands of those next me, and take my place in the ring to suffer and to work, taught by an instinct, that so shall the dumb abyss be vocal with speech. I pierce its order; I dissipate its fear; I dispose of it within the circuit of my expanding life. So much of the wilderness have I vanquished and planted, or so far have I extended my being, my dominion. I do not see how any man can afford, for the sake of his nerves and his nap, to spare any action in which he can partake. It is pearls and rubies to his discourse. Drudgery, calamity, exasperation, want, are instructors in eloquence and wisdom. The true scholar grudges every opportunity of action past by, as a loss of power.[1]

It is not a list. The actual cannot settle into either a list or a sequence.

Perhaps we make art to pluck some aspect from the actual, in its drifting temporal variety, and it is this aspect we call "the real."

We know it as "the real" because it is aligned to our understanding of what is true about the actual. Is this how the real and the true became inextricably intertwined?

The form of a thing, a poem: the condition through or by which it picks out its real: to structure possible meaning that might come out of the real.

But sometimes the presumed alignment between the real, extrapolated from the actual, and the true, which is our will to judge, is incommensurate, so that we are forced to reassess it.

If we have a strong sense of what is good and bad in the moral sphere, this sense is linked to other kinds of human experience.

When we think a work of art is "bad," we sometimes mistake aesthetics with morals, because the way in which it aligns the real with the true we think is false, a lie. The Robert Mapplethorpe pictures of homoerotic acts, extrapolating a real from the actual, and making it "true," because the photographs are convincing, and *beautiful* (as Dave Hickey has argued), caused some persons to be outraged because the photographs challenge the relation between what is actually happening among certain human beings, and the judgment of that activity by those who view this actuality as immoral.

One set of "values" is imposed on another set.

The good is linked to aesthetics by means of the beautiful.
The good is linked to ethics by means of happiness, the common good.

Can we say then, that
aesthetics is linked to the ethical via the concept of the good?

But neither happiness (the common good) nor beauty (good art) is fixed in time.
They cannot be wholly defined by convention.

When law, and science, are unlinked from the pursuit of the good, they lose their ethical ground.

Technology is morally neutral, it is not innately good or evil.

Reason is one way of aligning the real with the true. Jurisprudence, it would seem, is now the most persuasive and ubiquitous way in which we in America attempt to make an alignment between the real and the true, to make the actual come into alignment with values. But when law is in the hands of persons with strong opinions about values, about what should be "true" in the moral sense, it can be used to impose these values on the public.

Art cannot be reduced to its subject matter, any more than the actual can be, finally, reduced to a real. Surely this is one of the lasting insights of modernism. Cézanne's pictures are not "about" fruit, Stevens's anecdote is not "about" a jar, in the sense that a newspaper article is *about* a seventh-inning home run, or the stock market, or genocide in Rwanda (there's a list). Poems which can be reduced to their subjects too often fail to show the asymmetry between real and true, and so fail to elicit from the reader's imagination its capacity to interpret (or make judgments about) his or her "actual" world.

This gap is where the sublime might be hidden, the sublime as an insight into the discrepancy between what is (actual) and what might be (true). The sublime as a glimpse of the present lifted up on the will of the good.

You want to go somewhere away from what you know, this is a human instinct, the desire to discover some (-thing, -one, -place) else. Why else do we begin to crawl, noticing that to sit inside the perimeters of a scrap of cloth on the floor won't provide enough room to *find out more*?

Knowledge as an intimate fact, an intimacy that somehow finds its way across to the other, as if across two counties on a dark road, past dark shapes, hills, the black water onto which the moon has leaked a path.

A child came to me and said, "What is that path of light on the water?"

I think it must be the scarf of Venus, dropped as she was racing across the heavens.

"And what are the stars?"

I think they must be the sieve through which Eros pours his dust.

You search the whole night sky to find your heart.

The arc beyond the already known, a radiance that enters so you know you are porous, possibly even contaminated as the skin, touched, knows itself as that which is touched.

Jesus said *noli me tangere* to Mary Magdalene, touch me not, knowing that once touched it would be impossible to be

autonomous
in the face of love
in the face of betrayal

he would lose courage, his faith in the untouchable thing by which his immeasurable humanity had measured itself. Thomas, the Doubting Empiricist among the Disciples, insists, after the Crucifixion, that he put his fingers into Jesus' Wound. Jesus says:

Reach hither thy finger, and behold my hands; and reach hither thy hand, and thrust it into my side; and be not faithful, but believing. (John 27)

Jesus seems to be making a distinction between empirical knowledge and faith. He wants to say that there are some things, some truths, that are not self-evident, and these truths involve the principle of faith. Faith, then, is blind, and the blindness of faith and the blindness of love are related, since neither can be "proven" except by action, by a way of being toward the world, the Other of the world. Faith is knowable, that is, perceivable, only by example.

> The most useful investigator, because the most sensitive observer, is always he whose eager interest in one side of the question is balanced by an equally keen nervousness lest he become deceived. Science has organized this nervousness into a regular technique, her so-called method of verification; and she has fallen so deeply in love with the method that one may even say she has ceased to care for truth by itself at all. It is only truth as technically verified that interests her. The truth of truths might come in merely affirmative form, and she would decline to touch it . . . Human passions, however, are stronger than technical rules. "La coeur a ses raisons," as Pascal says, "que la raison ne connait point" . . .[2]

The conundrum of it, how it haunts the boundaries between us, which language attempts to negotiate. The crisis in the White House, protracted around the site of the body, its cravings, its alliance with touch, in the name of "love." The young intern, guileless and attracted to her hero, has no idea of the consequences of her actions, no sense of how the private space of the body can come undone and spill—the stain on the blue dress—into the public, where issues of virtue, responsibility, accountability, are assessed.

I am counting on you.

> The comedy begins with our simplest gestures. They all entail an inevitable awkwardness. Reaching out my hand to pull a chair toward me, I have folded the arm of my jacket, scratched the floor, and dropped my cigarette ash. In doing what I willed to do, I did a thousand and one things I hadn't willed to do. The act was not pure; I left traces. Wiping away these traces, I left others. Sherlock Holmes will apply his science to this irreducible coarseness of each of my initiatives, and thus the comedy might take a

tragic turn. When the awkwardness of the act is turned against
the goal pursued, we are in the midst of tragedy. Laius, in at-
tempting to thwart the fatal predictions, undertakes precisely
what is necessary to fulfill them. Oedipus, in succeeding, works
toward his own misfortune. It is like an animal fleeing in a
straight line across the snow before the sound of the hunters,
thus leaving the very traces that will lead to its death.[3]

Eros suspends and subverts the rules, in order to allow new rules to
come into being, a new vocabulary, a revised story, not quite so set within
convention—this first kiss will lead, ineluctably, to table settings, to the canon,
to decorum; habits and their calm pleasures, replication, reproduction.

The comfort of habit; the numbness of conformity.

Surely one way to argue for the necessity of art in a democratic society is
that it proposes change without violence, that it has the capacity to alter re-
ceived relations between each other, ourselves, and the world, without coer-
cion; to allow us

to see differently
less afraid of what we do not know
to include that which is, those who are, different from ourselves.

The common ground is not there waiting for us passively in the future,
nor is it back there, in a fictive agrarian reciprocity, labor to harvest; it is un-
der our feet in the present.

> The fundamental contradiction of modern man is precisely that he
> does not yet have an experience of time adequate to his idea of his-
> tory, and is therefore painfully split between his being-in-time as an
> elusive flow of instants and his being-in-history, understood as the
> original dimension of man. The twofold nature of every modern
> concept of history, as *res gestae* and as *historia rerum gestarum,* as
> diachronic reality and as synchronic structure which can never co-
> incide in time, expresses this impossibility: the inability of man,
> who is lost in time, to take possession of his own historical nature.[4]

The things I know

under the museum's cast

shadow format

    wondering what is to become of the dark night sky

what of these sayings

into the glass   fear

spoken into

        the ear

           so that there is the story

           genocide in Rwanda

could this be an example

as for example   eight hundred thousand

inside the community

could we ask

what is
eight hundred thousand

could I ask
what then is

what if
it is what you cannot say is.

      Under the eye's shadow

out of thin air

have we not
anointed Remorse

thou wing betokened
thou among dilemmas

cast in bewilderment
over the hill

and the cello blooms
and the mountain carves

above the bleak
above the slain

things in October happen
as if they were not recalled

and ask does this dilemma
have a common chart

is this a necessary divergence
why crave repetition

how is it this road is hot
this sky still sky

how is it the one leaves a trail
for the other to follow

in the humid days
where the leaves are adrift

or to ask is this reason
where I wake to your eyes

the precision of seeing
entering each

open again and once again
kept alive

the intimate seizure
iterating belief

and the Sad Girls
awaiting their heroes

what had we said
for what did we hope—

rapture of the blindfold
trust or terror.

This way to an embrace, this way to be shot at dawn.

A heap of stones.

A woman sitting next to her white pebbles picking out weeds one by one from her perfection, her lawn. Perfection, in human terms, is only another term for destruction. It is antithetical to the construct of beauty, wound like a vine around the stasis inheld at the core of change. The beautiful as only the advent of itself.

Poetry as the demonstration of this.

The voice in your ear, the sea in a shell.

And you see, as you do, that what is perfect is possible only as an approach, an anticipation, as when you look at the place where it isn't and you regard it happily because you are glad that the perfect has been delayed, offset, is, as it were, installed as incipience, as that which is not yet, as the lure of futurity. What completes the incompleteness of a perfect incipience? Another? Affirmed from elsewhere, from the grace of a different perspective or set, the one who comes along and says *that's perfect*, because the thing—event or thing—fits, or completes, what has been missing or incomplete over there, in that person's domain.

Blindfolded in embrace, one has an intimation of perfection.

Under threat at all times, under all conditions, and the only thing to do is to somehow abide the relation between the perfect and its demise, having and losing—to have a thing and long for it at once is fatal.

> But the newly initiated, who has had a full sight of the celestial vision, when he beholds a god-like face of a physical form which truly reflects ideal beauty, first of all shivers and experiences something of the dread which the vision itself inspired; next he

gazes upon it and worships it as if it were a god, and, if he were
not afraid of being thought an utter madman, he would sacrifice
to his beloved as to the image of a divinity. Then, as you would ex-
pect after a cold fit, his condition changes and he falls into an un-
accustomed sweat; he receives through his eyes the emanation of
beauty, by which the soul's plumage is fostered, and grows hot,
and this heat is accompanied by a softening of the passages from
which the feathers grow, passages which have long been parched
and closed up, so as to prevent any feathers from shooting. As
the nourishing moisture falls upon it the stump of each feather
under the whole surface of the soul swells and tries to grow
from its root; for in its original state the soul was feathered
all over. So now it is in a state of ferment and throbbing; in fact
the soul of a man who is beginning to grow his feathers has the
same sensation of prickling and irritation and itching as children
feel in their gums when they are just beginning to cut their
teeth.[5]

You learn to be patient.
So we write to keep the present present, keep it from moving away.
Hannah Arendt, writing about the gap between past and future, which
she calls, wonderfully, "thinking":

The gap, I suspect, is not a modern phenomenon, it is perhaps
not even a historical datum but is coeval with the existence of
man on earth. It may well be the region of the spirit or, rather, the
path paved by thinking, this small track of non-time which the
activity of thought beats within the space-time of mortal men and
into which the trains of thought, of remembrance and anticipa-
tion, save whatever they touch from the ruin of historical and bi-
ographical time. This small non-time-space in the very heart of
time, unlike the world and the culture into which we are born,
can only be indicated, but cannot be inherited and handed down
from the past; each new generation, indeed every new human be-
ing as he inserts himself between an infinite past and an infinite
future, must discover and ploddingly pave it anew.[6]

Why count? Hours, days, weeks, years. To each her age, his age; begin-
nings, middles, endings. Ascent and decline. The term. How many books,

pages, lines? The poems get longer, pushing against the short days. The great long poems of James Schuyler; *The Morning of the Poem*; *A Few Days*. John Ashbery's flowing charts of human perspicacity. Whitman's expansive meadow. Stein's reticulations, re/presentations of the present as wholly linguistic. These poets have no final horizon or frame, no fixed figure in landscape. American abstraction, proceeding from particular to particular, expanding as it goes. Imperialism and optimism. Sameness and difference.

> [Jackson] Pollock was asked once if he imitated nature, and he replied, "I am nature." Nature is various, though, and the nature that Pollock most closely resembles is not the ordered, driven, purposeful nature of biological form but the nature where momentary order is produced by the dialogue between chance events and ordinary material, the randomly generated nature of waves and winds and clouds. Pollock's poured pictures are ordered the way dunes and waterfalls are ordered, the way fire in the fireplace is ordered.[7]

Once I wanted to enumerate: first, second, third; one, two, three. I counted the steps for some reason. At my grandmother's house, where my mother and her four sisters were raised, the staircase curved at the top and at the bottom. Moving up, there was a powerful, indecipherable scent; the staircase was held by, enclosed in, a scent. *Ascent*. For as long as I was able to visit this house, the scent sent me into a dense indeterminate place without name, no single event affixed to it. It was as if I had access—a whiff—to a region outside of time, but which was also the accumulated patina of time, linearity collapsed; the event, unrecovered and unrecoverable, having left its excess, its trace.

The rational counting of the steps. The irrational accretion of experience into the as yet unnamed.

> *Obsessed, bewildered*
>
> *By the shipwreck*
> *Of the singular*
>
> *We have chosen the meaning*
> *Of being numerous.*[8]

Clearly, at the crux of our time is the problem of the subject. We are subjects. Then there are objects, alterity, the other side of the sentence. That there are subjects other than ourselves in the world is where Baudelaire's *flaneur* gets lost in the crowd. We wanted art to make an impact on the relation between a given subject and other subjects, to create, as it were, a community of subjects that recognize something human about or in themselves. Is this what Kant proposed: a core, shared human acknowledgment of the subjectivity of the subject?

We need art to prevent ourselves from making each other into objects. This is what our present condition seems to demand of us, it seems to want to persuade us to rid ourselves of our subjectivities so that we can be interchangeable, exchangeable.

If we are all to become ciphers, numbers, codes, then will we simply merge with the crowd and move aimlessly about, blind to one another?

Extremities of anonymity: the powerful, protected place of wealth; the abject, lost figure on the street.

What does it mean, to choose the meaning of being numerous?

In a recent encyclical, Pope John Paul calls for a rapprochement between faith and reason. He enjoins the modern world to allow faith to be the engine which guides reason toward good, away from evil. But his faith is one that invokes an ultimate Authority; faith, for him, *submits* to this Authority. But the last thing we need is submission; we need faith in ourselves and in our secular institutions, in the instruments that animate the reciprocity between ourselves and others.

The enlightened heart is not blind; the affective mind is not blind to the heart's capacity to enlighten.

Hi, Blake.

Hi, Ann.

I need your help.

Help with what?

With how to talk about love, without sounding like a daft teenager or a priggish convert.

It isn't easy. It takes a kind of willingness to be overt about stuff.

We can't do that here now for some reason.

Why not?

Because the world doesn't lend itself to the singularity of a voice anymore; it has become a chorus of competing voices, fractured and dissonant; and besides, the place of discourse—sorry about that word, it seems to have crept under the skin of language like a tick—has been debased, so we can't hear very well; we don't seem capable of a clear reception. We need to know who is speaking, but we also have become used to human speech without a particular human voice. As usual I am having a difficult time saying what I mean exactly.

I hear you.

I keep wanting to argue for the place of the poem, for poetry. I want to make the grand and perhaps grandiose assertion that poetry—that art—is essential and necessary. And I feel a disparity, a gap, or breach, a huge anxiety. I feel as if I had trapped myself in a corner, and the corner is the fact of faith itself.

To Mercy, Pity, Peace, and Love,
All pray in their distress:
And to these virtues of delight
Return their thankfulness.

For Mercy, Pity, Peace, and Love
Is God, our father dear,
And Mercy, Pity, Peace, and Love
Is Man, his child and care.

For Mercy has a human heart,
Pity, a human face,
And Love, the human form divine,
And Peace, the human dress.

Then every man, of every clime,
That prays in his distress,
Prays to the human form divine,
Love, Mercy, Pity, Peace.

And all must love the human form,
In heathen, Turk, or Jew;
Where Mercy, Love, and Pity dwell,
There God is dwelling too.[9]

Okay, thanks. It's getting dark, I think I'll go out for a walk now.

WHAT IS THE GRASS?
NOTES LEADING UP TO AND
AWAY FROM WALT WHITMAN

This piece originated as a talk given on March 26, 1992, at the City University Graduate Center in New York; it was subsequently printed in American Letters & Commentary, *no. 5 (Spring 1993), and in* Walt Whitman: The Measure of His Song *(Minneapolis, Holy Cow! Press). I have made some revisions.*

A Dutch journalist friend came to dinner the other night. He has traveled the world extensively over the last fifteen years with a small television crew, following the news. He says he is concerned about the future of Europe, that the same xenophobic extremism which now characterizes what was the Soviet Union is far more rampant in Germany, France, and his own Holland than we in the United States realize. Meanwhile, the borders between European countries no longer exist as they did, since the EEC has come into being. Another friend, an American of Norwegian origin, says that in Oslo, the Pakistani population "has taken the jobs that the Norwegians don't want," and that for the first time Norwegians are faced with their own racial resentments, fears, and prejudices.

Walt Whitman, *An American Primer* (c. 1853):

> For me, I see no object, no expression, no animal, no tree, no art, no book, but I see, from morning to night, and from night to morning, the spiritual. Bodies are all spiritual. All words are spiritual. Nothing is more spiritual than words. Whence are they? Along how many thousands and tens of thousands of years have they come? those eluding, fluid, beautiful, fleshless, realities, Mother, Father, Water, Earth, Me, This, Soul, Tongue, House, Fire.

George Steiner, *Real Presences* (1989):

The genius of the age is journalism. Journalism throngs every rift and cranny of our consciousness. It does so because the press and the media are far more than a technical instrument and commercial enterprise. The root-phenomenology of the journalistic is, in a sense, metaphysical. It articulates an epistemology and ethics of spurious temporality.

The journalistic vision sharpens to the point of maximum impact every event, every individual and social configuration; but the honing is uniform. Political enormity and the circus, the leaps of science and those of the athlete, apocalypse and indigestion, are given the same edge. Paradoxically, thus monotone of graphic urgency anesthetizes. The utmost beauty or terror are shredded at close of day. We are made whole again, and expectant, in time for the morning edition.

Monique Wittig, "The Mark of Gender" (in *The Poetics of Gender*):

The abstract form, the general, the universal, this is what the so-called masculine gender means, for the class of men have appropriated the universal for themselves. One must understand that men are not born with a faculty for the universal and that women are not reduced at birth to the particular . . . Gender is ontologically a total impossibility. For when one becomes a locutor, when one says "I" and, in so doing, reappropriates language as a whole, proceeding from oneself alone, with the tremendous power to use all language, it is then and there, according to linguists and philosophers, that there occurs the supreme act of subjectivity, the advent of subjectivity into consciousness. It is when starting to speak that one becomes "I." This act—the becoming of the subject through the exercise of language and through locution—in order to become real, implies that the locutor be an absolute subject. For a relative subject is inconceivable, a relative subject could not speak at all.

Jacqueline Rose, *Feminine Sexuality: Jacques Lacan and the Ecole Freudienne* (second introduction):

Subjects in language persist in their belief that somewhere there is a point of certainty, of knowledge and of truth. When the subject addresses its demand outside itself to another, this other becomes the fantasized place of just such a knowledge of certainty. Lacan calls this the Other—the site of language to which the speaking subject necessarily refers. The Other appears to hold the truth of the subject and the power to make good its loss. But this is the ultimate fantasy. Language is the place where meaning circulates—the meaning of each linguistic unit can only be established by reference to another, and it is arbitrarily fixed. Lacan, therefore, draws from Saussure's concept of the arbitrary nature of the linguistic sign, the implication that there can be no final guarantee or securing of language. "There is," Lacan writes, "no Other of the Other, and anyone who claims to take up this place is an impostor."

Terence Hawkes, writing about Shklovsky and the Russian Formalists in *Structuralism and Semiotics*:

> According to Shklovsky, the essential function of poetic art is to counteract the process of habituation encouraged by routine everyday modes of perception. We very readily cease to "see" the world we live in, and become anaesthetized to its distinctive features. The aim of poetry is to reverse that process, to defamiliarize that with which we are overly familiar, to creatively deform the usual, the normal, and so to inculcate a new, childlike, nonjaded vision in us. The poet thus aims to disrupt "stock responses," and to generate a heightened awareness: to restructure our ordinary perception of reality, so that we end by seeing the world instead of numbly recognizing it . . .

*

A child said, What is the grass? fetching it to me with full hands

The child *said*, the child did not *ask*. The child fully seen, his gesture vivid, his interlocutor invisible. Not "a child came to me and asked," which would emphasize the importance of asking *me*. We are flattered to be asked. The child and I are embarking on a conversation between equals, our difference almost unmarked—"fetching it to me with full hands"—an offering. The child has brought Walt Whitman *his book*: his hands are full of leaves of grass.

How could I answer the child?

The child's statement/question is answered with another question which asks about the possibility of answering. To whom is this question addressed? Not to the child, but to you and me, as well as to that part of Walt Whitman that wants to answer the child. The question is meant to awaken our interest in our own capacities to answer, as if to say, what would *you* say? You could, for example, say: "That is the grass, what you have in your hands, now go away and leave me alone." Once, my brother, when I was young and he was younger, asked me about a loud knocking noise as we were taking a bath in a strange house in Connecticut. "What is that?" he asked. I said, "I think it is the pipes." My brother was not happy with this explanation. He could not see the pipes, he could only hear something that bore no resemblance to the pipes he knew. (*Ceci n'est pas un pipe!*) So he asked again, as if he had not heard my explanation, "What is that?" So I said, "It's a dragon." This answer seemed to my brother to be much closer to what he had in mind.

> *I guess it must be the flag of my disposition, out of*
> *hopeful green stuff woven.*

Here we have an act of self-definition in the form of a supposition, a description of *Leaves of Grass* (all art is self-portraiture), a beautiful image of grass and, in the figure of the flag, the suggestion that "my disposition" flies under the common disposition of hopefulness. Whitman, guessing, again undermines his authority and instructs us on how to read. To guess is to "loaf and invite," a mild form of inquiry; to *guess* is to lift the lid off certitude, literalism, positivist sites of knowledge. In short, to *guess* is to acknowledge subjective uncertainty. *Guessing* is the opposite of journalism.

How is the grass a flag? It moves in wind, undulating. It is emblematic: one swatch of grass resembles another, elsewhere. Like "people," grass, singular, is made up of many individuals: leaves, persons. The flag stands as one for many. It is woven, it weaves the many—leaves, threads, persons—stuff, into a One. *Stuff?* Last week I was watching a program on TV called *Studs.* (Are you shocked?) There are two men, "studs," and three women. It's an entertaining program if you have an adolescent's mind, which I have, especially having spent the day pretending I don't. Hearts are strewn about with abandon. Anyway, one of the "studs" was talking and he kept repeating, "and stuff": "We went to a bar and had a few drinks and stuff." It was a general extension of the subject at hand. What you put into a turkey or a pillow to fill it: stuffing. "Stuff it!" we rudely retort. He's a real stuffed shirt. "Ambition should be made of sterner stuff." Raw, generic material. Franklin: "Time is the stuff which life is made of." Do your stuff. The right stuff. In the manufacture of paper, about which Whitman undoubtedly had knowledge, the paper stock, ground up and ready for use, is called "stuff." Also, in journalism (Whitman was, after all, a journalist) the copy; newspaper articles of any sort. Here, the colloquial "stuff" offsets the potentially high-toned "hopeful." So that hope might belong to anything, given a certain "disposition toward." Stuff, by virtue of being unformed, indeterminate, allows idealization (hope) to determine disposition. Disposition, hopeful, woven. O say can you see? Sounds weave flags in air.

> Or I guess it is the handkerchief of the Lord,
> A scented gift and remembrancer designedly dropped,
> Bearing the owner's name someway in the corners, that
> we may see and remark, and say Whose?

Now the child's wondering what grass is and Whitman's guessing blossom. The grass/flag falls, spreads out, verticality shifts to horizontality, an immensity of woven green which is what? a handkerchief! Remember, the child is holding the grass in his hands. ("He's got the whole world in His hands . . .") The Lord has dropped His . . . ? Is it "His"? Surely the Lord here is feminine. This charming custom, dropping flirtatiously (or, in Desdemona's case, disastrously, accidentally) one's scented handkerchief, is marked for gender. Yes, I think we must imagine the Lord as Female, Her initials stitched into the corners of the woven swatch of grass. Figures of Mother Earth and Father Lord conjoin; habits of gender assignment are broken. Property rights and ownership are evoked: Whose land is this? we ask, lifting the corners, scouting the boundary; whose plot? Who owns this grass?

Things are perceived in relation to other things; scale and possession migrate across the fluid indeterminacy of language: sameness, difference, woven flag, woven handkerchief. My hope, your doubt. My handkerchief, your flag. My plot of land, your grave. Your hands full of grass.

> that we may see and remark, and say Whose?

Does this grass handkerchief belong to someone?

A "scented remembrancer," to remind us it does not belong to us unless given by design. The handkerchief is dropped, we pick it up; ours, it is now also our responsibility to keep for a while, then return to its owner. The handkerchief brings us into relation with the Other, through Whitman's permutating tropes.

Or I guess the grass is itself a child, the produced babe of the vegetation.

Masculine authority continues to wane. Invoking the Lord, female or not, does not produce the Lord's Child but the child of vegetation, Nature's child. We have reached a kind of stasis, or doubling: child-grass-child. "We are the world." Toys "R" Us. Child now belongs to the earth's hopefulness. Harold Bloom: "A trope is . . . a way of carrying a perpetual imperfection across the river of Becoming . . . Rewriting is an invariable trope for voicing, within the poem, and that voicing and reseeing are much the same process, a process reliant on unnaming, which rhetorically means the undoing of a prior metonymy." Whitman doesn't exactly undo, he adds, making resonate, interlocked structures, in which particulars are brought into alignment with universals. A degree of abstraction is necessary. Philip Fisher: "American aesthetics is intrinsically an aesthetics of abstraction or, even more radically, an aesthetics of *the subtraction of difference*" [my italics].

> *Or I guess it is a uniform hieroglyphic,*
> *And it means, Sprouting alike in broad zones and narrow zones,*
> *Growing among black folks and among whites,*
> *Kanuck, Tuckahow, Congressman, Cuff, I give them the same, I receive*
>   *them the same.*

A hieroglyphic is sacred carving: here the linearity of grass becomes inscription, simultaneously individuating and uniting: a common denominator, ubiquitous, grass does not distinguish among those it gives and receives. *That all men are created equal*; Jesse Jackson: *common ground.* The meaning of the grass as text is to acknowledge and sustain difference in an ongoing reciprocity, giving and receiving "the same."

And now it seems to me the beautiful uncut hair of graves.

Guessing gives way to supposition—seamless seeming. Whitman omits the clumsy machinery of metaphor; things are not "like," they are. The act of perception subsumes the act of comparison. And so "beautiful uncut hair."

How many shampoo ads have you seen? Young girls twisting in false wind, their glossy tresses lifted into slow motion. But this beautiful hair belongs to graves, brought to mind by the receptivity of the grass, "receiving the same." Now the grass is a field, a graveyard, not the refined lawn of the Lord's handkerchief. Whitman here recalling the Indians, slaughtered by brute violations of territorial imperatives. Nobody asked, Whose? Art's job: to remind us of stupidity, cruelty, and death while somehow overriding them by acts of imagination. Whitman translates the grass. What is lost in translation?

> Tenderly will I use you curling grass,
> It may be you transpire from the breasts of young men,
> It may be if I had known them I would have loved them,
> It may be you are from old people, or from offspring taken soon
>   out of their mothers' laps

> And here you are the mothers' laps.

I guess, it seems. Diffidence, conjecture. Or, or, or. The grass, it seems, is capable of endless revision. But here Whitman begins to declare himself: "Tenderly I will use you curling grass." The line opens with an adverb, modifying "use," so that the sexual implications become overt, the hairs are from "the breasts of young men." To tenderly use. Is it useful? He used me. I used to go to the movies. What's the use? Cf. abuse, peruse, usurp, usury, utensil, utility. *Love me tender, love me true,* crooned Elvis back when. *Tender Is the Night.* Grass, flag, handkerchief, grave, curling hair of young men. American pragmatism. Legal tender. Desire. The lap of God, the lap of luxury. Would you like to sit on my lap? How many laps did you run today? I cannot remember; I have had a lapse, a relapse. Sons and lovers, mothers and sons. Ceremonies of innocence, or not.

> This grass is very dark to be from the white heads of old mothers,
> Darker than the colorless beards of old men,
> Dark to come from under the faint red roofs of mouths.

Dark, darker, dark. Where is the hopeful green stuff? Where is the unifying flag, its disposition? This grass is now as private as it once was public; the sun has gone down, the grass has turned black. The son has gone down. This is not beautiful uncut grass after all, not mother's lap, but the charged topos of oral eroticism. The poet has arrived at a place he perhaps had not intended to go. Joseph Brodsky: "A song is a form of linguistic disobedience and casts a doubt on a lot more than a concrete political system: it questions the whole existential order." Where is the child now? Now Whitman must recover his happy tune.

O I perceive after all so many uttering tongues,
And I perceive they do not come from the roofs of mouths for nothing.

Lear's despairing litany roils up from under the shadowy grass: "Nothing will come of nothing. Speak again." Anxiety about procreation, inheritance. Can these "uttering tongues" speak in such a way as to annul the nullity of desire without progeny? Can perception recover enough to bring us back from private erotics to public commons, make from intimate lyric moments of connection a chorus? A First Amendment?

I wish I could translate the hints about the dead young men and women,
And the hints about old men and mothers, and the offspring taken soon
out of their laps.

The answer is a qualified *yes*. The language is still partly private, hints that are less easily translated than the brightly generous and generative grass. Nevertheless, he will focus again on demotic inclusiveness, young and old, male and female, offspring taken from Whitman's lapse. Not for nothing. American optimism supersedes, subtracts from, the dark grass of difference.

What do you think has become of the young and old men?
What do you think has become of the women and children?

I do not know any more than he what has become of them. What's to become of him? we ask anxiously. A trope is thus *a way of carrying a perpetual imperfection across the river of Becoming*. American transcendentalism struggled to convert Christian "afterlife" into perpetual immanence; to conceive of an essential equanimity and reciprocity between and among beings and their souls. Whitman thought of words, language itself, as "spiritual"; he shifts its terrain from the Bible's originary and absolute Logos ("In the beginning was the Word") to a naturalized, demotic discourse.

I believe in you my soul, the other I am must not abase itself to you,
And you must not be abased to the other.

They are alive and well somewhere,
The smallest sprout shows there is really no death,
And if ever there was it led forward life, and does not wait at the end to
  arrest it,
And ceas'd the moment life appeared.

All goes onward and outward, nothing collapses,
And to die is different from what anyone supposed, and luckier.

The beautiful recursive moments of inquiry and supposition come to rest
with Whitman's vision of an unbounded temporal mobility: forward, onward,
outward. The luck of dying is the final subtraction of difference (of race,
gender, class, age) whereby all souls are equal, as the grassy graves' "smallest
sprout" attests.

Søren Kierkegaard, *The Present Age*:

> In order that everything should be reduced to the same level, it
> is at first necessary to procure a phantom, its spirit, a monstrous
> abstraction, an all-embracing something which is nothing, a
> mirage—and that phantom is the public. This abstraction has
> a way of crushing the individual, by means of the further ab-
> stractions that it produces—public opinion, good taste, and the
> like. In a deteriorating society, this public is the fiction of the
> press.

Chinua Achebe, *What Has Literature Got to Do with It?*:

> It is the very nature of creativity, in its prodigious complexity and
> richness, that it will accommodate paradoxes and ambiguities.
> But this, it seems, will always elude and pose a problem for the
> uncreative, literal mind . . . The literal mind is the one-track
> mind, the simplistic mind, the mind that cannot comprehend
> that where one thing stands, another will stand beside it.

The other night, quite late, I turned on the TV to see what Charlie Rose was up to. There, instead of the usual gaggle of celebrities and pundits, were poets! Sharon Olds, Allen Ginsberg, Galway Kinnell, and a fourth, whose face and name escaped me. As I tuned in, the poets were reading snatches of Whitman; favorite passages. Then Charlie Rose, in his mellifluous and, I often think, somewhat bogus show of interest, asked, "But what makes Whitman our *greatest* poet? Can you sum it up?" Sharon Olds murmured something about Whitman's humanity; Ginsberg, maybe for the first time in his life, was rendered speechless, stuttering. Charlie insisted, "Why is he *great?*"

Roland Barthes:

> The old values no longer transmitted, no longer circulate, no longer impress; literature is desacralized, institutions are impotent to defend and impose it as the implicit model of the human. It is not, if you will, that literature is destroyed; rather it is no longer protected: so this is the moment to go there.

As we set about strutting and preening over Walt Whitman, who may or may not be "America's greatest poet," we might consider that although Whitman is America's, America now is not Whitman's. As we once again face crises brought about by a growing tension for democracy—how to allow individual agency and identity to flourish within shifting global cultural economies—we might do worse than attend to Whitman's example. Here are some reasons, Charlie, why Whitman could be considered a great poet.

If you read *Leaves of Grass* with the same open curiosity as the child who asked, "What is the grass?" you will find:

a formal but fluid embodiment of the relation between conformity
    and its aversion; consensus and exception; sameness and
    difference; universals and particulars;
that the (masculine) fiction of a static coherent selfhood is subverted
    by a complex reading of the psyche as multifaceted and
    various, its "identity" released through linguistic contingency,
    and so
a writer's "authority" can be nonassertive, dialogic in structure and
    reciprocal in effect; that *doubt* is not the same as pessimism
    or indecision;
that belief does not belong only to those who Believe;

that our private dispositions, including our sexual preferences, are as
    defining as they are liberating;
that lists and catalogues can embrace inconsistency, thus renovating
    assumed ideas of order;
that how we name the world is a reflection both of how we perceive
    and what we wish it to be; that hope is not synonymous with
    either transcendence or optimism and can be configured into
    the most wretched reality;
that simple questions have multiple, complex answers.

What is the grass?

SLAVES OF FASHION

This piece was written in response to a request by the Boston Review *to contribute a response to* The Best of the Best American Poetry, 1988–1997, *chosen by Harold Bloom (New York, Scribner, 1998). I was dismayed that at the time, the valuable annual collections from which Bloom drew—*The Best American Poetry, *edited by David Lehman, who each year assigned a different poet to choose the contents—appeared to eschew the more innovative strains of American poetry.*

The slave revolt in morality begins when *ressentiment* itself becomes creative and gives birth to values: the *ressentiment* of natures that are denied the true reaction, that of deeds, and compensate themselves with an imaginary revenge. While every noble morality develops from a triumphant affirmation of itself, slave morality from the outset says No to what is "outside," what is "different," what is "not itself," and *this* No is its creative deed. This inversion of the value-positing eye—this *need* to direct one's view outward instead of back to oneself—is of the essence of *ressentiment*: in order to exist, slave morality always first needs a hostile world; it needs, psychologically speaking, external stimuli in order to act at all—its action is fundamentally reaction.

—Friedrich Nietzsche, *On the Genealogy of Morals*

There have been, of course, extraordinary anthologies. Take, for example, Alfred Kreymborg's beautifully titled *Others: An Anthology of the New Verse* (1916), a collection of thirty-six poets which included Pound, Eliot, Moore, Loy, Sandburg, Stevens, and Williams, as well as such figures as Man Ray and William Zorach, plus a host of persons now consigned to the infamous dust heap of history, many of them, I hasten to add, women: Mary Aldis,

Adelaide Crapsey, Alice Groff, Helen Hoyt, Hester Sainsbury, Marguerite Zorach. Their names alone suggest a devastating sorority. Or, just past mid-century, *The New American Poetry*, edited by Donald Allen and Warren Tallman, which brought together important strands of American poetry emanating from modernism by way of Pound, Stein, and Williams (but *not* Stevens; therein hangs a sad tale) and included poets associated with the Beats, the Objectivists, Black Mountain, San Francisco Renaissance, and New York schools. This volume was in some contrast to M. L. Rosenthal's *The New Modern Poetry: British and American Poetry Since World War II* (1967), an eclectic collection which foregrounded the confessional poets, but included such diverse poets as Elizabeth Bishop, Hayden Carruth, Robert Bly, Howard Nemerov, Robert Duncan, and Denise Levertov. In recent years, there has been a kind of anthology mania, as the milennium approached with the attendant desire to at once sum up the past and predict the future, ranging from Eliot Weinberger's contested but rigorous *American Poetry Since 1950: Innovators and Outsiders* (1993) to Paul Hoover's more catholic Norton Anthology, *Postmodern American Poetry* (1994). And now, just out from Talisman, Mary Margaret Sloan's magisterial *Moving Borders: Three Decades of Innovative Writing by Women*.

Of course none of these anthologies claims to be *the best*; each displays the preferences, the tastes, of its individual editors. But we live in a time when marketing schemes override critical nuance, when an individual's predeliction is not as compelling as the notion that something, some *thing*, is the best of its kind. To be the best implies there is an objective standard of judgment, some absolute way of measuring and knowing, and it is this idea which has, I think, contributed to the current crisis in aesthetics generally, and in critical responses to poetry in particular. And when there is a public that knows less and less about contemporary poetics, one feels a kind of cultural shudder—sadness mixed with fury—when only part of the landscape is illumined. For although there are many very fine poets and poems in these volumes, one cannot but notice an overall *distaste* for work by poets for whom the act of writing is a search for new structures, new forms, with which to meet a rapidly changing postmodern reality. Over in the unlit woods, the shadowy groves of the *unbest*, there are many poets, of varying degrees of accomplishment, who, in my view, have taken up the task which Emerson set for them, to give voice to "this new yet unapproachable America." Their virtual exclusion is a symptom of a condition which extends beyond the margins of poetry.

Which brings us to the issue at hand, and to Harold Bloom, whose behest

it was to reiterate *the best* into its resounding redundancy, *the best of the best.*
And who better qualified? He is, if not exactly our Old Testament God, at
least our Darwinian Freud, concerned with origins and etymologies, anxi-
eties and crossings, capabilities and canons, the Orphic Spin Doctor with a
whole lot of tools in his Survival Kit, midwife to the prolific American Muse.
He, among us, is free of the noxious toxins which have sullied the pure wa-
ters of aesthetic judgment, from the invading xenophobic French—down
with Kristeva! down with Derrida! down with Lacan!—to the factional fic-
tions of Identity—feminism, queer theory, multiculturalism—that have
made a turmoil of Lit Crit, as it was once quaintly monikered. A person of
impeccable discrimination, Professor Bloom knows a Giant when he sees
one, he has the requisite knowledge ("My mind was formed by Blake and
Hart Crane, and then by Wallace Stevens and Shelley," he modestly tells us)
to prise out, to cultivate, the essential *genius* of American poetry, to keep it
free from rampant weeds and vagrant winds of academic fashion and street
fad. You won't find Professor Bloom including a poem for impure reasons—
allegiances of religion, gender, race, institutional affiliation, not to mention
mere friendship; he is immune to such vulgar predicates. Professor Bloom
will not split the copulating atom of Truth/Beauty and wreak unholy havoc
on *the pure products of American poetry.*

My own Bloomsian Rant: I have just read *eighty-two* volumes of poetry (for
a prize), all first books, most of which have already won a competition in order
to be published. I must confess that the experience was not an especially en-
joyable one; not a feast, but a sort of bland diet of slightly sweet, sticky gruel.
Book after book, poem after poem, line after line, the center of concern is the
poet's *self*, his or her experience *in* life (not *of* life) transmuted into a language
one might imagine to be "poetic": a dressy, fussy, inflated diction. Most of
these writers rely on pictorial/narrative effects, and almost none seems to
want to explore either the aural possiblities of a line, except in its most tradi-
tional (When is a form not a form? When it is a new form! Jazz, anyone?) reg-
ister, or the corresponding material, physical pleasures of the page (I said
page, not *text*). The poems are dull: self-conscious and self-absorbed; most
are little prose essays, broken along their syntactical scaffolds into lines.
Somehow it is imagined (it is taught) that the main object of poetic ambition
should be a kind of discursive commentary, self-witnessing transformed into
picturing narrations of traumatic personal events. Next stop: *profundity, wis-
dom, pieties of essential truth!* They seem to be culturally and historically near-
sighted, undernourished, deprived. Some attempt to extend personal lives to
paradigmatic stature, believing, I suspect, that they are representative, but

they have neither Whitman's inclusive humanity nor Wordsworth's sense of historical centrality (not to mention linguistic gifts). In any case, these poets seem to be driven by (1) limited subject matter and (2) an idea of poetic diction and form which is as familiar as it is exhausted: mechanical monkey plays same old tune. They seem to accept the received idea of a poem as cultural decor, an accesssory, a small—nay, a tiny—entertainment. They seem unwilling to risk real play—the play that involves humor as well as eros—unable to ask the poem to tell them, and us, something they do not already know.

The poem as aspirin for the soul. Take two, you'll feel bettter in the morning.

What if truth and beauty are not eternal and static, but variable, and in an infinitely extendable and unstable equation? And what if it is precisely the *relation between* these two terms (truth as *form;* beauty as *hermeneutic)* which it is the task of a poet in any given time to manifest? And what happens when you begin to notice, as it began to be noticed as modernism began to wane, that there is no such thing as an aesthetic value which is not to some extent inflected, informed, by other values which, in turn, arise from particular, individual as well as cultural, ways of believing, perceiving, and knowing? What if, in fact, the aesthetic is the very site of turbulence and uncertainty through or by which an artist attempts to *come to terms* with the *various field* of human investment and experience, the choices, decisions, and judgments, which ratify a life? The aesthetic would then be the result of complex determinants, not fixed, not predetermined, not necessarily knowable in the first place, but always, definingly, a place of discovery.

Discovery, by its very nature, cannot be reduced to formulas, captions, or categories.

What, then, is the nature of this discovery? Or to put it another way, what is the source of *pleasure* which Professor Bloom continues, following Pater and Coleridge, to affiliate so closely with his understanding of the aesthetic experience? The pleasure of perspicacity, of insight, of seeing *into the life of things?* My own understanding is that there is, indeed, an ethics implicated in or by aesthetics, but it is not an ethics that can be realized or represented simply through assertions of specific content, or subject matter, what Charles Altieri has called "overt ideological claims or their value as social documentary." Citing Nietzsche, Altieri goes on to say that "what matters most about a culture emphasizing epistemic values is the difference between the questions that it allows itself to ask and the questions that it marginalizes. For those questions that are primary also offer the most pronounced and most powerful principles of identification and valorization within the culture."[1] On this reading, we might want to say that the new focus of attention in the field of literary studies reflect a much delayed, if much contested, adjustment to the questions the culture asks about itself. To blame and vilify the 1960s for these shifts is, I think, an act of revisionism not worthy of Professor Bloom's scholarship and humanism. To my mind, Emerson, Whitman, and Dickinson are radical, that is, original, thinkers, stunning innovators; they were, as well, profoundly generous; they would have been more tolerant of the anguish of the underrepresented, more patient with righteous, if short-sighted, zeal. They were, after all, nonconformists.

I love John Ashbery as much as the next guy, but every poet influenced by him is not a pale imitation of him, anxieties notwithstanding. His greatness has allowed many poets—from David Lehman to, say, Charles Bernstein, to name two not quite at random—to explore the territory he opened, some of which is, it would seem, directly attributable to his knowledge, not only of minor poets, but of literatures outside of Anglo-American descent; that of France, for example.

Bad poetry, I would submit, raises issues, makes complaints, marks territories. Bad poetry does not take on the more difficult task, where the question and its answer are as one. Good poems absorb into their formal and imaginative resources new questions which are as difficult to answer as they are to raise. Or put it this way: *the poem is an answer to a question or questions no one, including the poet, had thought to ask.* These questions are always in temporal, historical flux, responding to myriad collisions of information from every possible—they seem to multiply by the day—domain. The poem as answer to an unasked question puts pressure on the poet to be alert, vigilant, receptive, not just to the *past,* but to the weathers, internal and external, which characterize the day—"poems of our climate," indeed. The burden of knowledge is immense, but it is also messy and malleable; each time you reread Stevens's *Notes Toward a Supreme Fiction,* a new fiction will arise and the nature of its supremacy (its *bestness*) will alter. It is the critic's job to ask the question or questions which the poem elicits in its answering. As long as editors and critics are blindsided by the myopia of pre-existing conditions for good, better, and best (the latter a test only time can take), as long as they mistake subject for content, content for meaning, and form for that which *is* what *was,* much of the best of the best will remain invisible, and the real questions to their answers will go, as Shelley foretold, unacknowledged.

A rose, after all, is still only a rose, but it smells sweeter when there are three of them.

THREE INTRODUCTIONS

FANNY HOWE

This citation for Fanny Howe's Selected Poems (University of California Press, 2000), which won the Lenore Marshall Prize, was published in the Nation on February 4, 2002. The award is for the "most outstanding" book of the year.

In the days and weeks following the events of September 11th, one poet, one poem by one poet, seemed to come into circulation: W. H. Auden's "September 1, 1939." Set in New York, the poem's narrator, chastened by events into chill eloquence, speaks in slow rhymes, as formally reassuring as they are devastating in content. Like other modernists, Auden cultivated a poetics of narrative statement that gave public voice to private perception. It is a voice that turned the unruly emotions of sorrow, fear, and rage into ideas of order. But just as hot war tactics and cold war rhetoric feel outdated and dangerous in our new world, the pacifying sonorities of Auden seem strangely out of tune.

On the evening of September 10th, I met with my colleagues and co-judges, Elaine Equi and Bob Perelman, at my loft on Duane Street in TriBeCa to converse about our choices for finalists for the Lenore Marshall Prize. Over the summer, we had each read more than two hundred books, some, but by no means all, of the collections of poetry published in 2000. These books were written by poets of national stature and poets of only local repute; they included hefty life-works and slim first volumes. It was a daunting task, by turns exhilarating and infuriating. To choose from among them the "most outstanding" tested not only our individual judgments, but our shared belief in a poetics responsive to the contemporary moment.

The six finalists, John Ashbery, Charles Bernstein, Fanny Howe, Ed Roberson, David Trinidad, and Marjorie Welish, are remarkable writers. Together, they have contributed immeasurably to contemporary poetry in America: expanding formal range, resisting reductive subjectivity and its narrative claims, attending to the exigencies of both language and world. To select one from among them seems arbitrary, but there is only one prize to give. We have awarded the Lenore Marshall Prize to Fanny Howe for her *Selected Poems.*

Fanny Howe is the author of more than twenty books (poetry and fiction) published by some of the most adventurous and enduring small presses in America. This beautifully designed and produced book is the third in a series called New California Poetry from the University of California Press, edited by Robert Hass, Calvin Bedient, and Brenda Hillman. Until recently, Howe was Professor of American Writing and American Literature at the University of California, San Diego. She has now retired to her native New England.

Howe works in sequences of poems made of minimally punctuated short lines. The individual poems are untitled. This notational, almost diaristic format gives the impression of a seamless intimacy and urgency, as if the reader were present at the act of writing. A spare tonality moves against the density and complexity of her vision, where a classical lyric voice is annealed to a spiritual quest buffeted and embattled by resisting political and social realities. This tension is what gives the poems their power.

> Small birds puff their chests and feathers
> With the pleasure that they know better
> High morning clouds unload themselves
> On the world. Blue peeps through
> Sunny boys have spacious souls but killers
> Build war zones in the sky where they go to die
> Blue poems. Blue ozone. A V-sign
> Sails into the elements: an old ship
> Named Obsolete though Lovely is easier to see
> Now visualize heaven as everything around it

—from "Introduction to the World"

Howe's diction is not conventionally poetic, not dressed up, not avuncular, not pretty. It is peculiar, compelling, and provocative, with moments of absolute clarity adjacent to moments of mere glimpse. This quixotic, pulsating quality lends a sensuous mystery and scale to the landscape of her work, as if the lines were emanating from a lighthouse whose signal is blindingly bright one moment and scanning the horizon at the next. There is an asymmetrical oddness and frailty to her cadence that contributes to the dissonance between private and public event:

If goals create content stealth creates form

The air force hits space
With the velocity of a satanic wrist

How to give birth to children under these conditions
Favor the ghost over the father, maternalist

—from "Q"

Howe stitches into a single poem materials from diverse, often divergent, experience. Affective language is laid beside statement, but is not subsumed by it. The voice is personal, but there are no invitations here to bear witness to the concrete details of a life; or rather, that life's details are drawn through the poem as a thread in a fabric. In a world strewn with bare facts, Howe's reflective meditative lines are consoling, not for their content, which is as charged with pessimism as Auden's, but because they invite us, or remind us, to attend. The poems act on us like pilot lights, igniting the receptive synapse of language. She is compelled by the distinction between, and proximity of, history and story; her work brings us to the threshold of accountability.

Laughter—or slaughter—outside the door
And inside she was dying
To join in. So she had to go out
—a physical body

With subjective needs
Wing with the post-Christians. Her brow a headline
Reporting news of weather & mood

From masters of the military & amorous arts
Hide in her little close
Off the runway, or step into their story

—from "The Quietist"

On the dust jacket, one person compares Fanny Howe to Emily Dickinson, a comparison all too easily invoked in writings by women. But in this case, there is justification. Like Dickinson, Fanny Howe animates her work with an austere logic, in which aspects of a unique response, spiritual, emotional and intellectual, are held in an uneasy but necessary relation. She makes demands on her readers. If those demands are met, the rewards are as inestimable as they are real.

MICHAEL PALMER

Introducing Michael Palmer on the occasion of his reading at the 92nd Street Y in New York on December 18, 2000.

What does it mean to have poems which call themselves "Notes," notes for a place called Echo Lake? What does it mean to have poems with an odd epistolary address: "Dear M," "Dearest Reader," "Dear Lexicon." Who is or was Zanzotto? Where are we when we are *At Passages*? What are *The Promises of Glass*? What are we to make of a group of poems called "Autobiography" in which the "I" is barely discernible as someone who spends his days doing this or that? What are we to make of these numbers, these names: "Day One is called Trace," "Day Two is Map," "Day Three is X," "Name of X," "Name of N"?

In Michael Palmer's astonishing poems, we are invited to enter a *near* so close it converts to an almost unbearable *here*. *Here* one might presume a certain intimacy; a letter, after all, is a direct, personal address, to and from. "Sincerely yours," we write, and sign our name. But it is just at this juncture, at the signature of individual presence, that the "one" is evaded, or erased, or exploded—

He writes:

> *Call it Ones (split open)*
> *Call it A Scratch Band from Duluth*

He writes:

> *spilling names I had been-not I*
> *had been not lost I had seen you once*

Language not so much disembodied as set free and then recaptured *at passages* of a prolific, agile invention. The mind's own place. A deconstructive

will to displace, unname, is met head on by a constructive desire to reconfig-
ure: a world simultaneously orphaned and found. It is an exacting and per-
ilous economy.

Why does one find Michael Palmer's poems important and beautiful?
That is one reason, a relentless conversion.

Also: an unfettered interrogation by a mind beset by skepticism, in which
doubt and curiosity pivot around a vital, unsteady contingency.

FROM LETTER 3

> . . . I wanted to ask
>
> about dews, habits of poplar, carousel,
> dreamless wealth, nets, embers
>
> and folds, the sailing ship "Desire"
> with its racks and bars
>
> just now setting out. This
> question to spell itself.

An inquisition, then, at the level of language itself, as if life depended on it.
That is, as if the life of language and the language of life were the same:
idem. This acute anxiety and restlessness inflects and tests the reader's re-
sponsive agility, giving an uncanny, giddy pleasure, as if invited to witness a
perverse, belated Adam, back at his initial chore. Palmer's nominal play is be-
yond ideas of order, outside the captivity of the picture, the story's begin-
nings and endings. But these are not mere fragments, neither the arid games
of an exhausted repertoire nor the remnant ruins of our modernist shores.
This is not just a poetics of indeterminacy, but one of urgent, if unknowable,
consequence—

LETTER 7

> And you Mr. Ground of what, Mr. Text, Mr. Is-Was
> Can you calculate the ratio between wire and window
>
> Between tone and row, cop/ula and carnival
> And can you reassemble light from the future-past
>
> In its parabolic nest
> Or recite an entire winter's words,

—as if to release language into a temporal web of the most austere but mes-merizing music. That is another reason: to be this close to a gorgeous incipi-ence, witnessing the genome of linguistic matter, this far from the logics, rationales, and categories which shut us from both agency and reciprocity.

When, in 1931, Louis Zukofsky wrote that a poem should show a "desire for what is objectively perfect, inextricably the direction of historic and con-temporary particulars," that it should be "the detail, not mirage of seeing, of thinking with the things as they exist, and of directing them along a line of melody," he could not have anticipated the Penelope-like unweaving and reweaving of the English language that characterizes Michael Palmer's work. When George Oppen, in 1968, spoke of the "shipwreck of the singular" into the meaning "of being numerous," he could not have foreseen the intricate play of other voices and texts, drawn from the world community, that ani-mate Michael Palmer's work. And when, in a recent essay, Charles Altieri claims that the possibilities assembled in the Objectivist project remain "the road not taken" by contemporary American poets, he appears to have failed to look in the direction of Michael Palmer's generative revisioning of those potentials.

I had a vision, listening to Michael Palmer read some years ago, that he had a moat around him. That he was standing alone on a rock, speaking for us, or to us, I could not distinguish between these propositions, these prepo-sitions. I thought it was important and necessary either to join him on the rock or to get him off.

I was talking to Barbara Guest one day about poets of my generation. She commented, "You are lucky to have Michael." She meant "you" in the plural. "You" in the plural is "we."

ROSMARIE WALDROP

Introducing poet, translator, and publisher Rosmarie Waldrop for her reading at the DIA Foundation for Contemporary Art in Chelsea, New York, on December 7, 2002.

In thinking about the work of Rosmarie Waldrop, one is tempted to claims that might be perceived as extravagant.

But this temptation should be resisted, if only because one of the most salient traits of her work, as poet, translator, publisher, novelist, and teacher, is, exactly, restraint. This is not the restraint of the pious or the deprived, neither prim nor destitute, but of a complex precision; that of a mind articulating the vanishing point where reasoning language and sensuous world converge, a congruence at once detached and passionate, cerebral and visceral. Waldrop's linguistic world is elastic and intimate, built on the focus of a fragment and the viscosity and flow of sequence; clusters, intricate dissolution, moments of arresting perception, a poetics that is as subjectively charged as it is philosophically cool. Her work elicits sober awe, often punctuated by pleasures at her wit, warmth, and play, as if we were in a landscape where the predictable and uncertain are in such close proximity that cause and effect are estranged, and in this estrangement, this gap, precarious but exhilarating encounters occur.

Waldrop's poetry moves between austere lineation, where there is, as she says, "a refusal to fill up all available space, so that even if the words celebrate what is, each line acknowledges what is not," to poems made of sentences that defy their own logic. As she once put it, she wants to "accept the complete sentence (most of the time), but to do my best to subvert it from the inside, by sliding between frames of reference, especially pitting logic against the body. The body is, after all, our means to have a world—even to have logic." Indeed, in her great trilogy, *The Reproduction of Profiles*, *Lawn of Excluded Middle*, and *Reluctant Gravities*, Waldrop has reinvented the prose poem as a form of

exquisite tension and extension, in which moments of acute personal defini-
tion conjunct with questions of the limits of language. She writes:

> I badly wanted a story of my own. As if there were proof in
> spelling. But what if my experience were the kind of snow that
> does not accumulate? A piling of instants that did not amount to
> a dimension? What if wandering within my own limits I came
> back naked, with features too faint for the mirror, unequal to the
> demands of the night? In the long run I could not deceive ap-
> pearances: Days and nights were added up without adding up.

But the snows of experience have accumulated, the days and nights have
added up. Rosmarie Waldrop has given us more than a dozen books of po-
etry, two books of prose fiction, and a veritable library of translations from
German and French, including works by Jacques Roubaud, Paul Celan, Em-
manuel Hacquard, Elke Erb, and, most wonderfully, seven volumes of writ-
ings by Edmond Jabès. The presence of these writers in English has added
immeasurably to the landscape of contemporary American poetics. But her
generosity toward, and interest in, other writers has found its most extensive
manifestation in the publishing adventure Burning Deck, begun in 1961
with her husband, the writer Keith Waldrop. The authors they have pub-
lished and continue to publish constitute a pantheon of significant innova-
tive voices of the last half-century.

The fact that English is Rosmarie Waldrop's second language, the fact that
she is a German child of the Second World War, reared in Hitler's terror, only
intensifies our admiration. We begin to see that her poetry, often constructed
in and through dialogues with other writers—with Roger Williams in *A Key
into the Language of America*, with Ludwig Wittgenstein in *The Reproduction
of Profiles*, to cite only two—constitutes a kind of open house, a matrix of and
for language to be and become. In the recently published *Ceci n'est pas Keith,
Ceci n'est pas Rosmarie*, her "autobiography" inscribes and annotates a journey
through an extraordinary repertoire of encounters with place, person, book,
idea, music, voice, each contributing to an evolving poetics.

These "encounters with otherness" have given Rosmarie Waldrop, and
her readers, a way to make worlds within words. She has said, "I have always
thought of poetry as a way of building a world . . . Building a counterworld,
not better, but other." Some of us would argue that her counterworld is bet-
ter, made as it is of the singular materials of her articulating architecture,
built for humans, to live through, to think about, in which to love.

BARBARA GUEST: ARCHITECT OF AIR

These were the keynote remarks for a celebration, at the Art Institute in Berkeley, California, in June 2003, of the work of Barbara Guest on the occasion of the publication, from Kelsey Street Press, of her collection of essays on writing, Forces of Imagination. *I gave the address again at the Poetry Project in New York for a further celebration of her book on art and artists,* Dürer in the Window, *published by Roof Books.*

1.

Not long ago, I sat at a large table in a restaurant in New York with an affable contingent of poets, the remnant audience from a reading at Saint Mark's Poetry Project. At another, smaller table, in an adjacent room, another group gathered. This second group was younger, perhaps in their late twenties and thirties. At the first table, someone made a remark about generations, about the fact, or rather the impression, that the younger generation was eager for the older one to get out of the way, chomping at the bit, the bit of poetry. Meanwhile, at Bard College, where I teach, two poets read during the course of the year, John Ashbery and Robert Creeley. I have been thinking about Ashbery and Creeley and Barbara Guest, how their work has given not so much inspiration—a fleet thing—as sustenance to many of us, and how grateful I am to them. Each has given American poetry not just exemplary precedent, ways of going on, they have allowed us to know more about the energies by which the past enters the present and is transfigured. In their hands, the egotistical "I" has found its way to a liberated sublime; lyric has survived the cultivated noise of reductive platitude.

2.

It is not news that we are in a dispiriting time, one of personal and political cynicism, of unproductive doubt. Not what Keats had in mind as the poet's necessary capacity. This doubt has to do with a sense that there is not a way to assuage the mendacity of the world with the fact of our selves, our singularity. I want to say, for example, that the singularity of Barbara Guest's work has allowed us to gather around the fact of her work and to take from it the exception, our exemption, from convention's chosen wisdom, even as it dresses itself in newfangledness. The brittle fissures and shortsightedness of postmodernity become, under Guest's Midas touch, deep veins of ore: those *rocks on a platter* are gold, that foreground of defense shields rapture. Her reanimation and reconstruction are not reactionary, but are made from radical energies that find in the tidy lawn bumps that allow "the permissiveness of growing into variousness." A poetics that does not ask us to choose between Stevens's lush soliloquies and H.D.'s imagism, but to find in each the shaping ingredients of our particular needs as readers and writers. For Barbara Guest, activating the past has kept the present company, and given to the future an astonishing bounty.

3.

The fact is, Barbara Guest's work does what all art of consequence does: it invades time, breaks open narrative gloss, ruptures the static picture, imposes a counterharmonic. Her work is a kind of music. It enters the ear first, detonating interior space into cadences by which reality is destabilized and recuperated: angles and arches, objects and journeys, colors and scraps, the clear annealed to the obscure, the true chiaroscuro mystery of the human heartmind. Her work instructs us in the reciprocity of listening; to construct meanings there, at the site of listening. Guest converts the distancing conventions of the ekphrastic eye, with its scenic presentations, its effort at descriptive mimesis, into linguistic structures of the finest aural filament: the visual—paintings, objects, scenes—converted. This conversion she calls "plasticity," by which the poem stretches to include both lark and song. Words, she tells us, "need dimension. They desire finally an elevation in space. The poet of vision understands the auditory and emotional needs of the words and frees them so that the word becomes both an elemental and physical being, and continuous in movement." In Guest's work, image finds its way back to the house of the imagination.

Listen:

I want to speak about living out of oneself, as this will bring us
To the inner kingdom of the imagination

I want to insist that there is no conflict between realism and the
*   imagination*
Only imagination can return the texts to life

*   That it resists clear and absolute meaning*

*   It is rock*

Yet the unstableness of the poem is important

There is always something within poetry that desires the invisible

By whom or what agency is this decided, by what invisible architecture is
*   the poem developed?*

A pull in both directions between the physical reality of place and the
*   metaphysics of space.*

Driftwood of the unconscious

When the dark reaches of the poem succumb and shine with a clarity

Projected by the mental lamp of the reader, then

The shared vigilance

To arrange its dimensions

How splendid when a poem is both prospective and introspective,

Obeying tensions within itself until a classic plasticity is reached

To keep the poem alive after its many varnishings

To reach that surprise.

The fiction of the poet is part of restless twentieth century perception
Based on the discovery
That reality

Is a variable
And is open-ended in
Form and matter

The poet is unaware of the halo
Just as in the paintings
The persons are unaware of the halo

The halo has detected the magnetic field
Into which the energy of the poem is being directed

Away from the desk of a projected poem

To understand the auditory and spatial needs of a poem
To free it so that the poem can locate its own movement

Regard the poem as plastic

Moveable, touchable

4.

These passages are where my pencil itched its mark as I read through Barbara Guest's Writing on Writing collected in *Forces of Imagination*. I was struck by how slight the shift is between her prose and her poems. The same characteristics obtain: a diction stripped of ornament but structurally adamant, like Shaker furniture, so that what is evident is not necessarily obvious, what is honed is not bereft; an aesthetic both sure of its procedures and fretted with inquiry; an erudition that comes to us not as citation but as material source and resource; a subtle and canny wit—the barb in Barbara—

which is the sign of all great intellection; a sense of concentration that roughens the surface with surprise, where a single word or phrase torques a passage off its anticipated rails; a current of sensuous pleasure, a nearly erotic attachment to world as word, and so, most pervasively, an inextricable braiding of feeling's thought and thought's feeling into a single linguistic arc—"making song think and making thought sing," as the critic Rob Kaufman put it.

Revisiting Guest, I am struck also by a resonating pleasure, both awakened and calm, that I call gladness. This gladness, I like to argue, is our witnessing the construction of choice into art. When we love a person's work we experience this gladness, not just in or for the object before us, but because the choices of which it is made instantiate our own capacity to make choices in the work of life, the life of work. This analog of choice is, for me, the crucial social and political consequence and necessity for art as practice and presence: the apprehension of agency in the will to choose.

Barbara Guest's art, the sum of her choices, has the effect of a tuning fork, sending out exfoliating ripples that animate our connections to ourselves and to the world.

There are now, happily, numerous women poets who have eschewed the domestic household and its codified extensions as the domain of the poem. This is so, I think, in large measure thanks to Barbara Guest, who not only invokes Pound and Picasso, those prodigious villains of the modernist household, as her equals, but has been tenacious in a poetics whose versatility, daring, and strength attach the "fair" to realism, sexing it with, indeed, audacious power. This power has been acknowledged widely by contemporary poets, male and female. That so many of us have read her work, and written about it, tells us that it engages at the level of our own creative projects; we find a laboratory of poetic tools, even as she guides us away from the petty depredations of academic and careerist "moves" to a place free of cant, jargon, and brand-name coteries. In Guest's work, composition anticipates generational change as the objects of the world are released into linguistic orders that defy their settings. In her art, critical theory gets back where it belongs, following, rather than preceding, the inventive mind. She gives us weaponry with which to fight the dismissals and detractors who want our poems either to perpetuate a stale avant-gardism or to mimic mothers in tidy kitchens counting spoons. And so she can say this about Jane Austen:

> In writing concealed within a limited physical environment, as in the work of Jane Austen, the threat of claustrophobia hangs over

the whole body of the novels. In order to relieve this environmental tension, the writer with her strokes of genius elevates the characters above a physical dimension, so that although their persons appear to inhabit a close drawing-room they are actually removed from the interior to the exterior as they move beyond their limited space through the projection of the author.

They are persons who are capable in their minds, even in an obtuse mind, of looking outside themselves into another place, of shifting their persons. They are relieved of ordained claustrophobia, as is the reader, who might be stuck in that drawing-room, who is lifted by the author's inked quill, her euphemism for time, to project beyond singularity.

•

When the domestic does arrive in Guest's work, it might come via a journey to and from Byzantium, in which labor and its effects, in this case *silk*, enter our consciousness at the point of origin, or discovery, as the "serious and sophisticated weaving" at the bazaar in Mersan. The silk, purchased, gets turned into curtains and leads a domestic existence, "its history asleep, much as a poem enters an anthology." The critiques embedded in this swiftly told anecdote show how masterful Guest is at writing through more than one lens; her work has the restless perspicacity of a prism.

I think of the beautiful Frank Gehry building that has arisen on our campus at Bard, with its undulating, reflecting roof somehow capturing both the luminosity of the nearby river and the musicality of the interior performances it will house. How did this shape come into being? Someone told me that Gehry makes a drawing, and a computer figures out how to make from it something that can actually be dimensional in space. And so the idea is lifted, transported.

I thought: Barbara Guest, architect of air.

To call it a piece of air, to let it sing, then to conclude it is rare

A halo rescued from life

The rustle of silk in Mersan evoked the noise of the imagination.

6.

Art that matters is generative. By which I mean that it engenders our atten-
tion, captures our focus, and then allows for the pleasure of discovery: of it,
of course, but also of ourselves. It opens itself, its boundaries, to our own
boundaries, and we find the core of our capacity to change through the en-
counter with what we are not. This is a precious and profound enactment,
whereby what is strange becomes familiar, what is different stretches our
sense of solitude, of exile from ourselves and from the world, into, as she has
it, wounded joy.

The wound is

another aspect of the art

this essence has no limits

this need for delimiting

this beautiful balance between the hidden and the open

a little ghost

*leave this little echo to haunt the poem, do not give it form, but let it
    assume its own ghost-like shape. It has the shape of your own soul as
    you write.*

*The presence of a hidden anxiety about a poem might be a necessary
    prodding to go intensely into the poem. A poem should tremble a little.*

The poem's midnight
*The poem lies quivering on its page, its contents wounded, yet the poet is
    joyful.*

7.

The riddle of the image, how it conquers the mundane, "beyond the tenure of the brush, shell, or escapist sail." The tantalizing dance between what is written and what is spoken, between page and voice, between the materiality of the painting and the temporality of music; the quest to collapse these separations into the true contingency that poetry absolves and experience honors, so that "a severe distance is established between her realism / and his anxious attempt to define it." The understanding of form as an expression of our deepest and most constant dream, to include passional registers of affect and spirit in the ongoing project of Enlightenment. This is what Barbara Guest's achievement has given us.

> To introduce color to form
> I must darken the window where shrubs
> Grazed the delicate words
> The room would behave
> Like everything else in nature,
>
> Experience and emotion performed
> As they did within the zone of distance
> Words ending in fluid passages
> Creating a phenomenal blush
> Dispensing illusion

It is nightfall. It was the longest day of the year, the summer solstice. It rained and rained and rained. But, as Barbara Guest tells us, quoting the songwriter Johnny Burke, "Imagination is funny. It makes a cloudy day sunny."

All quotes are from Barbara Guest, *Forces of Imagination: Writing on Writing* (Berkeley, Kelsey Street Press, 2003).

ON DAVID SMITH'S LANGUAGE:
THE POETICS OF IDENTITY

On October 2, 1999, there was a symposium on American sculptor David Smith at the Storm King Art Center in upstate New York, where his work was on view. The curator of the symposium, Michael Brenson, along with Peter Stevens, the administrator of Smith's estate, asked me to write about Smith's use of language in relation to his sculpture. The quotations are drawn from David Smith by David Smith: Sculpture and Writings, *edited by Cleve Gray (London, Thames and Hudson, 1968), and* David Smith, *edited by Garnett McCoy (New York, Praeger, 1973). All quotations are from these two sources.*

David Smith was working and writing about his work before language about art and art about language became inextricably webbed, spawning a wilderness of meta-languages. Reading him today, one is struck by the absence of these mediating discourses; one feels as if he were writing closer to nineteenth-century Romantic understandings of the relation between artist, artwork, and culture than to our highly contested and elaborated dramas of postmodern self-consciousness. When Smith uses the word "identity," it does not come trailing clouds of rhetoric around questions of gender, class, and ethnicity. For Smith, identity and politics are related, but there is no sense of "identity politics," where academic wars are fought over texts and contexts, narratives and canons, exclusions and inclusions. For Smith, "identity" was a code word to signal a *summa* of his being and bearing fully realized in the process of making sculpture.

> I never intend a day to pass without asserting my identity; my work records my existence.

> I feel raw freedom and my own identity. I feel a belligerence to museums, critics, art historians, aesthetes and the so called cultural forces in a commercial order.

It is natural that artists know more about art than non artists. It is their total identity, they live it and make it.

My sculpture is part of my world; it's part of my everyday living; it reflects my studio, my house, my trees, the nature of the world I live in.

If you ask me why I make sculpture, I must answer that it is my way of life, my balance, and my justification for being.

The truly creative substance in the work of art is the artist's identity.

It is identity, and not that overrated quality called ability, which determines the artist's finished work.

In his introduction to *David Smith by David Smith*, Cleve Gray remarks: "David's handwriting was clear, bold, generous, unpretentious, masculine, large, energetic, and consistent. Looking at it one sees no smallness, nothing cramped, erratic, flaccid, affected, or fanciful." Reading this description, I felt slightly cornered, as if the whole issue of David Smith's writing might turn out to be an open-and-shut case of classic male identifications—the egotistical unsublimated sublime. Given Smith's own powerful sense of working-class origins, his love of machines and factories, iron and steel, trains and cars, I wondered if there were anything to be said that might contradict or complicate this totalizing picture. Certainly, one could say that much of Smith's use of language is straightforward to the point of an abrupt, brute assertiveness. He had a fondness for nouns, and used modifiers sparingly. He often repeated phrases. He liked lists and catalogues. In its syntax, Smith's writing is declarative and additive, rather than discursive or paratactic: it wants to get where it is going without having to digress or linger. It eschews ambivalence. At times it is awkward, giving it a rough eloquence. His writing is stylistically unselfconscious. Often, it registers emphasis, urgency, certainty.

One thing that David Smith was most certain about was an acute antipathy to words, especially words about art. Over and over, he asserts the primacy of visual over verbal language; over and over, he fulminates against analytical/historicist/critical readings of art.

"In childhood," he rails, "we have been raped by word pictures. We must revolt against all word authority. Our only language is vision."

> Tradition comes wrapped up in word pictures, these are traps which lead laymen into cliché thinking. Art has its tradition, but it is a visual heritage.

> To the serious students I would not teach the analysis of art or art history—I would first teach drawing; teach the student to become so fluent that drawing becomes the language to replace words. Art is made without words. It doesn't need words to explain it or encourage its making.

> We have all let anthropologists, philosophers, historians, connoisseurs and mercenaries, and everybody else tell us what art is or what it should be. But I think we ought to very simply let it be what the artist says it is. And what the artist says it is, you can see by his work.

> Generally speaking, aesthetics in verbal form are a bastardization of the creative artist's beauties.

Given these strong objections, the question might arise: what compelled David Smith to write at all, especially about art? He was not Robert Smithson, whose writings are the record and residue of an essentially ephemeral practice; he is not Donald Judd, for whom writing was a conceptual correlative to the material severity of his sculpture. David Smith's works have such resolute clarities, such physical command of the spaces in which they occur, one would think that they needed no auxiliary support from their creator, especially given his overt disdain for words. And yet, David Smith wrote, not just letters and the occasional "talk," but curiously intense and often lyrical poemlike verbal elaborations of his process, from conception to production to reception. It is as if he were anxious that something about his work, about his identity, would be misread, some crucial aspect of it would be ignored. But what?

What I noticed first in reading David Smith writing about David Smith is an extraordinary economy, not in the sense of frugality, but in the sense of a powerful relation between means and ends. Like another major modern figure, the irascible Ezra Pound, Smith was grounded by an ethic in which the idea of *use* was paramount. In his famous prescription for imagism, Pound says: "Use absolutely no word that does not contribute to the presentation." For Smith, everything was potentially part of an economy of use. He writes, "My method of shaping material or arriving at form has been as functional as making a motor car or a locomotive." He repeats the phrase, with slight variations, once again, saying, "My aim in material function is the same as in locomotion building: to arrive at a given functional form in the most efficient manner." The relation between form and function has a long history, as we know, and Smith's desire to inscribe his formal procedures with attributes of function was certainly embedded in his own affiliations with nitty-gritty factory work. But there is a difference between a train or a car and a piece of sculpture, and this difference is something Smith was both profoundly aware of and constantly attempting to articulate. His writings frequently draw attention to the significance of an abstract visual language in relation to the concrete realities of objects.

> The objects I had worked with in the factory were abstract. They
> were always functional pieces, having relationships, but were not
> objects of realism, gears, cross members, brackets, the triangle in
> a circle, spare tire carrier etc., were all abstract parts.

In this passage one feels Smith wanting to make a distinction between the functional, pragmatic uses of the objects in the factory—what he calls their "realism"—and his own sense of them as "abstract parts." Once an object—a gear or a bracket—ceases to be purely utilitarian, it becomes "abstract" in the sense that it enters a visual, an aesthetic, language. Smith wants to create and maintain a dual conceptual space, in which a work of art's social and aesthetic functions are inseparable. At the core of this idea is an ethical vision. As he told a *New York Herald Tribune* forum in 1950: "The freedom of man's mind to celebrate his own feeling by a work of art parallels his social revolt from bondage. I believe that art is yet to be born and that freedom and equality are yet to be born." For David Smith, art was not something which simply took its place among the myriad objects of desire which capitalism proffers. The act of art making was a declaration of one's personal freedom, which meant a kind of absolute conviction—"I challenge everything and everybody," he proclaimed.

In "Self-Reliance," Ralph Waldo Emerson had written, "To believe your own thought, to believe that what is true for you in your private heart is true for all men—that is genius." David Smith would concur. If one believes in this relation of personal conviction to universal application, then the nature of what is beautiful is embedded in an ethics. For Smith, the world around him was the source of beauty; his job was to transform it into a new order.

He wrote:

> ... *beauties come*
> *to be used, for an order*
> *to be arranged*

Arranging the beauties of the world, which came to David Smith as an unceasing diverse flux—what Emerson called "the embarrassing variety"—was for Smith a consummate, a consuming process. His horizon of receptivity was limitless. In this he reminds me of another modern figure who also wrestled with dichotomies between verbal and visual expression. In *Notes Toward a Supreme Fiction*, Wallace Stevens wrote:

> *He had to choose. But it was not a choice*
> *Between excluding things. It was not a choice*
>
> *Between, but of. He chose to include the things*
> *That in each other are included, the whole,*
> *The complicate, the amassing harmony.*

David Smith had an immense appetite for "the whole, the complicate, the amassing harmony." It is as if, in order to keep his avidity for existence in check, he had to constantly collect and transform each individual thing, from the most mundane junk to the most exalted mountain, into what he called "the adventure viewed." The world seems to have presented itself to Smith as a kinesthetic array of sensuous events, whether these events were in city time or country space.

> At 11:30 when I have evening coffee and listen to WQXR on AM I never fail to think of the Terminal Iron Works at 1 Atlantic Avenue, Brooklyn and the coffee pot nearby where I went same time, same station. The ironworks in Brooklyn was surrounded by all night activity—ships loading—barges refueling—ferries tied up

at the dock. It was awake 24 hours a day, harbor activity in front, truck transports on Furman Street behind. In contrast the mountains are quiet except for occasional animal noises. Sometimes Streever's hounds run foxes all night and I can hear them baying as I close up shop. Rarely does a car pass at night, there is no habitation between our road and the Schroon River four miles cross county. I enjoy the phenomenon of nature, the sounds, the Northern lights, stars, animal calls, as I did the harbor lights, tugboat whistles, buoy clanks, the yelling of men on barges around the TIW in Brooklyn. I sit up here and dream of the city as I used to dream of the mountains when I sat on the dock in Brooklyn.

But for Smith the process of making sculpture was not solely dependent on the constant influx of the world's stimuli. What he emphasizes in his writing, over and over, is the "intuitive and emotional" content of his working process. "The creative artist should not be impressed by the written directives, for his are intuitive and emotional," he told an audience in Woodstock in 1952. "To make art, the artist must deal with unconscious controls, controls which have no echo but which guide him, direct and first-hand."

Smith wrote to Edgar Levy about the "flowing groove," about an "emotional long flow," about a "stream plan." He says, "One gets subject to emotional fears in the process, like poverty forcing one to give up work for a while—death, the years are numbered." Elsewhere, he says, "I've put in years at machines dreaming aesthetic ends—one never becomes oblivious to the surrounding order—in concentrated work alone under ideal conditions—outside vistas intrude like sex—hungers and assorted fears, fears in survival, lonesomeness for my children, many waves intrude during the most ideal set up—one works with one's nature—sets his own equilibrium, develops his resources, evens up his rage in whatever conditions present . . ."

I want to suggest that Smith turned to language partly to draw attention to those aspects of his identity that were most difficult to describe in words and which were not obviously manifest in his sculpture, but were essential to its realization. These are aspects which, traditionally, belong to the language of poetry.

Art is made from dreams and visions and things not known and least of all from things that can be said. It comes from the inside of who you are, when you face yourself. It is an inner declaration of purpose.

The truly creative substance in the work of art is the artist's identity. How he comes about this is personal. It is internal, secret and slow-growing.

David Smith's code word for the necessary disposition of an artist toward this "inner declaration of purpose" is "affection." In "The Sculptor and His Problems" he writes:

> The stingy logic of the philosopher, his suspicion that the irrational creative menaces the will, excludes the all-important element of art-making which I will call affection. This feeling of affection which dominates art-making has nothing to do with the philosopher's need for rationalization.

And again:

> We must speak of affection—intense affection which the artist has for his work—an affection of relief, proudness, belligerent vitality, satisfaction and conviction.

And again:

> Does the onlooker realize the amount of affection which goes into a work of art—the intense affection—belligerent vitality—and total conviction? To the artist it must be total to provide satisfaction. Does the critic, the audience, the philosopher even possess the intensity of affection for the work which its creator possessed? Can they project or understand this belligerent vitality and affection which contemporary art possesses? Or do they deal in the quality at all? Is this emotion too highly keyed—or is it outside their lives? Or are they too skeptical?

What seems at issue for Smith here is some anxiety or doubt that his sculpture—that art—might find itself misread, misinterpreted, lodged within an arid critical vocabulary of judgments which would not include the "intensity of affection" neccesary for its making and for its reception: all clarity and no grace, all use and no beauty, all prose and no poetry. Clement Greenberg, for example, in an introduction to the 1964 exhibition of Smith's work at the Philadelphia Institute of Contemporary Art, speaks about Smith's use of materials, his surfaces, about the "three clearly demarcated veins" of geometries, about an unevenness in the output. He writes, "In the Voltri-Bolton Landing series, as elsewhere in his art, his drawing takes on more and more of geometrical regularity. It becomes more and more the kind of drawing that moves from the elbow or shoulder rather than from the wrist or fingers. And it converges with the newest developments in abstract painting, where the smears and squiggles of painterliness are ceding to cleaner, more anonymous handling." Greenberg further comments: "The regularity of contour and surface . . . are there in order to concentrate attention on the structural and general as against the material and specific, on the diagrammatic as against the substantial; but not because there is virtue in regularity as such." In conclusion, Greenberg makes this curious remark: "I am not going to talk about the content of Smith's art because I am no more able to find words for it than for the ultimate content of Quercia's or Rodin's art. But I can see that Smith's felicities are won from a wealth of content, of things to say, and this is the hardest, and most lasting, way in which they can be won. The burden of content is what keeps an artist going, and the wonderful thing about Smith is the way that burden seems to grow rather than shrinking."

Here we find a leading critic shying away from directly engaging in the "wealth of content" of David Smith's work, judging it largely in terms based on formal values in a language as abstract as it is vague. Greenberg wants the work to become more regular, less idiosyncratic, less varied. He wants virtually nothing to do with its "burden of content."

If, for David Smith, making art reflected a host of affective registers, each one of which is dependent on and reciprocal to the others—affection for the things of the world, affection for the materials of production, affection for oneself as inward repository and generative agent, affection for the work of art itself—then one begins to understand why he wrote. He used words at least in part to give names to passages of his identity which were as passional and volatile in his life as they were essential to his art making; he used words to refute, deflect, and augment reductive readings of his sculpture and, by extension, all art, readings that would ultimately strip it of its force as identity, with all the complex personal, social, and political efficacy he connected to that term.

Responding to his dealer Marian Willard's request for statements about his work to accompany an exhibition in 1947, David Smith came up with three categories: "The Landscape," "Spectres Are," and "Sculpture Is." He tells Willard that "they are not fancy, nor poetry" but "the words, notes, and thoughts which I've taken out of my workbooks," what he calls "verbal working controls." Force fields of historical, mythic, fictive, and personal associations, they evoke the peculiar disparate impulses and images with which Smith approached his subject:

THE LANDSCAPE

I have never looked at a landscape without seeing other landscapes.
I have never seen a landscape without visions of things I desire and despise
lower landscapes have crusts of heat—raw epidermis and the choke of vines
the separate lines of salt errors—monadnocks of fungus
the balance of stone—with gestures to grow
the lost posts of manmaid boundaries—in moulten shade a petrified
paperhanger who shot the duck
a landscape is a still life of Chaldean history
It has faces I do not know
its mountains are always sobbing females
it is bags of melons and prickle pears
its woods are sawed to boards
its black hills bristle with maiden fern
its stones are assyrian fragments
it flows the bogside beauty of the river Liffey
it is colored by Indiana gas green
it is steeped in veritable indian yellow
it is the place I've traveled to and never found
it is somehow veiled to vision by pious bastards and the lord of Varu the
nobleman from Gascogne
in the distance it seems threatened by the destruction of gold

You might say that these compendiums are signs or indicators of the very "content" that Clement Greenberg could not bring himself to address. Here we see how language helped Smith to suggest both the variety and regress which propelled his work, and the intensity of feeling which everywhere informed it.

"Sculpture Is" ends:

> *the dialectic of survival*
> *everything I sought*
> *everything I seek*
> *what I will die not finding.*

But he did find it. For David Smith, as for so many artists, both those whose work is primarily visual and those whose work is verbal, the process of seeking is ongoing, and the object—the poem or the painting or the sculpture—is simultaneously an end and a beginning.

When the critic David Sylvester asked David Smith if he had any preconceptions about his work, this is what he replied:

> I try not to have. I try to approach each thing without following the pattern that I made with the other one. They can begin with any idea. They can begin with a found object, they can begin with no object. They can begin sometimes even when I'm sweeping the floor and I stumble and kick a few parts and happen to throw them into an alignment that sets me off thinking and sets off a vision of how it would finish if it all had that kind of accidental beauty to it. I want to be like a poet, in a sense. I don't want to seek the same orders. Of course, I'm a human being, I have limited ability, and there's always an order there.

Or, as Wallace Stevens put it:

> *He imposes orders as he thinks of them,*
> *As the fox and snake do. It is a brave affair.*

And it was.

GERHARD RICHTER: "THE ENIGMA"

I was invited by Peter Stevenson to participate in a panel on the German artist Gerhard Richter during a retrospective of his work at the San Francisco Museum of Modern Art on November 16, 2002. The poet and publisher David Breskin had edited a book, Richter 858, *for which he had asked a number of writers, myself included, to respond to Richter's painting.*

1.

Until his retrospective last year at MoMA Manhattan, Gerhard Richter was for me a peripheral figure. I could recall seeing only the Baader-Meinhof sequence, his stunning retro-real noir contribution to the iconography of political violence that has occupied so much of our visual landscape.

When the drums began to beat for the Richter retrospective I was caught off guard. I did not know that Gerhard Richter was, as the Sunday *New York Times Magazine* put it, "Europe's greatest painter." They called him, alluringly, "the Enigma." I wondered to myself who Europe's greatest poet is, and if she, too, had made a journey from the depredations of the Communist East into the welcoming free-enterprise zone of the West of the coattails of American late modernism.

I am old enough and have been hanging around the art world long enough to remember when German artists began to be players in the international contemporary art world. I remember early days of Joseph Beuys, whose catalytic subversive insurgency crumbled distinctions between politics, performance, and a mystical, if not transcendent, aesthetic. I remember, later, the arrival of Sigmar Polke and Anselm Kiefer. I have a book by Lisa Saltzman called *Anselm Kiefer and Art After Auschwitz*. She takes up the historical conundrum of Adorno's remark "after Auschwitz to write a poem is barbaric." She argues that Kiefer's work expresses the historically inexpressible, as if he could simultaneously extend and refute German Romanticism.

2. Fragment, Detail

When the poet David Breskin phoned to ask if I would contribute to a Richter book, I accepted. I have learned that as a poet, it is a good idea to say yes when asked, even if you are not sure of the ground.

David and I agreed that I would write not to a painting but to a detail.

I use the word "to" because I am not interested in description per se. I am interested in dialogue. The poems I have written in relation to paintings are essentially dialogues, as if the painting were a form of speech that I could answer. When works of art cause me to begin to speak, that is, to think, I am drawn toward them or into them. Also, I knew I would not be looking at an actual painting, and so I thought a reproduction of an enlarged detail would be more honest than a reproduction of an entire painting. I thought about the simple difference between verbal and visual arts in an age of electronic reproduction; how what I write can be transported anywhere without alteration of scale, color, surface, and so forth.

But the more substantive reason I wanted to write to a detail of a Richter painting is because my own practice has led me to think about the idea of a whole fragment. To think about Richter's work in terms of whole fragments is interesting, as we might see each genre or style as a kind of example or sample. An example, a fragment, a detail.

The notion of the whole fragment had come in part from thinking about Robert Ryman's *white,* his paintings as fragments of *whiteness,* and about how some abstraction can be perceived as an accrual of individual marks each of which is, on its own, a whole fragment.

I think that we need to bring ourselves into a celebratory idea of the fragment, not to lament a spurious, imagined whole. This is how I construe the present. Perhaps similar to the way Richter eschews a single genre, I have come to believe that ideas of discursive progression, linear narrativity, endemic to history and to language, are constructs which can constrict our reading of where we are and how we act in relation to where we are.

That Richter has refused to be genre-specific is pleasurable; to see an artist who does not have a brand, a way of making a mark, a way of transforming world into style is exhilarating.

3. Presence, Event

Richter's retrospective at MoMA New York left me dazzled, wanting to locate within its array a perspective or point of view that was not simply an assertion of formidable capacity, not a retrenchment, not only art about art.

Arthur Danto, in his review of the show, suggests that Richter takes on history itself, history, as he put it, in a blur. Danto, who compares Richter favorably with Warhol, comments, "One often has to look outside his images to realize the violence to which they refer." Danto continues:

> But what the show at MoMA somehow makes clear is that there
> finally is a single personal signature in Richter's work, whatever
> its subject, and whether the work is abstract or representational.
> It comes from (a) protective cool . . . a certain internal distance
> between the artist and his work, as well as between the work and
> the world, when the work itself is about reality. It is not irony. It is
> not exactly detachment. It expresses the spirit of an artist who
> has found a kind of above-the-battle tranquility that comes when
> one has decided that one can paint anything one wants in any
> way one likes without feeling that something is given up. That
> cool is invariant to all paintings, whatever their content.

The idea that the twentieth-first century, with its roiling hot terrors, should open with a celebration of a painter whose signature quality is "cool" is disturbing. The artist as production machine, confident, indifferent, cool. There is in these values a reprise of modernist models of masculine genius.

My sense is we need to come into contact with art that brings us closer to the possibility of human engagement, agency, and response, not to be reminded at how distant we are from the actual. Part of our exhilaration as spectators comes from an inner acknowledgment of possibility; that by witnessing an artist's choices we are brought into contact with our own capacities to act, to choose, to decide; finally, to judge. This is what I call gladness. When I look at Gerhard Richter's work, I do not cross the threshold into this gladness, but am kept at bay; I come away with an immense admiration for his practice, but no closer to my sense of agency as a result of that admiration. This is not a critique in any real sense of the word. I have been looking at pictures long enough to know that what one resists is often what one comes to love.

Richter's terms are set, and they are not the terms of presence, or event. Richter is not concerned with signs of presence, he is concerned with the sign of absence, as if the work were the object of a nonsubjectivity. He confers on his art an absence of presence, presenting us with potential tragedy, one that consigns individual agency to the dust heap of the future. The world as we know it is mediated, and Richter seems to fully accept and enforce this mediation, the *blur*, the cool of re/presentations. Richter's world is direct in its mediation. In "The Man on the Dump," Wallace Stevens imagines a world stripped of image, of the typography of presence which syntax, and Stevens's modernist anxieties, demanded. The poem ends, horribly, with the words "The the." The specific without its specificity, the empty sign, the no thing of the replication of the definite article: "The the." Richter makes us enter this world, but instead of the stripped bleakness of *the the*, there are many representations, many "thes," but no representer. It is pure materiality.

JOHN CURRIN: PRESSING BUTTONS

In the spring of 2004, I gave a practicum on writing for graduate students at the Curatorial Center at Bard College. The focus of the course was on subjective and objective sites of critical investment and assessment, and I asked the class to write on current exhibitions in which these basic issues might be addressed. The young American artist John Currin was enjoying a considerable critical success. Many of the students, particularly the women, found it difficult to articulate their ambivalence; I decided to try my hand.

With John Currin, whose mid-career retrospective at the Whitney Museum recently closed, movers and shakers of the art world again yielded to the seductive strut of a bad-boy wunderkind hawking new toys. This time, a dirty-blond Yalie with Twenty-fourth Street smarts, a fashionista wife, and a baby with balls (see Richard Avedon's picture accompanying the Currin profile in the *New Yorker*), showing his prowess with painterly technique, appropriated Old Masterish composition, and transgressive subject matter.

Currin's paintings tell of a soured American idealism, of a sacred native goodness fallen to a curdled profane. Where once there were John Singer Sargent's luminous portraits of long, imperious women in satin dresses, now there is haggard and disappointed *Ms. Omni* (1993), her eyes dully sated. Where once there were Norman Rockwell's scenes of domestic coziness, or Andrew Wyeth's calendar-perfect rural landscapes, now there are strained encounters with suburban domesticity gone awry and astray. Wyeth's talismanic, if mawkish, Christina has turned, long tresses bleached blond, Keane-eyed as a Paris Hilton doll, to face "her"—that is, our—world. Where once there were Warhol's portraits of a transfigured, mythic Marilyn, now there is the ordinary face of TV star Bea Arthur above an ordinary middle-aged American woman's naked torso. Where once high aesthetic technique and inventive finesse—say, Johns, or Guston, or de Kooning—stood for a complex and replete Americana, now it serves the dubious retro-fit of a canny virtuoso. This

212 THE NIGHT SKY

isn't Kansas anymore, or the magical mystery tour of urban New York; we're in a redundant faux Oz, where the wizard is Larry Gagosian and the magic is the sound of rushing casino coin. This is George W. Bush's America, where, according to the *New York Times*, we are back in the culture wars *big time*.

I don't quite buy the idea of the "grotesque" which such stellar critics are Robert Storr and Robert Rosenblum are promoting as a way to think Currin. It feels too much like a means to insinuate a troubling oeuvre into the fabric of historical narrative. Of course we cannot argue that the work doesn't come from some place, no one wants to claim that kind of originality anymore; but the grotesque doesn't seem quite right. I think Currin is closer to a reactionary social critic, a kind of *Vanity Fair* guy who listens to Howard Stern while he writes insider scoop. He has some of the simplistic shtick of the maven of shock, where attitude is everything, putting the other at a disadvantage by the sheer force of the in-the-know putdown. Currin has something, too, of the cartoonist's distorted mark, and of the pop pornographer's detached voyeurism—Hugh Hefner's friendly stare. But his work lacks the torque either of true parody or of satire; it's too perfunctory, too silly and obvious, not droll and trenchant like, say, R. Crumb's, or Jeff Koons's at its best. One might evoke Hopper, but there is not a shred of pathos in this work, and neither is there nostalgia for a lost anything. Many of Currin's female subjects have the same stilted smile and vacuous stare, lifted from advertising; his work seems joyless, sarcastic, and glib, and it is difficult to come round to the idea that he is actually sympathetic to the curiously inadvertent subjection of his subjects (one could think here, perhaps, of the roiling conversation around Diane Arbus's freaks). Something about this work makes us feel creepy and embarrassed, as if we were caught like a teenager rummaging in our parents' underthings; we feel awkward, ashamed and giggly. This is not only for the obvious reasons found in such macabre works as *The Wizard*, depicting a gloved Howdy Doody–esque figure groping, or manipulating, the immense breasts of a blonde; it is pictures like *Minerva* and *The Activists*, where Currin's disdain is crudely palpable. Minerva, otherwise known as Athena, goddess of wisdom, is shown as an hysterical crone with maple leaves stuck in her hair; the "activists" are pathetic seniors, grandmas and grandpas left behind in the milllennial dust. (It is no stretch to imagine this picture in the living room of, say, Donald Rumsfeld.)

Currin's claim to fame seems to be an adolescent's sense of uncouth subversion combined with the student's desire to ingratiate his teachers. The straight married white guy *will* make spoofy pictures of gay couples in domestic bliss, of overly endowed middle-aged women; he *will* portray young

African-American women and flimsily clad silk-skinned ingenues; he *will* insinuate his own features onto those of a girl, playing with sexual identity as if it were a sort of New Age set of Lego. He *will* portray Nadine Gordimer, the South African Nobel laureate, with a huge head, lachrymose and overburdened, on a desexualized, emaciated body. He *will* take the iconic thin society matron and show her to be a grim combination of material privilege, vanity, and spiritual destitution.

Compositionally, Currin's work is often stilted and vapid; interior pictorial space is broken up by edges of mirrors and frames, bland objects, and traces of vague landscape elements which do nothing to conduct or connect the viewer's eye into a circuit of details that might lead to an interpretive insight. His figures are adrift in an uninflected habitat without anything that signals their personal sense of belonging: work, house, landscape. They abide in a drained, inanimate, placeless place, a mall of the soul. Further, the three features where portraiture is traditionally revelatory of a subject's character—hands, eyes, and mouth—are remarkable in Currin for their homogeneity. His subjects' hands, in particular, are invariably slender, long-fingered, and limp (male or female), as if drawn from studies of mannequins for women's gloves. Currin excels, however, at the details of garb: his brush finds nuance in the ribbings, texture, and drape of cloth. (There is good reason why his name is dropped so frequently on the fashion pages of the *New York Times*.) At the heart of all Currin's images is a platitudinous superiority that houses a distaste for the difficult uncertainties of intimacy or attachment. The yellow-brown murkiness of his palette drains vitality; his head-shot portraits merge into one ubiquitous stare. None of his subjects is animated by the individuation of personal agency; they all seem, even those who are not "invalid," halted, inert. Under this inertia is a sense of impending violence. One imagines his next body of work to be themes of mayhem and slaughter, when the comparisons to Goya will be more apt.

But what about Currin's much-touted painterly expertise? These claims seem exaggerated, brought about by deprivation, as if everyone had been starving and someone came up with some carrot sticks. There are countless passages in this work which look either uncertain or overwrought; his surface is by turns glossy and built up, pocked; often he seems unsure of the relation between drawing and paint. In any case, contra McLuhan's mantra, here the medium is decidedly not the message. It is precisely the disconnect and clash between Currin's attention to, and proclaimed love of, the act of painting, and the crude assertiveness of his subjects, that captures our attention, confuses our habits of seeing. Like a pirate, he steals booty off the good ship

PC and sails off on a sleek old schooner, replete with polished teak and brass fittings. (Those naked *Fishermen* in their laden dinghy are headed out to a very cool yacht parked at the Vineyard. Trust me.) He has hoisted the academic flags of postgender-feminist-colonial-multiculturalisms on their own postmodern discourse-saturated petards, all the while letting the ship fill with the brine of an ostensible universality. For Currin, equality is not a complex ratio of opportunities, but a flat transaction, an economy of reductive semblances. Currin's in-your-face rejection of ideology- and theory-driven models for art experience is, I think, what has caused aestheticians like Peter Schjeldahl to react with inebriated joy. Schjeldahl's sine qua non is pleasure, the delirium of a sensuous high from which, later, language and its conceptual demands ensue. Still a poet at heart, Schjeldahl wants to fall in love and tell about it later in rapturous prose. And so Currin's combination of art-historical savvy (where Schjeldahl and *frères* can strut their stuff), painterly finesse, and subversive topicality adds up to a rave.

It is, perhaps, the very *materiality* of Currin's work, the fact that they are paintings, that most confuses the issue. If these were manipulated glossy prints or video investigations of identity (Cindy Sherman, Bruce Nauman) or narrative hybrids (William Kentridge), they would attract little attention, since Currin has no imaginative flair for either subjective introversion or cultural complexity, and he is no ironist. (He is sincere! He is ironic! He is sincerely ironic!) But compared to the peculiarly haunting and charged portraits of Gerhard Richter, another master of the lost art of painting, whose works engage us in a subtle and wily sensibility, steeped in multiple layers of (biographical, art-historical, historical) narrative, Currin's work is simplistic, repetitious, banal.

We have been taught to see through the subject, as if it were a mere transparent veil pulled across the glories of paint and its surfaces. This teaching begins the story of modernism, where the how always overode the what; where form subsumes subject. When is a flag not a flag? When it is a picture by Jasper Johns. When is an apple not an apple? When it is in a painting by Paul Cézanne. Just remember: *Ceci n'est pas un pipe*. Signifiers and signifieds, referents and signs. Along the way, the "subject" disappeared entirely into the halls of abstraction and formalist critique, culminating in this country with, say, Brice Marden's transcendental sublime, or Frank Stella's grand colored gears. Sooner or later, painting began to lose its edge, to falter before the hot new performative techno-installation-video-sound Matthew Barney/Damian Hirst extravaganzas. Of course painting went on, and painters like Leon Golub or Alex Katz or Amy Sillman or Frank Moore continued to find in the peopled and thingy world subjects for their work. Critics nattered about representation and narrative, but the hot spots were clearly over there, with Ann Hamilton's poetics of architectonic scripture or Sarah Sze's fantasy digs. If painting was alive and well, it had left these American shores and returned to its first home in retro Europe, where people are still allowed to smoke.

If content inheres in the dissolution of subject and form, and if meaning is derived from our contemplation of this dissolution, what are we to make of John Currin's effort so far? In Currin's work, form and subject do not dissolve to release content; they remain obdurately separate, and we are forced to look through disparate lenses at the same time, distorting our vision. Asked to find meaning in the very cut that opens between these forms and these subjects, we cannot talk the formalist talk without falling on our faces in front of a frothy "heartless" ingenue, a disastrous Thanksgiving. If you read the critics, none has found a way to speak about this work without separating, so to speak, the yolk from the white.

It has been a while since we were asked to address the full affective registers of visual art, to find ourselves reassessing our stake in its ability to interpret and illuminate, beyond the playground of lifestyles, hot tickets, and market allure. (I have been reminded, often, of another artist whose work caused similar outbursts of hyperbolic acclaim and derision, Julian Schnabel. Twenty years later, Schnabel is still a celebrity, but he dumped the art world for greener pastures.) When I first saw Currin's show, I gave it the most generous of interpretations, wanting to imagine Currin with a sympathetic gaze, depicting women, for example, as fashion victims, still beholden to outmoded cosmetic pressures and ideals. But the reading did not hold; it collapsed into wishful thinking. Currin pushes us away as he draws us toward, like a roadside crack-up or tabloid headline. He elicits our interest at the cost of our care. What if *all* he cares about is painting, if his subjects are only in service to a supreme indifference, verging on scorn? Are we complicit with this indifference, this contempt? Is every *other*, every alterity, merely a pretext for self-serving self-esteem? We are back, then, to modernist manners stripped of their consequence: James Joyce and T. S. Eliot, paring their fingernails, writing sonnets.

We pass the accident, glad that we are safe and sound in our SUV, just as targets are bombed from above, and the survivors left to their own blasted emergency.

So it might seem that this is Currin's game: to marry high "European"-derived painterly technique and historical quotation to banal American illustrative pictorialism, and to let us, his viewers, suffer the indignities that result. No matter how much jargon of authenticity we muster in protest, the rich win at their own aura-denuded game, and the rest of us teach. Can we see through Currin's subjects to his "gorgeous" surfaces, and ignore our desire to rescue them from a vindictive and puerile schoolboy stare, in thrall to butt and bust? Does Currin unsettle us, as Emerson would say, by placing us in an uncomfortable contradiction between masterly artifice and demeaning tableaux? That is, does he tell it like we are, trapped in a toxic homegrown brew of material-techno plenitude of expertise and power, reality TV's exploited and exploded private/public space, and the resulting damned fantasies of the "good life"?

We do not want to believe that someone as heralded as John Currin is a slick literalist of the imagination. A culture gets the artist, and the art, it deserves. The eagle soars over a destitute and cynical landscape.

REMEMBERING JOE BRAINARD

When I first returned to New York from London in the early 1970s, I became friends of the poet and lyricist Kenward Elmslie and his partner, the artist and writer Joe Brainard. In the ensuing years, until his death of AIDS in 1994, Joe became one of my most cherished friends; I often visited him and Kenward at Kenward's house in Calais, Vermont. What follows is excerpted from my journal. In 2000, there was a panel on Joe at the Studio School that included Bill Corbett, Ron Padgett, Carter Ratcliffe, and myself. My remarks are included.

October 23, 1993

It is six in the evening, a Saturday, perfect weather. The sun is just going down; my curtains are still open; the blue is delphinium. At around two today I went to see Joe, who has come back from Vermont after an anguished summer. He had told me about his bile ducts, and about an ulcer; he had a procedure a few weeks ago; he told me he had lost a lot of weight. Kenward had written a note to ask me to tell a few of his close friends that he was undergoing this procedure, which I had done. Joe told me a few years ago that he had tested negative and I of course believed him; even when he came down with a bad case of shingles, which someone said is often a prelude to AIDS, and even when he got awful throat infections, despite his scrupulous care with his body. I think I did know, or begin to know, because I dreaded going to see him today as much as I wanted to see him, and was confused about what to bring him. One is always confused about what to give Joe, because he never seems to want anything, although when he is given something he appreciates it; whatever the "it" is, it never seems "good enough," because his own immense thoughtfulness toward the "it" of others is unfailing and unstinting. He gives with an uncoerced ease, and seems never to expect anything in return. For years, he has been the standard to or for me of goodness: loyal, generous, unself-serving; forgiving, responsive. He brings to mind words we never think to say anymore: "gracious" and "abiding." So today I go to see him, and I bring him some groceries: fresh fish and broccoli from the market, pasta from Dean & DeLuca, a piece of sweet bread, and some yams. He said he didn't want most of it, since he doesn't cook; somehow I thought that because he is staying at home, he was cooking, because he sometimes cooks in Vermont, but I was wrong. He kept the pumpkin ravioli, but I think he will probably throw them out. His loft was, as usual, absolutely spare. Bed on the floor, couch with a pillow and an Indian blanket we had bought together at the flea market (he bought it), his two antique cloth black dolls. There is a beautiful table on which is a white vase with some semidried stuff in it; a single mirror on the wall hanging from a wire; on the table in front of the couch nothing but a small album Kenward had made for him and an ashtray. He asked me to sit in the chair, not on the couch. He looked beautiful, he is beautiful, and I didn't really register how thin he is, since he is thin. I sat down and I suppose some words were said; he asked me how my day had been so far, and I said I was too busy, and had too many stupid things to do—my usual litany of complaints that he has heard for years, and to which he always responds with a kind of sweetness that is without judgment, always solicitous. Then he said, "I have something to tell you I am a lot sicker than you think I have AIDS." Pretty much like that, without skipping or pausing.

I think I said, "I was afraid you would tell me that," although it was only then that I admitted to the fear. Then we talked and I told him stuff, but it was hard to concentrate; he told me he had to take medicine intravenously, and I looked over to the shelf and saw all these medical supplies. He said, eventually, that he hoped he wouldn't suffer too much, that he felt very lucky, that he was fifty-one; he said he hoped he would not become blind. He said he would move to a place in the village to be closer to Kenward, because he probably wouldn't be able to climb the stairs. At some point I couldn't really stand it and I went around the table and sat on the couch and fell toward him and put my arms around his very thin shoulders and wept. He wept also; we were I suppose grieving for each other.

January 25, 1994

Late evening; after some hours spent with Joe at the hospital. His skin is luminous and slightly transparent; his eyes large and clear; his brows more pronounced against his gray hair and thin face. He moves slowly and not easily; you can tell there is almost nothing to him; his lean muscular body is now a thin layer of skin over bones. He is hauntingly beautiful, if this is an allowed perception; that is, if beauty is here somehow augmented or made evident by illness.

The situation is not good. He has CMV, he has an ulcer, his pancreas is not functioning, and now he has some stomach virus, for which he has to take immense pills, four at a time, on top of endless infusions and no real food, none. This kind of sensual deprivation is intense for someone like Joe, who has so fully enjoyed without greed or excess the pleasures of food: orange juice, corn, peas, bread, pasta, chicken. He has a quiet swoon about the world of sensuous pleasures; he makes a kind of sound, part groan, part sigh, when the world gives out its loveliness and he is included in it. It has, I suppose, to do with welcome and with gratitude.

I sat with him on the fourteenth floor while he was infused; some hours. The wide river was there. We talked. Sometimes about his situation, but only the physical real, not the spiritual unknown. At the end of the day, Pat (Padgett) had arrived, and we went back to his room where he wanted to rest on his bed and I offered him a cold washcloth on his forehead, which he accepted, and that was nice for me, to give him something simple and needed.

January 29, 1994

Joe said when I left tonight, "You should have been a nurse." I brought him some magnolia branches, which made the room smell glorious, and John's new book, *And the Stars Were Shining*. I asked Joe if he wanted some music, and he said no, music made him too sad, it was too beautiful. Jan Hashey arrived, with Frank Moore. Then Ron came, and there was a constant patter of conversation on the fourteenth floor while Joe was infused, falling in and out of being there. At one point I looked at his face, and he seemed peaceful, and feminine for the first time. Odd.

Joe believes that he still has some time with clarity ahead. It would be so wonderful if he could eat again. It makes you so aware of how precious it all is, the taste of things, the smell, the touch. Now it is a cigarette, and the cold washcloth across his brow: these are his pleasures.

February 12, 1994

Extremity persists: huge snow today, all day, many hours of which were spent in Joe's room watching it: the extremity, the snow. He begins, now, to look caged, caught; when I smile he looks at me wondering why it is I am smiling; his smiles are running out. He maintains his great courtliness; he kisses my hand. I feel loved by him even as he is trying to leave with dignity and grace. Waking from his morphine sleep, which isn't really sleep since, he says, it is on the surface, he gets up, quickly, startled to find himself still here or there. "What are you reading?" he asks. "Horace," I reply. "Huhm," he says, "it's probably good for you." Pause. "Like spinach."

May 25, 1994

Joe is dead.

There is lightning and thunder; I told Kenward, since it started to storm just after we left the hospital and went to Greenwich Avenue, that this was a greeting for Joe. Last night I flew in from Denver, and the moon came out, full and brilliantly gold, just as we landed, after a tempestuous and worrying flight. I got home around 10 p.m., and there was a message from Ron saying that Joe's condition had worsened, that time was getting short, or some such gentle message of emergency: Ron, ever the great captain of the good ship life. I had not eaten and had taken Valium to get across the country, but I called and left a message, and then he called to say he and Pat had just come from the hospital and were probably going to return.

So I knew I had better go, and I did, riding in the night with the moon full, but now eclipsed, as if a hand or cup had come across its face. When I went into Joe's room on the seventeenth floor Kenward was there sitting at his side holding his hand, and John [Joe's brother], and the night nurse. Kenward instantly rose and we left and went to sit in the outer room, looking over the river, and the moon was there, still eclipsing. Kenward was lucid and calm, but I was molten, and he told me I had to be strong and I wept on his great shoulders, and he said things about the days. Finally, we returned to Joe's room, and we sat with him, and Ron and Pat arrived and we sat, holding Joe's hands. Kenward asked me about my sister's death, and about my mother's and father's deaths, and it seemed peculiar to have him ask these questions just then, and kind. Joe's hands were warm, his eyes open but not in focus, although I thought when I said I was there he seemed to know it. I said, "I am wearing your necklace."

We were there through the night, and Joe came out of his morphine sleep suddenly and was anxious and agitated and said something, and I thought he said "Shut up," but what he said was "Sit up" and again "Sit up," almost impossible to understand under the ghastly oxygen mask. So they raised the bed almost upright, and so forth.

I left at dawn, the light incredible, the color of dark delphinium, and the huge peach-colored moon globe low over the river. I slept for four hours and got up and went back. Ron and I had lunch in the cafeteria and talked about Jackie Kennedy, and then went back. Joe's hands were cold, and the vital signs were beginning to diminish on the machine. I left at 2:25 to go to my therapy appointment, where I wept, and then I went back to the hospital and went back into room 1752, and John and Caroline were there on one side and Kenward was on the other, and Ray, the nurse. The numbers on the machine were lower, and Joe was an awful gray color, and his hands were white and cold. I was there for maybe six or seven minutes, maybe ten. He died.

John closed his eyes.

I went back into the room when they had taken the mask off his face.

I could still see the beautiful face.

I kissed him on the forehead.

When I went to see him last Monday in the hospital he was all hooked up to a million things and he had the mask on. When I left I said "I love you, Joe" and he said "I love you too, Anni." This is what I get to keep.

October 20, 1994

Last Friday, I flew up to Burlington. Kenward and I had arranged to meet at an inn not far from there, to spend the night, and to drive to Calais the next day. We had dinner in his room and talked, mainly about Joe, and about plans for the remembrance at the Poetry Project. Saturday was a day of archetypal autumnal clarity: cool, cloudless, and augmented by the vivid display that belongs only to New England. The drive across to Montpelier, which is the nearest town to Calais, is one I have taken before, with its mountain vistas in the distance and its redolent near, punctuated by farms, cornfields, and sudden splashes of river. Kenward's house sits on a hill overlooking a pond, where Joe and I would swim, Joe walking slowly in, wearing his skimpy black suit, his skin burnished and gleaming, and then sink down and come up, letting out a groan of pleasure. Nobody knew better how to take pleasure in such simple acts; Joe loved objects and was more discerning about them than anyone else I know, but he did not let them mediate the sensuous world; he did not know the world through its objects; he did not know himself by his possessions. Once, when I was working on Greene Street in a gallery, he came in, wearing jeans and a white shirt and sneakers and a sports jacket. It was probably spring or fall. "Anni," he said, "I have something for you," and he reached into his pocket and drew from it a silver necklace from which hung many charms that he had collected over the years, which he poured into my hand.

When we drove up to the house and parked next to Kenward's studio, which sits across the road from the house, I was afraid to get out. I have so many mental images of Joe coming out of the orange door and loping with his agile stride across the grass to take my bags; I can hear his voice still so clearly in my mind's ear. "Hi, Anni, this is Joe." Can we describe a voice? His was soft at the edges; never anxious, quietly anticipatory, with a slight whispery sensuality to it, a sort of caress; it had natural warmth, and a melodic quality without being theatrical. I can't imagine it shrill or enraged or cruel. Kenward and I sat for a while in the car, to gather ourselves away from the sad dread, and then we went in. We had a light lunch of salad, fresh from the market, and some delicious egg rolls. The odd chandelier that hangs over the table was festooned with leaves which Kenward had put there last year; it looked like a kind of autumnal crown. The purpose of this visit was to climb up the hill behind the house to Joe's stone and to strew some of his ashes.

After lunch, I went outside for a cigarette, as Joe and I had many times, sitting on the bench overlooking the pond; Joe with his Trues and I with my Merits. When I went back in, Kenward was holding a round aluminum pot with a top on it. He told me that in the pot was a glass. "The glass is yours," he said, "and the ashes are yours also." (Several persons have made this journey over the summer: Ron and Pat Padgett, Anne Waldman, Bill and Beverly Corbett, John and Caroline Brainard, Anne Dunn, Peter Gizzi, and Elizabeth Willis among them.) We walked slowly up the wooded path, past some brilliant red berries the names of which neither of us knew. It was like walking against a tide. At one point we stopped and held each other, and began to weep, and went on. Joe's stone is white quartz, almost oval, about two feet long and a foot and a half high. It had been outside his studio, where Joe could see it easily from his many windows. Kenward has had it placed in a grove of white pines which sits in a rough meadow toward the top of the ridge. When we got there, a bird began to make rapid drumming sounds. Kenward handed me the pot, we hugged, he left. I stood for a while in the lovely air. Kenward had told me that people were bringing objects to leave; I had brought a pearl from my mother's broken necklace, a button from my secondhand Armani jacket, and a third shell button. I set the pot down, and then I took off the lid and lifted out the heavy goblet. *Rip, rip, rip*, said the bird, and the hand is astonished to let go.

January 18, 2000 (The Studio School)

Despite the lapse of some years since the death of Joe Brainard, I find it difficult to disengage the heart's desire for protracted eulogy, to move from the subjective terrain of loss to the more objective place of detachment which would offer some enlightenment or insight to those in the audience who did not have the luck to know him. This situation aggravates the need to extrapolate the person from his work, from his paintings, poems, writings, collages, collaborations. The personal and the critical are at odds. What could I say that would keep these two opposing modes from collapsing into reveries of praise of not much use now to anyone? In thinking about this evening, my mind kept turning toward a conversation, or maybe more than one conversation, not about making art but about not making art. This is how one tries to accommodate absence.

The compensations of a flawed memory are not much help. Events that were separate in time and place become slowly annealed to each other. Where were we, and when was it, that Joe and I sat at a bar and I had the temerity to ask him why he had stopped making art? I think it must have been in the mid-1980s, when I was still working in art galleries, feeling increasingly scared, trapped, and remote, not having any real sense of how I was going to move on. I think it was during the pre-Christmas season, since Joe and I often went shopping together, wandering through the Village and SoHo, until we had had enough and would stop for a drink or dinner.

There were two parts to Joe's answer. The first part was startling in its benign confession. He said he didn't think he was good enough. This may seem to have been an indirect request for contradiction, for praise, but I think for Joe it was his objective assessment of the truth. Joe rarely dissembled. He wasn't really capable of the ego management which would corral support by feigning weakness. He was naturally discerning; he made careful and constant assessments, which he somehow managed to communicate, without appearing to be either competitive or judgmental. It was a peculiar knack of his soul. But he thought things should be the best they could be, and "things" included everything from poems to persons to rings to food to dolls to paintings. This had nothing to do with a rote perfectionism. It was instead a form of economy, the economy of vigilant excellence wherein there wasn't any point in adding to the stuff of the world just for the sake of it. Thus he could decide, by some internal estimation, the work he made was inferior. Inferior to what or to whom? Giorgio Morandi? Fairfield Porter? Andy Warhol? Joseph Cornell?

The second part of his answer was a remark about ambition. Joe said he wasn't ambitious enough to be an artist. This second remark was more important, more telling, for me at the time. I think it had to do with the turn in the art world, where one began to feel that in order to be successful as an artist one had to have an extra dose of ambition, or a new kind of ambition, not just for the goodness of one's work, but also within the world of commerce, where affection, affiliation, and admiration were subtly distorted into strategies of alignment and agencies of contact. Joe wanted nothing to do with these new determinants, whether or not he was actually capable of them. He wasn't a moralizing prude and he didn't condemn those who were good at being players in the new art game: he knew perfectly well that it was possible to be an opportunistic rat and still make good art. I think the new atmosphere simply spoiled his sense of pleasure and fun, and his desire for a tacit community of mutual reciprocity.

As an artist, I think, Joe Brainard believed that the familiar could not be exhausted. Like Jimmy Schuyler and Rudy Burckhardt, he believed in the radical power of perception when it settles on subjects of common ubiquity in a person's life—a cigarette in an ashtray, a comic book, a pet, a flower, many flowers, a vase of flowers. Perhaps he felt that in the new art world, such connections, such an artifice of direct observation, would be seen as insufficient, or trivial, or banal. Perhaps he thought his peculiar combination of exuberance and restraint, his post-pop, nonironic celebration of the ordinary, would be seen as belated or callow.

I think Joe Brainard at heart was a classicist. For him, art making was an act of simultaneous preservation and discovery, one pointing toward the past in the form of recollection, or retrieval, the other toward the future as structure distilled and revealed, each collapsing into the other to create a present, a presence, of consummate clarity.

9/11

WHAT IS A DAY?

9/11 is in two parts: "What Is a Day?" was written in October 2001 to try to capture some of the immediacy and urgency of my experience of the events of September 11th; "After the Fall" was written for a special section of the journal American Letters and Commentary, "Beyond Extremis: Seven Essays on Language and the Imagination," *issue no. 14, 2002.*

1.

To narrate oneself into a catastrophe with unknowable global consequences seems trivial, or vain, or both. What does it matter where one was or what one did or how one reacted or felt or what one thought, if thinking occurred at all, during or afterwards?

Why should one insert oneself into a cataclysm after *the shipwreck of the singular?*

> *One plus one equals two.*
> *One plus one equals eleven.*
> *One plus three thousand equals three thousand and one.*

> *The eleventh day of the ninth month is an emergency.*
> *In an emergency call 911.*

Satan the Joker.

Flight 11 drove overhead, engines so close it could have been inhaling the air, so one was being sucked up into the roar, had become the roar.

Out of sleep into nightmare, out of sleep into the recall of earlier times when every plane carried a bomb, when the night sky was nothing if not a seedbed of danger. In New York, in Lower Manhattan, during the Second

World War, during the Korean War, during the cold war. Bombs. Planes with bombs.

Rolled or fell or jumped down onto the floor, covering the head.

Silence for seconds.

Then a great thump, a muted swallowing sound. Not a big crashing sound, but the sound stealth might make on its way to annihilation. A giant rat swallowing a giant snake.

One could see nothing, or rather one could not see the Something that had just transpired, because my south-facing windows no longer looked out, but only *at* the backs of buildings recently constructed into the view. It took months for these buildings to go up, the workers only a stone's throw away: scaffolds, hard hats, reverberating tools. Bit by bit, the sky was removed, the view of the Towers sealed under the collage of progress, under the sign of a swollen prosperity. When I first moved in, twenty-odd years before, the view included the Hudson River and the Woolworth Building and the Twin Towers. The days and nights were quiet. The moon came up and stood visible in the framed sky before going on. Sunlight streamed through the big south-facing windows, carrying the glittering façades with it.

In the first place, and until a few years ago, the first floor was a hum of activity all night long, long yellow trucks, men loading and unloading foodstuffs—eggs and butter and cheese—to deliver to the restaurants in the city. Now the downstairs is called ROOM; it is filled with smart cool furnishings. Across the street, there are chairs hanging by threads in the window. They cost, according to the *New York Times*, $140,000 for a set of twelve. Slender women in tight pants and slim pointed shoes stand on the loading dock with their cell phones, speaking with French accents. They do not smile when one passes them carrying one's groceries.

The neighborhood seems overtaken by a throng of well-dressed young persons who move as if blind, barely noting the parts of the world that do not directly address their needs or intentions or designs; they walk as if the world were put there for them, is a result of their desires. They seem to have no sense of time, as if nothing existed before they arrived, and nothing will exist when they leave.

One siren.

Another siren.

Make coffee, get dressed. One is alive after all, after *whatever that was.* Turn on the television. One never turns on the television in the morning, in the day, but *something* just happened. A bright female voice is talking to a male voice who is describing sitting on his balcony in Union Square, sipping his morning coffee, and seeing a jet come in low, too low, calling to his wife, "Hey, honey, come look at this jet so low over the city." One sees the image of a shadow plane, the plane's silhouette like a cutout, peculiarly dematerialized.

The body and mind in discreet places, wires crossed, thinking one should get to the basement, take cover, thinking about tornadoes, hurricanes, huge winds, and bombs. Confused between accident and intent, acts of nature and acts of man.

One does not remember at what moment *terror* took on motivation, pulled the cause into the effect, the effect into the cause.

Pictures of a tower in flames.

Still, one does not quite register that the plane was that plane, the towers those towers. One is at the place that the tiny TV screen is making into an image. See! Look there! Where? *At passages.* The actual collides with its images.

The cat goes into the closet.

One goes upstairs to the neighbors. We are not good neighbors to each other, we are poor denizens, neither friendly nor unfriendly, who have lived with a floor between us for more than twenty years. The neighbor is wild with worry for her son. Her teenage daughter tries to look as if nothing is happening. Her television is blasting; one hears the word "Pentagon."

One goes downstairs. M. is standing near the elevator. She lives on the top floor with her three sons and her husband, S., the landlord, son of Harry, who started his butter-and-eggs business here decades ago. She is wearing a pretty dress. One mentions the basement; M. stares; she mentions the school. We are not in each other's company. The trajectories of fear do not intersect; words spoken fly into the dead space of incomprehension.

One goes out. One looks to the right, where a small crowd has gathered on the northeast corner of Hudson Street, everyone looking up, looking south. One walks to the corner and looks south. The tower is in flames, orange flames licking out of the edges as if one had thrown a box into a fireplace.

There are no comparisons. It is not *like* anything.

One is back in the house. There is an explosion, the windows rattle, the building shimmies. A sudden wash of pale grayish particles rains down. The TV picture turns into a spray of splinters and the sound shreds into a shimmer of agitating vibrations.

One goes back onto the street. More people, moving and gathering. One walks to the other corner, the west side. One looks up, the other tower is in flames. It looks like the first tower. Symmetry.

Persons scream, point.

Above, tiny figures are emerging out of the windows into the blue air.

Slowly turning out, seemingly weightless, like paper dolls.

Persons below are crying, running.

Now the whole city is a Siren, an Engine heading downtown.

> *Tyger, Tyger, Burning Bright*
> *In the Forest of the Night*
> *What Immortal Hand or Eye*
> *Could frame thy Fearful Symmetry?*

Even as a little girl, I refused to watch newsreels of war.

2.

My nephew Richard phones; I tell him I am frightened. He says his friend David is at home across the street. Richard has recently married; he works for ABC News. David has recently married; he makes films. They are both in their early thirties. I leave with a bottle of water and my purse; I do not shut the windows. I go across the street, ring David's doorbell. David gives me some scotch, says he is going to pack a bag and walk north, find his wife who is in the Village.

It takes a village.

David says, "We can go across the street and close your windows and you can pack a bag." I say, "I am too frightened to go back, let's just leave." We leave, walk north, through pockets and eddies of persons looking bewildered and scared, some of whom start to run in panic. The sirens are now at a steady pitch, billowing downstream into the maw of it. I do not look back.

Don't look back.

David keeps saying, "I just want to see my wife." He says, "Now we are refugees."

At Bank Street, where David's wife is with some of their friends, I do not want to watch the big TV screen in the small apartment. I do not want to see any more of it, but I do see the towers collapse like so many gossamer threads. I do see the shadow shape of the airliner plunge into the tower. I see the huge orange ball of fire coming out of the side of one of them, immense flaming innards from a ruptured body.

Everyone in the world is seeing these images.

A wholly phallic rape, the plane penetrating the material verticality of the erected.

> *How big is yours?*
> *I have two.*
> *One minus one is zero.*

I never liked the Twin Towers. I was working on Broome Street in SoHo in the early 1970s, as a waitress, shortly after they were completed, and I saw them each day as I walked to work. I found them totemic and graceless, not so much minimal as monolithic. If this is world trade, then why are they the same? Where is the reciprocity and recognition of difference? What or where is the Other between two identical objects?

If this is world trade, then why are they so anonymous, uninflected by the human, so brutely abstract? What are these colossal vertical plinths, dwarfing all else, meant to mean to a city of pedestrians, island wanderers, immigrants? Where is the space of dream, the vicissitude of hope and disappointment, the contemplation of the space between action and consequence?

If this is the World Trade Center, then where is the world, where is the trade, where is the center? Where is the turn of the tide, the humility of looking back from far off in space, tiny blue and white ball in a great sea of change? Where is the horizon's distant line that gives definition to days and nights, figures the man and the woman, the beasts of burden, road from town to town, from wilderness to city, voyages, discoveries, routes from China, from Spain, from England, over, and from, sea to shining sea?

Giant step for mankind.

Not trade but power, not exchange, but Capital on its hegemonic march.

Upward mobility.

Out of *scale* with everything around it.

Scale, n. a drinking vessel; a bowl; a cup.

The obsolete definition gives way to the two dishes of a balance or a machine for weighing.

Things weigh in the balance.

The figure of Justice with her *scales*.

When, twenty years ago, my friend Jennifer had her wedding supper at the Windows on the World restaurant, I felt the tower shift like a dry reed in wind.

Eventually, I learned to love the weather play against them, the sapphire blue of long Manhattan twilights, the dark pewter gauze of cloud or fog or mist covering their tops like an ethereal hem, the setting sun splashing its scarlet against their surfaces.

I thought they were like fish leaping from the water. I saw them then, imagined them, plunging down, into the Hudson.

Late in the day I go uptown by subway with another nephew, Jack, who is an architect. He has walked down from his office to Bank Street to get me. We sit outside together, just down the street from Saint Vincent's Hospital, which is strangely quiet. I can see a crowd of white-uniformed doctors and nurses milling about, waiting. David and his friends try to give blood, but the lines are too long.

When the fighter jets begin to streak overhead, I cover my ears.

Friendly fire.

3.

On Wednesday morning, my friends Peter and Susie and I set out from their house on Eighty-fifth Street. The city is quiet, no traffic, the stores are closed. We find a gypsy cab, whose driver tells us he can only go as far as Fourteenth Street. We zip down Ninth Avenue. In the unencumbered distance, we can see the cloud of orange-tinged smoke rising, filling the bright blue southern sky.

We are stopped by a police barricade. I say I live on Duane Street and need to get my cat. The policeman is gentle, and tells us to go to the next corner, where I show my ID, and we continue south. We pass a wrecked car covered in white dust. We stop at Citibank to get some cash. I keep saying, "There is no way the garage is going to be open. I will not be able to get my car." All I want to do is to leave the city.

Fight or flight.

The air is thick with gritty particles. We run into the poet Jackson MacLow and his wife, composer and poet Anne Tardos. They are trying to buy some food but do not want to go farther south because the air is too bad. Jackson looks small and recessed and ashen.

The building where I live is dark and vacant; a sign on the downstairs door says that my landlord suggests the tenants evacuate because there is no electricity or gas.

Madonna, my aged cat, named for the pop star, comes out from her hiding place in the closet. She looks betrayed and resentful.

To the south, where there had been the aspiring pillars, a massive pile steams and heaves like a beached whale, its great belly engorged with sorrow and waste.

The man who is always at the Kinney Garage is sitting on a chair where he always sits, at the entrance ramp. He has ebony skin and a kind, chiseled face. I say the obvious in disbelief: "You are open!" He says, smiling, without irony, "We are open twenty-four hours a day."

From, for example, the 11th of September until the 12th of September, 2001. I am thinking, *What is a day?* He says he cannot take credit cards or a check, only cash. I borrow money from Peter.

4.

Now it is October. The days move away from the Day, but the Day stays near, does not move back in time. It feels as if it wants to attach itself to another day, equally terrible. There are flags everywhere, messages of condolence from anonymous companies in the paper, scraps of paper on buildings with pictures of missing persons. People in the neighborhood seem to be moving more slowly, with less sureness of where they are going. On the weekend, a steady parade of persons streams past, cameras around their necks, to stare at the wreckage. There is a smell of burning, acrid and gritty, rubbing against the bright autumnal air. The sky where the towers were is empty, as if time had rolled backwards. The Woolworth Building looks taller, less archaic, like an elderly relative called to stand in for the dead.

AFTER THE FALL

A day spent *at* the garden. Not, certainly, *in,* as *in* suggests a kind of Bloomsburian ease, trimming and admiring, taking out a few stray weeds, adding a little mulch to the roses. No, *at*. Obsessive, violent actions, based on intuition, augmenting and shifting and bending and digging until the throat is dry, the back aches, the hands are a fund of dirt. And then a bath, but before the bath, looking out, a bluebird flits through the late sunlit air, quick, quick, the blue of it almost a mirage against the grass.

Prepositions count. The United States has declared war *on* terrorism. This phrase, in which "with" is replaced by "on," is reminiscent of other recent wars, the one *on* drugs, the one *on* poverty. These are conceptual wars, front-loaded with their own assent. They are wars without borders and without clear identifications or markings—"you there, you look like a terrorist, we will detain you." They are wars that allow extreme authority to those who declare them. They are "good" wars, on the side of incontestable right. But this current war is more pernicious than the ones on poverty and drugs, which were social and domestic, using the ultimate language of combat against inequity and abuse, to incite and motivate political action. To declare war on terrorism is to subsume the violence of war into the violence of terrorism: the two terms merge across the innocuous "on." A terrorist can be anyone, anywhere, at any time. The war on "it" has no limit.

Terrorism is a way of surprising persons with death.

Isolated in the hyperbole of unmeasured contamination, breach, pleas from other languages, sets, beliefs not to be excluded, arrested, ignored; to notice the distortion of hope's boundary, asymmetries of goods, wealth cascading through the openings of unlimited power, spirit congealed and trapped, grief leaving its white dust on every cup; to duck when the bombs fall, when the towers collapse, when the temple is broken, submerged or merged into the nightmare affiliations of infinite reprisal—

Since the eleventh of September, when I was thrown from sleep by the close proximity of a plane overhead, I have had constant dreams of annihilation. This, despite Ritalin for concentration and Paxil to keep me even-keeled. I have abandoned the city I love, because the sound of planes, Delta or American, flying overhead still ruptures into fear. Because now the neighborhood is inundated with tourists on their way to Ground Zero, who may or may not stop at Century 21 for a few garments.

The twenty-first century, dating from the birth of Christ. Christ, the Semite Jesus, was an interesting fellow. He had some good attributes. He was courageous and he was humble and he was scared when faced with annihilation—"Let this cup pass from me," I think he said. He allowed himself a certain luxury, the luxury of belief, a belief in the possibilities of the human. He was not a terrorist, but some who followed him were and are. Many among us in the West seem to have forsaken some of his signature traits, some of his teachings, his words. He was not the only wise man to inaugurate spiritual traditions, and he shares with many of them an understanding that language has more than one way to intercept reality.

Theodor Adorno's remark connecting poetry to barbarism after Auschwitz comes back to haunt us. But to borrow from history, to attach a reduced vocabulary, like a slogan, to the present, is a specious and dangerous game, one at which politicians are all too adept, and one about which Adorno was particularly conscious. The world seems, now, a place for barbarism to take hold like a weed, turning civility into rampant opportunism, with or without poetry.

What, I want to ask, would Adorno say now? Might he say: "Poetry, after September 11th, is necessary for survival?"

Poetry cares for the local; for incident, increment, detail; for tendencies, measures, mysteries, margins, dialects; for exceptions, boundaries, games, memories, transitions, translations; poetry is less interested in plots, more interested in epistemology as an ongoing retrieval of, and quest for, the unknown: that which is omitted or conceived as the yet-to-be. Poetry foregrounds the indissoluble relation between how words are used and what they might mean; it trains us to listen for the moment when tears commence to be intellectual things. Poetry makes *logos* responsive to both reason and faith, if by "faith" we mean an acceptance of that which cannot be used in evidence. If post-Enlightenment language is an instrument of the rational, poetry augments sense-making to include those aspects of existence which elude cognitive logics. Poetry, as a mechanism of survival, takes into its reckoning the abject rancor of those who are convinced that human life is not worth saving. Poetry continues to elucidate the vital topography between individual and historical accounting.

Of course poetry, like terrorism, is without agency, volition, will; there are poets and there are terrorists. How easy it is to fall into the language trap, animating, or declaring war on, abstractions!

But if we have, as George Oppen wrote, chosen the meaning of being numerous in the shipwreck of the singular, what does this imply for those of us who continue to write poems? Oppen for a long time chose silence, believing that poems could not be reconciled with the exigencies of political action. He resisted polemics. Then he found a way to make poems that would allow an ethical relation between poetics and the world, in work that fretted the "I" and the "we" through the difficult lens of "clarity," which Oppen attached not to visual transparency but to personal limit. He refused the luxury of transcendence, and in that refusal took up the difficulty of secular belief. In the world of global capital, it is difficult to know who is speaking. Poets always acknowledge who is speaking, whether or not they use the word "I." Without this simple accountability, the distance between intention and action is inevitably blurred, and discourse becomes a free-standing, untethered, nondialogic sign.

I no longer watch television. After the screen became a rash of noise and splinters as reception was lost along with the thousands of humans surprised by death, I stopped watching it. Now I listen to the radio. Sometimes I hear midday talks, eloquent and vivid recitations about the state of the world. Talks on the environment, on architecture, on politics and health and education. Nothing about poetry, nothing about art. Nothing that connects political, ethical, and aesthetic ideas. I heard Robert F. Kennedy Jr. the other day, articulate and impassioned about the land and the water, enraged at corporate malfeasance and greed: General Electric ("We bring good things to life") and PCBs in the Hudson, for example. Kennedy did say the word "poetry," it was on a list of things we care about, which constitute, he said, our cultural inheritance. I heard someone talking about slow time, how nature works its changes slowly, but corporations work on speed, the speed of profit, where time, as is said, is money. Reading poems, like writing them, also takes place in slow time. The slow time of reading and writing works against the fast time of profit, the catastrophic time of terrorism.

The forms of freedom are not without restraint. If we do not know how to restrain, retrain, our desires, then we will not know how to align our power to the limited resources of the world. If we do not begin to reimagine our power, we will use it to constrain others. How to convey the urgency of making choices and decisions which lead to forms of life that do not impinge on others, bully them into agreement, mock context, trivialize faith, thwart rights, waste resources, collude need with want? Poets, I want to say, are expert at the complex ratio of limit to possibility.

Poetry, I want to suggest, is one way to not be surprised by death.

AFTER EMERSON:
OF GENERAL KNOWLEDGE
AND THE COMMON GOOD

When I left the City College of New York in 1998 to become a full-time member of the faculty at Bard College, Martin Tamny was Dean of Humanities. Since then, he has retired, but he asked me to speak in May 2004 to the initiates to the City College chapter of the Phi Beta Kappa honor society.

When I asked Dean Tamny what people talk about when they talk to the Phi Beta Kappa Society, he said, "Well, no one talks about the life of the mind or anything like that." He was probably trying to put me at ease, letting me know that I could talk about snow in spring if I so chose. It is snowing now and it is almost spring. Today's snow seems more ferocious than any this winter; the flakes are as big as dimes and they are falling rapidly, as if from a casino jackpot. There is a stiff wind coming from the north. I am sitting at my desk, facing west, and just beyond the small hemlocks in the foreground there is a graveyard that dates from 1710. Many of the stones in it have been rubbed smooth, so you can no longer read the name of the person buried there.

Just now I can hear the train as it moves along the Hudson River, heading either to Canada or to New York City, I cannot tell which direction. In the graveyard two small American flags are blowing in the wind. I saw a PBS special the other night—well, it wasn't a special, it was a promotion, as they were in their fund-raising mode—and the special guest was Peter from the folk-music group Peter, Paul and Mary. During the show, there were many film clips of Peter, Paul and Mary in their heyday, when they sang, for example, in Washington during the great march at which Dr. King gave his seminal address. Watching these tapes, it was difficult not to feel, once again, a sense of loss for the unanimity of a crowd brought together by the power of an idea and a belief in the possibilities of change. I thought, watching the flags wave in the graveyard, of Bob Dylan's melancholy refrain: "The answer, my friend, is blowin' in the wind / The answer is blowin' in the wind."

Not long ago, I was at a small dinner after a poetry reading at Bard College, where I teach. There was a lively and articulate young Jamaican-American student there. She had protested the imminent war in Iraq last year, and she had joined in the enthusiasm for Howard Dean. The fact that these efforts had failed left her thinking there wasn't any point in voting next fall; she was thinking of becoming an anarchist. Her short-sighted impatience alarmed me; it seemed symptomatic of a general cultural habit, a curtailed investment in process, a desire for quick-fix answers before difficult questions are asked, for goals met almost before quests are undertaken.

I have chosen as my guiding spirit today the nineteenth-century American philosopher/poet Ralph Waldo Emerson. When I was an undergraduate in the 1960s at the University of Wisconsin, I took a year-long course called American Intellectual History, taught by William Appleman Williams, who had, in turn, studied with the great Harvard historian Perry Miller. In the decades since then, this course has stood in my mind as crucial to my understanding of the relation between American ideas, social behavior, and political will; that is, the ways in which language mediates, imagines, and reflects these unstable but essential dynamics. The materials for the course were almost all primary; we read contemporaneous speeches and journals, essays, letters, sermons, narratives, autobiography. This exposure to original texts, unusual at the time, animated history, rendering it less a matter of factual event, narratives of linear cause and effect, than a matrix of oppositional and irresolute forces, where those that were dominant were often shadowed by those that were recessive. The notion that America was itself an idea, an experiment, formulated largely in two written documents, gave me a sense of its frailty as well as its peculiar optimism. It was in this course that I first read Emerson.

Why Emerson? He was born in Boston in 1803, into the millennial cusp of the nineteenth century, as we are at the millennial cusp of the twenty-first. His father, pastor at Boston's First Church, died when Emerson was eight, leaving eight children to be raised by his mother, Ruth, and his eccentric aunt Mary. He went to Harvard College, where he, like so many other undergraduates since, waited on tables and taught school to help defray costs. He kept a journal. After graduation, he continued to teach, but often felt dejected and at a loss. He had eye troubles and other physical symptoms of distress. He fell in love and married Ellen Tucker, but she died, age nineteen, in

1832. By then Emerson had become junior pastor at Boston's Second Church.

By the time he was thirty, Emerson has rejected a profession in the church, calling it "antiquated," and, in poor health and already a widower, he traveled to Europe, to Rome and Paris and London, where he met the philosopher John Stuart Mill as well as the great Romantic writers Coleridge and Wordsworth and Thomas Carlyle. Returning to America to settle in Concord, he writes in his journal, "I wish I knew where & how I ought to live." From this moment on, he undertakes to answer these questions. By 1837, he has begun to lecture, on nature and history and the lives of great men. In that year, 1837, he gives a celebrated address, later titled "The American Scholar," to the Phi Beta Kappa Society at Cambridge.

But why Emerson?

Emerson was committed to the idea of human life as a deep reciprocity between a given self and the world. "The eye is the first circle; the horizon it forms is the second," he wrote. "The world—this shadow of the soul, or other me—lies wide around. Its attractions are the keys which unlock my thoughts and make me acquainted with myself." At the heart of Emersonian thought, for me, is an almost constant desire to reconcile what he called "polarities" into manifestations of flow, circuits and cycles, relation and concordance. I think this urge came from his wish to bring his spiritual faith into alignment with his equally strong belief in reason. Within this typology of reconciliation comes an immense intellectual permission to explore the moody and mercurial shapes of life, to be digressive and uncertain. He writes, "There are no fixtures in nature. The universe is fluid and volatile. Permanence is but a word of degrees." This perception of the instability of things leads him to distrust what he called "the false good" of immediate rewards: "Men, such as they are, very naturally seek money or power; and power because it is as good as money . . . And why not? For they aspire to the highest, and this, in their sleepwalking, they dream is highest. Wake them, and they shall quit the false good." Writing, for Emerson, is a constant exploration of relations, fueled by a conviction that knowledge itself is both the means and the end of the true good. "Fear," he comments, "always springs from ignorance."

One feels in Emerson the pressure of affective thought finding its way to a practical outcome; his writing is less a display of erudition than an exploration of how knowledge might infuse and influence ordinary, daily action. He continually stresses his desire for a uniquely American culture, one that rises from the low, the common, and the near. A person of some social and economic privilege, he situates himself within his own writing as much student as teacher, as much lay person as preacher. One feels that his convictions are at risk, his conclusions not foregone. He writes to find out what he knows about what he knows. He was, along with William James, one of our first "public intellectuals," giving talks and addresses to large crowds. He was one of our first celebrities, an intellectual rock star.

But, as Philip Fisher has pointed out in his book *Still the New World*, this template of speaker and audience is not in essence democratic. Fisher writes:

> Performer and audience define the world of both entertainment and professionalism, along with the larger worlds of mass politics and religious revival, and even the world of radical politics, from the time of the abolitionists, through the temperance movement, the civil rights and anti-Vietnam movements of the 1960s. This antidemocratic space of speaker and audience has been, as the example of Martin Luther King, Jr., would show, decisive even where the goal has been a more democratic social life. Even American philosophy was invented in public by Emerson and William James as lectures given to crowds.

What is missing, of course, is conversation, dialogue, the expressing and sharing of thoughts and ideas across the social space, so that the mute acquiescence of the many is not relinquished to the authority of the one. American social space is not a fluid transparency; it is ruptured—in Fisher's word, "damaged"—by institutionalized inequities that begin with slavery and continue as endemic racism, economic disparity, uneven distribution of social services, medical care, education, and so on.

Emerson was not unaware of these disparities; the fact that he is able to construct an optimism from personal griefs and public dismay is one of the reasons I continue to consult him. "This time, like all times, is a very good one," he comments wryly, "if we but know what to do with it." It is difficult for me, as I am sure it is for you, to accept such an optimistic dictum. Our time seems saturated with both fear and ignorance. The daily rhetoric seems contaminated with words pulled loose from their moorings. There is a kind of indiscriminate evocation of such potent abstractions as "freedom" and "evil" that move through our public discourse with promiscuous abandon. A confusion between the true and the real percolates up from the core; dissimulation is stitched into the fabric of our sense of events so that correction, if it comes, is often too late, too hidden from public view, to alter our perceptions.

I often find myself thinking about the fact that we seem to know the world through a system of contraries; the English language itself embraces one of the most fundamental, the one between subject and object, and its extension into subjectivity and objectivity. For writers, the conversion of subject into object is perhaps our most basic and perplexing task: how to conceive of words as not locked within the self awaiting liberty, but as freely circulating outside of the self, waiting to be taken in, transformed, and sent back out. Emerson says, "The scholar of the first age received into him the world around; brooded thereon; gave it the new arrangement of his own mind, and uttered it again. It came in to him, life; it went out from him, truth." The modernist poet Wallace Stevens understood that imaginative work is the work of truth; that fiction aspires, in the form of "a new arrangement," to tell a truth which is not necessarily fixed on fact, but on the interpretative motions of a perceiving mind. In *Notes Toward a Supreme Fiction* Stevens makes of duality a kind of hymn to change:

> Two things of opposite natures seem to depend
> One on another, as a man depends
> On a woman, day on night, the imagined
>
> On the real. This is the origin of change.
> Winter and spring, cold copulars, embrace
> And forth the particulars of rapture come.
>
> Music falls on the silence like a sense,
> A passion that we feel, not understand.
> Morning and afternoon are clasped together
>
> And North and South are an intrinsic couple
> And sun and rain a plural, like two lovers
> That walk away as one in the greenest body.
>
> In solitude the triumphs of solitude
> Are not of another solitude responding;
> A little string speaks for a crowd of voices.

The partaker partakes of that which changes him.
The child that touches takes character from the thing,
The body, it touches. The captain and his men

Are one and the sailor and the sea are one.
Follow after, O my companion, my fellow, my self,
Sister and solace, brother and delight.

Recently, I heard a talk by the environmentalist and journalist Bill McKibben. He was talking about issues of global significance, about the destruction of the ecosystem and about the possibilities of human cloning. He wasn't interested in talking about the sacred space of human individuality as such, but rather the way cloning might make of human life yet another commodity. He said, in answer to a student's question about what makes humans human, that we are the only animals for whom there is a decision to make when faced with desire; we know the word "no." No, not as an order from another, but from the inner self, the part of the self that says "You have had enough" or "Don't do that."

The narrator of the great South African Nobel laureate J. M. Coetzee's novel *Waiting for the Barbarians* speaks about a certain colonel.

> Since his second day here I have been too disturbed by his presence to be more than correct in my bearing towards him. I suppose that, like the roving headsman, he is used to being shunned. (Or is it only in the provinces that headsmen and torturers are still thought of as unclean?) Looking at him I wonder how he felt the very first time: did he, invited as an apprentice to twist the pincers or turn the screw or whatever it is they do, shudder even a little to know that at that instant he was trespassing into the forbidden? I find myself wondering too whether he has a private ritual of purification, carried out behind closed doors, to enable him to return and break bread with other men. Does he wash his hands very carefully, perhaps, or change all his clothes; or has the Bureau created new men who can pass without disquiet between the unclean and the clean?

In detailing atrocities at the Abu Ghraib prison, an American soldier repeatedly refers to one of the Iraqi detainees as "it." This use of a tiny two-letter word, in which a person is turned into an object, a thing, is as reveal-ingly abhorrent as any of the horrific images that have surfaced. Like Emer-son, I believe that words are a form of action; their use, and abuse, can travel with stupendous speed into our hearts and minds. This is why the words that are uttered by persons in power are of such critical significance. I want to say that the ubiquitous application of universals, such as freedom, terror, and evil, unmoored from both context and concrete example, move with weedy rapaciousness to contaminate both their meanings and acts committed in their name.

Aristotle writes, in book 3 of the *Ethics*, "For an irrational being the ap-petite for what gives it pleasure is insatiable and indiscriminate, and the ex-ercise of the desire increases its innate tendency; and if these appetites are strong and violent, they actually drive out reason."

Emerson says, "The ancient precept, 'Know thyself,' and the modern pre-cept, 'Study nature,' become at last one maxim."

The radical American modernist Gertrude Stein commented, "I am I be-cause my little dog knows me." Stein makes a charming elastic shape out of the ingredients of self-knowledge, different, for example, from the Cartesian formulation which makes thinking, or consciousness, the necessary con-struction of the I Am. Stein's writing is permeated with what we might call a deliberate strangeness or alienation, one that does not allow the reader an immediate access to a normal real. Her self rarely appears in the guise of the first-person pronoun. Her amusing comment "I am I because my little dog knows me" suggests that we are constituted by the ways in which we are known by others, and that this recognition is based on our behaviors toward them. She anticipates recent theories of personality that suggest we are not static and stable entities, but fluid and varied, that we change somewhat ac-cording to whom and with whom we are communicating, which in turn in-fluences and affects how we measure our self-knowledge. I am not quite the same when I am teaching a class as when I am holding my friend Terry's daughter in my arms or paying for my groceries at the local market. We change depending on what we are doing in our lives. "Where do we find our-selves?" Emerson asks at the opening of his essay "Experience."

For many people, poems are understood to be tidy linguistic utterances that emit from a given self, as if poets were like those pretty Italian pots that fizz and spurt tiny cups of thick, bitter truths about life. On this model, po-ets are curiously exempt from accusations of narcissism, since the poet's self, his or her "I," is somehow meant to give to the mute and inarticulate reader linguistic counters for the inexpressible. On this reading, the subjectivity of the writer is rendered objective through a sort of threshold of mutual, perhaps cathartic, identifications. But in our age of rampant information and exploited privacies, such self-examinations, however dressed up in pretty language, are insufficient. We want our life lessons in the form of scandal and exposé; we want our happy endings, our sweet closures, as a kiss at the end of a film, a victorious lawyer in *The Practice*.

I want to return here to how Emerson sought to find common ground between religious faith and secular reason. He did not, in his writings, forfeit his use of the word "God," and he speaks frequently of spirit and of souls. But at each turn, God exists not as an authority, not as supreme being, but as an initiating animation or energy from which nature, and ourselves, evolve. Responsibility is in the minds and hands of persons: "In proportion as a man has any thing in him divine," he writes, "the firmament flows before him and takes his signet and form. Nor he is great who can alter matter, but he who can alter my state of mind."

In the Divinity School Address, he says, "The time is coming when all men will see, that the gift of God to the soul is not a vaunting, overpowering, excluding sanctity, but a sweet, natural goodness, a goodness like thine and mine to be and to grow."

Emerson's notion of "natural goodness" which connects humans to their environment, to be and to grow, rests at least in part on a concept of the local, the near, the particulars and peculiarities that form immediate experience. His rhetorical strategies move quickly between flares of roiling heightened eloquence to simple pronouncements and memorable epithets, as if he were always wanting to return to the vitality of the actual, to touch the immediate, acknowledge the proximity of his audience. He writes:

> It is a great stride. It is a sign,—is it not? of new vigor, when the extremities are made active, when currents of warm life run into the hands and the feet. I ask not for the great, the remote, the romantic, what is doing in Italy or Arabia; what is Greek art, or Provençal minstrelsy; I embrace the common, I explore and sit at the feet of the familiar, the low. Give me insight into today and you may have the antique and future worlds.

This turn toward the local, the near, is one of the dominant traits of nineteenth-century American aesthetic and cultural vision, as it comes to replace European classical, often hierarchical, orders, and begins to find in the proliferation of local incident a way to articulate and map the complex ratios between the One and the Many. The still-new country would come to embrace a new paradigm where the coordinates of time and space were marked by the here and now of an individual presentness and presence. Thoreau's *Walden* becomes the template for this universe of particulars, what Ezra Pound would later call "radiant details." By the mid–twentieth century, this idea would express itself in a unique abstraction, built up by single gestures, as in much Abstract Expressionist painting, where each mark is absorbed into the panoply of a diverse but unifying field.

There was, not so long ago, a categorical non-category, "of general interest." I am not sure now where it appeared—in bookstores, on newspaper lists. It assumed something about the public, about the needs of the public to be generally informed about things that did not necessarily apply to a particular person's interests, his or her stuff. The non-category of the category "of general interest" suggested that there were things about the world, in the world, of the world, which persons without specific expertise might find useful or stimulating or even necessary. This category has vanished, to be replaced by the generic "nonfiction," which covers everything from superstring theory to, say, *The Unconquerable World*, Jonathan Schell's study of strategies of war and peace.

In a recent issue of the *New York Review of Books*, there is an essay about the Marxist literary critic Terry Eagleton's new book, entitled *After Theory*. The reviewer gives it scant, provisional praise: "*After Theory*," he writes, "is an ambitious and thought-provoking book as well as an exasperating one, but it overestimates the importance of Theory outside the academy." He then adds, "But to anyone outside the arena [of the academy]—the educated general reader, for instance—the excruciating effort of construing this jargon-heavy discourse far exceeded the illumination likely to be gleaned from it, so they stopped reading it, and nonspecialist publications stopped reviewing it, which was bad for both academia and culture in general."

This decision on the part of nonspecialist publications, general-circulation magazines, and daily newspapers to stop writing about theory is also true for poetry, and the result is also, in my view, bad for both academia and for "culture in general." A certain disdain prevails, a sense that poetry, like theory, takes too much effort to be worth the time. But poetry, unlike theory, has never been, until recently, confined to the academy. For Emerson, the poet represented the epitome of articulated hope and vision. He called poets "liberating gods," whose work was the "ravishment of the intellect by coming nearer to the fact."

But American culture has moved quickly from such heralds and avatars;

poems, neither pure information (nonfiction) nor pure entertainment (fiction), are seen as remnant vestiges of a dying literary culture. Poems rub against the prevailing need for pragmatic expertise, for sharp focus, single study, the idea that we should all find our subject and stick to it: the writings of Niccolò Machiavelli; the life cycle of the round worm. This bias toward the expert, the professional, has been in the works for a long time, and has slowly erased such quaint notions as "of general interest," "the general educated reader." General interest now finds itself erupting in the degraded form of reality TV, such strangely disorienting fake-news shows as *Dateline*, or bogus, delirious fantasies like *Extreme Makeover* and *The Bachelor*. These shows parody "of general interest."

In perhaps his best known essay, "Self-Reliance," Emerson writes: "Whoso would be a man must be a nonconformist. He who would gather immortal palms must not be hindered by the name of goodness, but must explore if it be goodness." This insistence on the necessity for each person to undertake his or her own moral exploration is a key to the radical nature of Emersonian ethics. From the standpoint of our present moment, it is almost beyond what we can imagine: that the public, one by one, can and will think outside of the proscriptions and prescriptions of political and social commerce and commentary; that each of us is both willing and able to find our way out of received ideas that govern so much of our discourse. Emerson writes:

> If I know your sect, I anticipate your argument. I hear a preacher announce for his text and topic the expediency of one of the institutions of his church. Do I not know beforehand that not possibly can he say a new and spontaneous word? Do I not know that, with all this ostentation of examining the grounds of the institution, he will do no such thing? Do I not know that he is pledged to himself not to look but at one side,—the permitted side, not as a man, but as a parish minister? He is a retained attorney, and these airs of the bench are the emptiest affectation. Well, most men have bound their eyes with one or another handkerchief, and attached themselves to some one of these communities of opinion. This conformity makes them not false in a few particulars, author of a few lies, but false in all particulars. Their every truth is not quite true. Their two is not the real two, their four is not the real four; so that every word they say chagrins us, and we know not where to begin to set them right.

This is not the voice of a true believer, but of someone who has agreed to move through his world with the open demeanor of doubt. I want to suggest that for Emerson, doubt was a prerequisite of reason, of knowledge as well as of faith. He had inherited the Enlightenment, where skepticism was part of what it meant to be human. I think what most deeply frightened him was a burgeoning sense of American entitlement, God-given, invincible, irrefutable, where freedom would be conceived as unfettered self-interest, opportunity as unlimited choice, and success as one or another form of acquisition and victory. Doubt, for Emerson, was the engine of curiosity, curiosity the path to knowledge; and knowledge, itself unsteady and plural, both agent and receptor of experience.

Emersonian knowledge rarely steadies itself into certitude. He says:

> But lest I should mislead any when I have my own head and obey my whims, let me remind the reader that I am only an experimenter. Do not set the least value on what I do, or the least discredit on what I do not, as if I pretended to settle any thing as true or false. I unsettle all things. No facts are to me sacred; none are profane; I simply experiment, an endless seeker . . . People wish to be settled; only as far as they are unsettled is there any hope for them.

This idea of being unsettled resonates now as it must have when Emerson first wrote it. America, we say, was "settled" by the early pioneers. On the West Bank and Gaza, there are "settlements." We tell our children to "settle down," and we, in turn, wish to settle into the safety of our homes, to come to rest in a secure setting. To remain unsettled, then, goes against the ways in which our hope for happiness is pictured to us. To be unsettled is to join the great diaspora of the world.

I took this contrary, unsettled, path: the precarious was, for me, more dependable than the secure. As time went on, an at times reckless commitment to instability and uncertainty migrated into a form of perception, and from perception into an interest in the limits of order, the outer rims of sense. These became the basis for a poetics. I came to want to write poems that did not offer the reader, or listener, calmly composed reflections, neat epiphanies of recognition or identification, but instead poems that ruptured, confused, suspended, the charmed solace of such expectations. As I write this, I realize it sounds both perverse and elitist, the worst kind of deliberate obfuscation. But this is not the case; I want my work to exhilarate, to awaken and stimulate; indeed, to unsettle. I want to invite readers and listeners to the edge or boundary of their assumptions about how language constitutes, or reconstitutes, the self and the world, and how these in turn constitute how we use language. It is this essential reciprocity that guides what I do.

I am by nature restless and impatient, and in order perhaps to accommodate these character flaws and deficits, I have given myself permission to think of my job as a kind of scanner. I net language from its free-floating, ubiquitous circulation and make for it a matrix in which musical phrase and spatial display are coordinates. My poems are often destabilized narratives, where moments of connectivity are placed against fragments, abbreviated notes, pieces of linguistic thread that are not woven into the substance, but act as floating remnants, leftovers, frayed edges. These loose constructions sign to me and I hope to my listeners and readers a kind of layered indeterminate field, from which incidents erupt and consequences—the great syntactical order—sometimes, but not always, obtain. I want to convey that making sense and finding meaning are what we do when we use language, but that these senses and these meanings are never stable and fixed, but responsive to temporal and spatial conditions, to the specificity and particulars of context. Each person in this room has a different notion, a different picture, to go with the word "tree."

In choosing to be a poet, I took a path that led toward the unknown, perhaps to the unknowable. My future had only the most furtive of shapes; my aspiration, the most chancy, digressive routes. Language came to me as the most potent, and yet most ephemeral, of commitments. To this day, I am not sure what a poem is. Each time I write one, it becomes the particular, the example, but the next one may not resemble the one before it, or the one to come. Poetry, like so much else in life, can be known only by example. To write a poem is, in the first place, to be curious about what a poem is.

As we witnessed the demise of an active readership, a general public, for all but the most trivial and obvious poems, I and many of my peers have retreated into the protection of the academy, there to teach another generation how to love, if not poetry, at least language. I have had moments of doubt. "What are poets for in a destitute time?" the German philosopher Heidegger asked; and the great cultural critic Theodor Adorno commented that "after Auschwitz, writing poetry is barbaric." It is often difficult, given the state of the world, to believe that there is any merit, any reason, in making another poem. And yet, poets and books of poems and little magazines devoted to poetry proliferate; readings occur in small towns and large cities across the nation, often to only a handful of persons, all under the radar of general interest, out of the searchlight of celebrity exposure, million-dollar book deals, late-night chat shows. A discipline of extraordinary variety and hybridity, moving between fact and fiction, narrativity and fragment, formal orders and chance operations, poetry foregrounds at all times the value of the single word. As the poet Lyn Hejinian has commented, "Writing develops subjects that mean the words we have for them."

There is a far-flung but enduring community of poets, who connect with each other not only on the Internet, but in person, where hands and faces, tones of voice and gestures, contribute to the nuance and intricacies of a shared interest in each other and in each other's work. Poetry is a culture of presence and immediacy, of gathering around, listening, exchanging, thinking aloud. It constitutes an oddly familiar community, inflected with small-town gossip and meanspirited jealousies, love affairs, marriages, and deaths; we write to and for and about each other, often with admiration, pleasure, and joy. We are on the whole lucky to spend our lives in such close proximity to the primary engine of human communication. This intimacy, this primary attachment to language, is convertible to the needs and ambitions of persons who may not be poets, may not want to become poets.

The core of our moral shape begins with our finding out to what we are attached by birth, geography, disposition, intellect, talent. Our initial attachments lead to others, and those to others still; and as we age, we become more clear about those that were given to us and those that we choose. If we are lucky, they eventually merge, the given and the chosen, into forms of attention that can be communicated to others. These habits of mind, of predilection and practice, are the most valuable tools of a life well spent.

But as long as works of imaginative response and interpretation—by which I mean not just poems but all creative work, painting and music, dance and sculpture, film and fiction—are viewed by the culture at large, the general public, as either decorative entertainment or private, elitist distraction, and not, to borrow Emerson's phrase, as "beautiful necessity," then we are in danger of a perfunctory, reductive literalism. We lose our bearings, become mere tokens of political or commercial expedience. Imaginative work is grounded in thinking about, and thinking through, the immediacy of events, both private and public, in order to draw from them objects, materials rendered into forms, that bring us closer to our sense of connection, our personal agency. Art asks to be interpreted, not just consumed; it asks us to suspend our judgment while we engage our senses. If the so-called "real" world of events is always remote, no matter how close our computer and TV screens, then our sense of engagement and response is in danger of shutting down. Art is a language which anneals individuals to each other through experiences that are uniquely human, that demand connection at the level of making meaning. If we lose our ability to make meaning—that is, to interpret, to find form in the raw materials of life—then we stand in danger of having meaning made for us, a rupture between what is said and what is done, between false intentions and disastrous consequences.

If the word "freedom" begins to sound hollow in our ears, if every person who is not one of us is against us, if restraint is confused with constraint, and liberty with unregulated self-advancement, regardless of consequences, then the experimental poem called America is at risk. If scholars withdraw into the protective worlds of their scholarly pursuits, if the academy is perceived by the rest of the public as a place of dubious benefit, with too-long holidays and too-high salaries, if art is cordoned off as somehow relevant only, if at all, to the consuming rich, then our great experiment is at risk. As I think Emerson understood, the power of faith must be turned toward the world as it is, to its secular institutions, both public and private, its schools and colleges, libraries, museums, parks, hospitals, laboratories, its local communities and their local associations. We—and this "we" now includes you—need to have faith in these, to bring to them our resources, our curiosity and knowledge, our purposes and protections. As Emerson writes at the end of "Experience," "Never mind the ridicule, never mind the defeat: up again, old heart—it seems to say, there is victory yet for all justice; and the true romance which the world exists to realize, will be the transformation of genius into practical power."

ACKNOWLEDGMENTS

Books that are made from a collection of writings written over a long time, in this case nearly twenty years, owe much to many. One thinks of the moment in the awards ceremony when the winning actress thanks everyone she ever knew. I will try to avoid such an outpouring, tempting as it is.

I did not really find my bearings until I began to teach.

Many students, in a variety of contexts, have given me moments of un-surpassable pleasure, in the intensity of their commitments, the value they give to creative work, their openness to and curiosity about ideas, as well as their patience with the idiosyncrasy of my own thought processes and the proximate nature of my knowledge. I feel myself to be more than lucky to find, in the demanding articulations of teaching, perpetual exhilaration. This book owes its existence to my hopes for them.

I was working part-time in art galleries in New York when John Ashbery asked me to teach his poetry workshop at Brooklyn College while he was re-cuperating from a serious illness. I am grateful to him for that, as for so much else. In 1986, while working at the Joan Washburn Gallery in New York, Robert Towers invited me to teach a class at Columbia. Bob was as subtle and judicious as he was kind, and he helped me to negotiate all manner of doubt.

My experience at City College and at the Graduate Center was seminal in many ways; to Paul Sherwin, Joshua Wilner, Martin Tamny, Joe Wittreich, William Kelly, I owe particular thanks. The experience of teaching with them continues to inform my thinking and writing.

When in 1995 I taught a semester at the Writers' Workshop in Iowa City, one of my colleagues was the poet Arthur Vogelsang. It was Arthur who asked me to write a series of columns for the *American Poetry Review*, of which he is an editor. These became the seven "Night Sky" pieces at the center of this collection. Without Arthur's invitation, they would not have been written.

I joined the Writing faculty at the Milton Avery School of the Arts at Bard College in 1991. My admiration and affection for Arthur Gibbons, the Direc-tor, is beyond qualification. The Faculty has provided me a community whose conversation, humor, intelligence and dedication has been a source of constant comfort and inspiration. Among them: Lynne Tillman; Stephen Frailey, Stephen Westfall, Peggy Ahwesh, Leslie Scalapino, Jeffrey DeShell, Lydia Davis, Matt Sharpe, Richard Teitelbaum, Amy Sillman, Nayland Blake, Blake Raine, Les LeVec, Nancy Shaver, George Lewis, David Levi Strauss.

Since 1998, I have been Ruth and David Schwab II Professor of Languages and Literature at Bard College. For David and Ruth, and for the President of Bard, Leon Botstein, I have deepest esteem, affection, and gratitude. I cannot imagine a more exhilarating and rewarding place to work.

Conversation is at the heart of these works. Many are ongoing and crucial; some are occasional but still crucial: with Diana Michener, Jonathan Schell, Thomas Neurath and Constance Kaine, Joan Retallack, Charles Bernstein, Peter and Susan Straub, Kenward Elmslie, Ed Barrett, Carla Harryman, Tom Dumm, Michael Palmer, Augusta Talbot, Norma Cole, Nan Graham, Mark Costello, Ann Hamilton, Charles Altieri, Brenda Hillman, Marina Van Zuylen, Stacy Doris, Chet Weiner, Mei-Mei Berssenbrugge. All lists are incomplete.

Tom Johnson has taught me the meaning of intimacy within the insoluble paradox of time. For him and to him, my profound, delighted love and thanks.

To my family, attenuated through loss, but remarkably resilient, this work is offered as one version of our ongoing experience: my brother David and his wife Andree; my cousins Michael, Margot and Stevenson Carlebach, Nathaniel Tripp and Reeve Lindbergh; my uncle Bill and aunt Priscilla, who took me in in the midst of their own bereavement: these persons constitute courage in the face of life's most obdurate challenges. My sister Jennifer, who died far too soon, and her two remarkable sons, Jack and Richard, and Richard's wife, Katherine Pope, have been life-sustaining presences.

My poetry editor for many years at Penguin, Paul Slovak, has been both generous and persevering; I am truly indebted to him for supporting this project. My agent, Lourdes Lopez, has managed, with the greatest discretion and grace, to keep many of my demons at bay. Without her, this book would not have come to fruition.

To John Brainard and Ron Padgett, my thanks for the use of Joe's collage on the jacket.

I want to thank Camille Guthrie, Ethel Rackin, and Stuart Krimko for labors far below their talents.

Finally, two colleagues, Joan Richardson and Michael Brenson, have offered perpetual encouragement and inspiration. Their intellectual and critical acuity, personal conviction, and abiding friendship have made this work possible. This book is dedicated to them.

NOTES

INVENTING UNREALITY

1. Sigmund Freud, "Mourning and Melancholia" in *General Psychological Theory* (New York, Collier Books, 1963), p. 166.
2. Norma Cole, "Conditions maritimes," in *Counterfact* (Elmwood, Potes & Poets Press, 1966), p. xxv.
3. Giorgio Agamben, *Stanzas: Word and Phantasm in Western Culture* (Minneapolis, University of Minnesota Press, 1993), p. 59.
4. Giorgio Agamben, *Language and Death: The Place of Negativity* (Minneapolis, University of Minnesota Press, 1991), p. 86.
5. Rainer Maria Rilke, "Dolls: On the Wax Dolls of Lotte Pritzel," *Essays on Dolls: Heinrich von Kleist, Charles Baudelaire, Rainer Maria Rilke* (New York, Syrens, Penguin Group, 1994), p. 33.
6. Susan Stewart, *On Longing: Narratives of the Miniature, the Gigantic, the Souvenir, the Collection* (Durham, Duke University Press, 1993), p. 136.
7. Jacques Derrida, *Aporias* (Stanford, Stanford University Press, 1993), p. 74.
8. Wallace Stevens, "The Irish Cliffs of Moher," *The Collected Poems of Wallace Stevens* (New York, Alfred A. Knopf, 1964), p. 501.

THE NIGHT SKY I

1. Roberto Calasso, *The Ruin of Katsch* (Cambridge, Belknap Press, Harvard University Press, 1994), p. 92.
2. John Donne, "Song," in *Elizabethan Lyrics from the Original Texts*, ed. Norman Ault (New York, William Sloan Associates, 1949), p. 244.
3. SBD should not be confused with SPD, Small Press Distribution, where you may order almost any book of poetry published by a small press: 1-800-869-7553.
4. "All the little nouns are the ones that I like the most: the deer, the sun, and so on. You say these perfectly little words and you're asserting that the sun is ninety-three million miles away, and that there is shade because of shadows, and more, who knows? It's a tremendous structure to have built out of a few small nouns. " George Oppen interviewed by L. S. Dembo in *Contemporary Literature*, vol.10, no. 2 (Spring 1969), pp. 162–163.
5. The following quotations are from the following authors, not necessarily in the following order: Ron Padgett, C. D. Wright, Frances A. Yates, Samuel Beckett, William Shakespeare, Keith Waldrop, Mina Loy, Bernadette Mayer, Harold Brodkey, Henry David Thoreau, Raymond Roussel, Peter Straub, Kamau Brathwaite.
6. *New York Times* Sky Watch: January 21, 1996, p. 28.
7. George Steiner, *Real Presences* (Chicago, University of Chicago Press, 1989), p. 139.
8. Ibid., p. 148.
9. Theodor Adorno, *Aesthetic Theory* (London, Routledge & Kegan Paul, 1970), p. 120.

10. Jonathan Schell, "Politics in an Age of Distraction," *Newsday*, January 21, 1996, p. 38.
11. Wallace Stevens, *Notes Toward a Supreme Fiction*, in *The Collected Poems of Wallace Stevens* (New York, Alfred A. Knopf, 1964), p. 404.
12. Martha C. Nussbaum, *Poetic Justice: The Literary Imagination and Public Life* (Boston, Beacon Press, 1995), p. 2.
13. John Ashbery, "Soonest Mended," in *The Double Dream of Spring* (New York, E. P. Dutton & Co., 1970), p. 19.
14. W. H. Auden, "The Sea and the Mirror: A Commentary on Shakespeare's *The Tempest*," Part 3: Caliban to the Audience, in *Collected Poems* (New York, Random House, 1976), p. 331.
15. Richard Rorty, *Contingency, irony, and solidarity* (Cambridge, Cambridge University Press, 1989), p. 48.
16. Donne, op. cit.

THE NIGHT SKY II

1. Richard Feynman, *QED: The Strange Theory of Light and Matter* (Princeton, Princeton University Press, 1985), p. 10.
2. Ralph Waldo Emerson, "Circles," *Emerson: Essays and Lectures* (New York, The Library of America), p. 412.
3. Susan Howe, *Frame Structures: Early Poems, 1974–1979* (New York, New Directions, 1996), p. 62.
4. Both quotes are from the *New York Review of Books* for August 8, 1996. The first is from James Fenton on Pisanello, the second from David Lodge's review of *Granta 54: Best of Young American Novelists* (Summer 1996).
5. Rosmarie Waldrop, *Lawn of Excluded Middle* (Providence, Tender Buttons, 1993), p. 11.
6. Averil Cameron, *Christianity and the Rhetoric of Empire* (Berkeley, University of California Press, 1991), pp. 60–61.
7. Sacvan Bercovitch, *The American Jeremiad* (Madison, University of Wisconsin Press, 1978), p. 23.
8. Emerson, op. cit., p. 236.
9. Richard Rorty, *Contingency, irony, and solidarity* (Cambridge, Cambridge University Press, 1989), p. 33.
10. Leslie Scalapino, *The Front Matter, Dead Souls* (Hanover, Wesleyan University Press, 1996).
11. William James, *Principles of Psychology I*, pp. 275–276.
12. Barbara Johnson, *A World of Difference* (Baltimore, Johns Hopkins University Press, 1987), p. 15.
13. Philip Fisher, "Democratic Social Space: Whitman, Melville, and the Promise of American Transparency," *Representations* 24 (Fall 1988), p. 62.
14. Michael Palmer, "Letter 3," *At Passages* (New York, New Directions, 1995), p. 5.
15. John Cage, "Lecture on Nothing," *Silence* (Middletown, Wesleyan University Press, 1973), p. 111.

THE NIGHT SKY III

1. Ludwig Wittgenstein, *Philosophical Investigations*, trans. G. E. M. Anscombe, third edition (New York, Macmillan, 1953), p. 114.
2. Michel Leiris, *Brisees: Broken Branches*, trans. Lydia Davis (San Francisco, North Point Press, 1989), p. 27.
3. Stephan Mallarmé, "The White Water-Lily," in *Mallarmé: Selected Prose Poems, Essays & Letters*, trans. Bradford Cook (Baltimore, Johns Hopkins Press, 1956), p. 6.
4. Giorgio Agamben, *The Coming Community*, trans. Michael Hardt (Minneapolis, University of Minnesota Press, 1993), p. 50.

5. Stanley Cavell, *The Senses of Walden* (Chicago, University of Chicago Press, 1992), p. 63.
6. For a historical exploration of debates about private and public discourse, see Rochelle Gurstein's *The Repeal of Reticence: A History of America's Cultural and Legal Struggles over Free Speech, Obscenity, Sexual Liberation, and Modern Art* (New York, Hill and Wang, 1996).
7. Vaclav Havel, "The Power of the Powerless," in *Open Letters: Selected Writings, 1965–1990* (New York, Random House, 1992), p. 133.
8. Thomas L. Dumm, *Michel Foucault and the Politics of Freedom* (Thousand Oaks, Sage Publications, 1996), p. 16.
9. Wallace Stevens, "Anecdote of the Jar," In *The Collected Poems of Wallace Stevens* (New York, Alfred A. Knopf, 1964), p. 76.
10. Wittgenstein, op.cit., p. 139.
11. Wittgenstein, op.cit., p. xxx.
12. Joan Retallack, "Uncaged Words: John Cage in Dialogue with Chance." Published with minor differences as a monograph in the metal-box catalogue for Cage's *Rolywholyover A Circus*, Museum of Contemporary Art, Los Angeles (New York, Rizzoli International, 1993). I take the quote from a manuscript copy, p. 6.
13. "Centering Marginality," organized by Serge Gavronsky, November 15–16, 1996.
14. Charles Olson, "Projective Verse," in *Charles Olson: Selected Writings*, ed. Robert Creeley (New York, New Directions, 1966), p. 24.
15. Charles Olson, "Equal, That Is, to the Real Itself," in *Charles Olson: Selected Writings*, p. 49.
16. Charles Olson, *In Cold Hell, in Thicket* (San Francisco, Four Seasons Foundation, 1967), p. 35.
17. John Ashbery, "A Blessing in Disguise," in *Selected Poems* (New York, Viking, 1985), p. 62.
18. Giorgio Agamben, *Stanzas: Word and Phantasm in Western Culture*, trans. Ronald L. Martinez (Minneapolis, University of Minnesota Press, 1993), p. 59.
19. For a brilliant, dense discussion of abstraction and modernist poetry, see Charles Altieri's *Painterly Abstraction in Modernist American Poetry* (Cambridge, Cambridge University Press, 1989).

THE NIGHT SKY IV

1. Jacques Derrida, *Aporias*, trans. Thomas Dutoff (Stanford, Stanford University Press, 1993) p. 21.
2. Nathaniel Tripp, *Father, Soldier, Son* (Hanover, NH, Steerforth Press, 1997), p. 40.
3. Bob Perelman, *The Marginalization of Poetry: Language Writing and Literary History* (Princeton, Princeton University Press, 1996), p. 40.
4. Maurice Blanchot,"The Song of the Sirens: Encountering the Imaginary," in *The Gaze of Orpheus*, trans. Lydia Davis (Barrytown, Station Hill, 1989), p. 112. I am grateful to Arthur Vogelsang for reminding me of this extraordinary essay.
5. Jacques Derrida, *Specters of Marx*, trans. Peggy Kamuf (New York, Routledge, 1994), p. 75.
6. For a lucid discussion of William James's Pragmatism, see Frank Lentricchia's *Aerial and the Police* (Madison, University of Wisconsin Press, 1988).
7. This only slightly facetious suggestion and much of what follows were largely precipitated by a panel held at New York's Segue Performance Space, organized by Dan Machlin and Sean Killian, on Bob Perelman's book cited above. The participants were Perelman, Ron Silliman, Steve Evans, Juliana Spahr, and myself.
8. Hal Foster, *The Return of the Real* (Cambridge, MIT Press, 1996), p. xiv.
9. Julia Kristeva, "The Father, Love, and Banishment," in *Desire in Language: A Semiotic Approach to Literature and Art*, ed. Leon S. Roudiez (New York, Columbia University Press, 1980), p. 150.
10. Henry James, *The Complete Notebooks of Henry James*, ed. Leon Edel and Lyall H. Powers (New York, Oxford University Press, 1987), p. 10.
11. Giorgio Agamben, *Infancy and History*, trans. Liz Heron (New York, Verso, 1993), p. 25.
12. *New York Times*, March 30, 1997, p. A16. This was part of the coverage of the Heaven's Gate suicides in California.

13. Agamben, op. cit. p. 42.
14. Ibid., pp. 49–50.

THE NIGHT SKY V

1. Paul Celan, "The Meridian" (speech on the occasion of receiving the Georg Büchner Prize, Darmstadt, October 22, 1960), in *Paul Celan: Collected Prose*, trans. Rosmarie Waldrop (Riverdale-on-Hudson, New York, Sheep Meadow Press, 1986), pp. 49–50.
2. Robert Smithson, "The Spiral Jetty," in *Robert Smithson: The Collected Writings*, ed. Jack Flam (Berkeley, University of California Press, 1996), pp. 146–147.
3. "Constantinople, the Coveted City," in *Lands and Peoples: The World in Color*, ed. Gladys D. Clewell (New York, Grolier Society, 1929), p. 264.
4. Ibid.
5. Rebecca Solnit, "The Garden of Merging Paths," in *Resisting the Virtual Life: The Culture and Politics of Information*, ed. James Brook and Iain A. Boal (San Francisco, City Lights Books, 1995), p. 229.
6. George W. S. Trow, *Within the Context of No Context* (reprint; New York, Atlantic Monthly Press, 1997), p. 55.
7. *The Concise Oxford Dictionary of Current English*, Fifth Edition, 1964.
8. Ralph Waldo Emerson, "Experience," *Ralph Waldo Emerson: Essays & Lectures* (New York, Library of America, 1983), p. 487.
9. Ibid., p. 492.

THE NIGHT SKY VI

1. Lydia Davis, "Paring Off the Amphibiologisms," in *Joyful Noise: The New Testament Revisited*, ed. Rick Moody and Darcey Steinke (Boston, Little, Brown and Co., 1997), p. 197.
2. Don DeLillo, *Underworld* (New York, Scribner, 1997), p. 280.
3. Emily Dickinson, *The Poems of Emily Dickinson*, ed. Thomas H. Johnson (Cambridge, Belknap Press, Harvard University Press, 1955) no. 258, p. 185.
4. Henry Louis Gates Jr., "The End of Loyalty," *New Yorker*, March 9, 1998, p. 44.
5. Patrick McGrath, review of Martin Amis, *Night Train*, *New York Times Book Review*, February 1, 1998, p. 6.
6. Jean-Luc Nancy, *The Sense of the World*, trans. Jeffrey S. Librett (Minneapolis, University of Minnesota Press, 1997), p. 25.
7. *The Concise Oxford Dictionary of Current English*, Fourth Edition, 1964.
8. Laura Kipnis, "Adultery," *Critical Inquiry*, vol. 24, no. 2 (Winter 1998), p. 321.
9. Lewis Hyde, *Trickster Makes This World* (New York, Farrar, Straus and Giroux, 1998), p. 7.
10. John Keats, *The Letters of John Keats*, vol. 1, (Cambridge, Harvard University Press), p. 193.
11. Sylvia Plath, *Letters Home*, selected and edited by Aurelia Schober Plath (New York, Harper & Row, 1975), pp. 222, 234, 244. Please note: all ellipses are in the text.
12. Ted Hughes, *Crow: From the Life and Songs of the Crow* (London, Faber and Faber, 1970), p. 14.
13. Gilles Deleuze, "Michel Foucault: Life as a Work of Art," *Negotiations* (New York, Columbia University Press, 1995), p. 98.
14. Jennifer Wardwell Lauterbach, "In Search of an American Youth Movement: A Study of the Political Life of the Young in America 1905–1940," B.A. thesis (Honors in History), Smith College, 1962, p. 68.
15. Marcia Westkott, *The Feminist Legacy of Karen Horney* (New Haven, Yale University Press, 1986), p. 179.

THE NIGHT SKY VII

1. Ralph Waldo Emerson, "The American Scholar," in *Emerson: Essays & Lectures* (New York, Library of America, 1983), p. 60.
2. William James, "The Will to Believe," *William James: Writings, 1878–1899* (New York: Library of America, 1992), pp. 471–472.
3. Emmanuel Levinas, "The Ambiguity of Contemporary Ontology," in *Entre Nous: Thinking-of-the-Other*, trans. Michael B. Smith and Barbara Harshav (New York, Columbia University Press, 1998), p. 3.
4. Giorgio Agamben, *Infancy and History: The Destruction of Experience*, trans. Liz Heron (New York, Verso, 1993), p. 100.
5. Plato, *Phaedrus and the Seventh and Eighth Letters*, trans. Walter Hamilton (New York, Penguin, 1983), p. 58.
6. Hannah Arendt, *Betweeen Past and Future: Eight Exercises in Political Thought* (New York, Penguin, 1993), p. 13.
7. Adam Gopnick, *New Yorker*, October 19, 1998, p. 80.
8. George Oppen, "Of Being Numerous," in *George Oppen: Collected Poems* (New York, New Directions, 1974), p. 151.
9. William Blake, "The Divine Image," in *William Blake: A Selection of Poems and Letters* (London, Penguin, 1958), pp. 33–34.

SLAVES OF FASHION

1. Charles Altieri, "Poetics as 'Untruth': Revising Modern Claims for Literary Truths," unpublished manuscript.

INDEX

Achebe, Chinua, 173
Adams, John, 94
Adorno, Theodor, 15, 207, 233, 246
Agamben, Giorgio, 14, 16, 93
Alcott, Louisa May, 126
Aldis, Mary, 176
Allen, Donald, 177
Altieri, Charles, 179, 186
Andre, Carl, 93
Arbus, Diane, 212
Arendt, Hannah, 161
Aristotle, 241
Arthur, Bea, 211
Ashbery, John, 38, 43, 56, 92, 93, 104, 162, 180, 181, 189
Astaire, Fred, 126
Ataturk, 120
Auden, W. H., 181
Austen, Jane, 193
Avedon, Richard, 211

Bach, Johann Sebastian, 126
Barthes, Roland, 174
Bates, Milton J., 37
Baudelaire, Charles, 1, 76, 112, 163
Baudrillard, Jean, 6
Beatles, 29
Beckett, Samuel, 3, 25, 43, 88, 108, 126, 162
Bedient, Calvin, 182
Beethoven, Ludwig van, 126
Benjamin, Walter, v, 1, 15, 116
Bercovitch, Sacvan, 9
Bergen, Candice, 54
Bergson, Henri, 89
Berlioz, Hector, 128
Bernstein, Charles, 8, 104, 180, 181
Berryman, John, 141
Beuys, Joseph, 207
Bishop, Elizabeth, 177

Blake, William, 27, 135, 146, 163, 178, 228
Bloom, Harold, 170, 176, 177, 178, 179, 180
Bly, Robert, 177
Boal, Iain A., 114
Brahms, Johannes, 126
Brainard, Caroline, 221, 222
Brainard, Joe, 217–24
Brainard, John, 219, 220, 221, 222
Brenson, Michael, 8, 102, 197
Breskin, David, 207, 208
Brodsky, Joseph, 58–59, 153, 172
Burckhardt, Rudy, 224
Burke, Johnny, 196
Bush, George H. W., 37
Bush, George W., 212
Bush, Laura, 2

Cage, John, 93
Carlyle, Thomas, 237
Carroll, Lewis, 126
Carruth, Hayden, 177
Cartier-Bresson, Henri, 102
Celan, Paul, 55, 115–18, 188
Cézanne, Paul, 154, 214
Chaplin, Charlie, 20, 21, 53, 126
Charles, Ray, 126
Chernoff, Maxine, 19
Chomsky, Noam, 8
Clay, Cassius (Mohammed Ali), 86–87
Clinton, Bill, 41, 123, 139–41
Coetzee, J. M., 240
Cohen, Marvin, 144
Cole, Norma, 13, 89
Coleridge, Samuel Taylor, 179, 237
Columbus, Christopher, 46
Corbett, Beverly, 222
Corbett, Bill, 217, 222
Cornell, Joseph, 223
Crane, Hart, 178

Crapsey, Adelaide, 177
Creeley, Robert, 104, 189
Crumb, R., 212
cummings, e. e., 141
Currin, John, 211–16

Danforth, John, 69
Danto, Arthur, 209
Davis, Lydia, 131
Dean, Howard, 236
Deaver, Michael, 36
de Kooning, Willem, 93, 211
DeLillo, Don, 132–33
Derrida, Jacques, 17–18, 95
Descartes, 35, 110, 119
Dewey, John, 8
Diana, Princess of Wales, 140
Dickens, Charles, 76
Dickinson, Emily, 1, 35, 93, 94, 107, 180,
    183
Donne, John, 1
Doris, Stacy, 10
Dostoevsky, Fyodor Mikhaylovich, 76
Douglas, William O., 21
Duchamp, Marcel, 119
Ducornet, Rikki, 12
Dumm, Thomas, 114, 135
Duncan, Robert, 91, 177
Dunn, Anne, 222
du Plessis, Rachel Blau, 89
Dylan, Bob, 128, 132, 235

Eagleton, Terry, 243
Eliot, T. S., 34, 42, 104, 141, 145, 176, 215
Elmslie, Kenward, 217, 218, 220, 221, 222
Emerson, Ralph Waldo, 4, 6, 9, 23, 28, 32–33,
    34, 35, 57, 66, 104, 129–30, 152, 153,
    180, 200–201, 216, 235–48
Emerson, Ruth, 236
Epicurus, 114
Equi, Elaine, 181
Erb, Elke, 188

Fisher, Philip, 170, 238
Flanagan, Dennis, 20
Fleischer, Cornell, 121
Foster, Hal, 106
Foucault, Michel, 36, 37, 89–90, 149
Francis of Assisi, Saint, 57, 112
Franklin, Benjamin, 169
Fraser, Kathleen, 89

Freud, Sigmund, 12, 71, 177
Friedman, Thomas, 140–41
Frost, Robert, 105, 141

Gablik, Suzi, 91
Gagosian, Larry, 212
Gehry, Frank, 194
Ginsberg, Allen, 57, 106, 174
Gizzi, Peter, 222
Golub, Leon, 215
Gordimer, Nadine, 213
Goya, Francisco José de, 213
Gray, Cleve, 197, 198
Greenberg, Clement, 203–4, 205
Gregory, Andre, 2
Groff, Alice, 177
Guccione, Bob, 139
Guest, Barbara, 89, 186, 189–96
Guston, Philip, 94, 126, 211
Guthrie, Woody, 126, 128

Hacquard, Emmanuel, 188
Hamill, Sam, 2
Hamilton, Ann, 93–94, 215
Hashey, Jan, 219
Hass, Robert, 182
Hawkes, Terence, 167
H.D., 190
Hefner, Hugh, 212
Hegel, Georg Wilhelm Friedrich, 16
Heidegger, Martin, 16, 99, 100
Hejinian, Lyn, 19, 247
Hepburn, Audrey, 126
Herblock (Herbert Block), 21
Hickey, Dave, 62, 154
Hillman, Brenda, 182
Hilton, Paris, 211
Hirsch, Ed, 152
Hirst, Damian, 214
Holiday, Billie, 72, 126
Hoover, J. Edgar, 19
Hoover, Paul, 19, 177
Hopper, Edward, 212
Horace, 220
Horney, Karen, 150
Howe, Fanny, 181–83
Howe, Susan, 89
Hoyt, Helen, 177
Hughes, Ted, 132, 140–51
Hussein, Saddam, 139
Hutchinson, Anne, 97

Ives, Burl, 126

Jabès, Edmond, 188
Jackson, Jesse, 170
Jackson, Michael, 57
James, Henry, 101, 109
James, William, 6, 101–2, 238
Janik, Allan, 38–39
John Paul, Pope, 163
Johns, Jasper, 93, 211, 214
Johnson, Barbara, 40
Jordan, Michael, 86
Joyce, James, 24, 25, 215
Judd, Donald, 199
Justinian, 120

Kafka, Franz, 162
Kant, Immanuel, 90, 112
Karr, Mary, 104
Katz, Alex, 215
Keats, John, 1, 190
Keillor, Garrison, 60
Kennedy, Jackie, 140, 221
Kennedy, John F., 141
Kennedy, Robert F., 234
Kentridge, William, 214
Keyes, John, 90
Kiefer, Anselm, 207
Kierkegaard, Søren, 38–39, 173
King, Martin Luther, Jr., 235, 238
Kinnell, Galway, 174
Kitaj, R. B., 91
Kline, Franz, 126
Koons, Jeff, 212
Kreymborg, Alfred, 176
Kristeva, Julia, 108, 178

Lacan, Jacques, 166–67, 178
Lehman, David, 176, 180
Leiris, Michel, 81
Levertov, Denise, 177
Levy, Edgar, 202
Lewinsky, Monica, 139
Lorca, Federico García, 152
Lowell, Robert, 141
Loy, Mina, 176
Luce, Henry, 19, 86
Lyotard, Jean-Francoise, 44

McCourt, Frank, 104
McCoy, Garnett, 197

McGill, Ralph, 21
Machiavelli, Niccolò, 244
McKibben, Bill, 240
MacLeish, Archibald, 125
MacLow, Jackson, 230
McLuhan, Marshall, 213
McQuade, Molly, 8
Madonna, 57
Malebranche, Nicolas de, 116
Mallarmé, Stéphane, 81
Mapplethorpe, Robert, 153–154
Marden, Brice, 93, 214
Martin, Agnes, 93
Matisse, Henri, 126
Melville, Herman, 90
Middlebrook, Diane Wood, 140
Mill, John Stuart, 237
Miller, Perry, 236
Milton, John, 47
Miró, Joan, 81, 126
Mohammed Ali (Cassius Clay), 86–87
Monroe, Marilyn, 126, 211
Moore, Frank, 176, 215, 219
Morandi, Giorgio, 223
Moriarty, Laura, 89
Mottram, Eric, 91
Moyers, Bill, 10, 59
Mozart, Wolfgang Amadeus, 126
Murray, Elizabeth, 94
Myung Mi Kim, 89

Nancy, Jean-Luc, 116
Nauman, Bruce, 214
Nemerov, Howard, 177
Nicholas, Saint, 121
Nietzsche, Friedrich, 149, 179
Niles, John Jacob, 5
Nussbaum, Martha, 56

O'Hara, Frank, 59, 104, 105
Olds, Sharon, 174
Olson, Charles, 89, 90, 91
Ondaatje, Michael, 93
Oppen, George, 48, 186, 233
Orwell, George, 35
Ovid, 5, 131–32

Padgett, Pat, 219, 220, 222
Padgett, Ron, 217, 219, 220, 221, 222
Palmer, Michael, 104, 184–86
Pascal, Blaise, 156

Pater, Walter, 179
Perelman, Bob, 181
Peter, Paul and Mary, 235
Picasso, Pablo, 193
Piel, Gerard, 20
Plath, Sylvia, 132, 140–51
Polke, Sigmar, 207
Pollack, Jackson, 93, 126, 162
Polo, Marco, 46
Porter, Fairfield, 223
Post, Steve, 82
Pound, Ezra, 2, 34, 42, 44, 176, 177, 193, 200, 243
Presley, Elvis, 126, 171
Price-Williams, David, 121–22
Prideaux, Tom, 25
Proust, Marcel, 3, 88, 112, 162

Quercia, Jacobo della, 204

Rabinowitz, Anna, 31
Rankine, Claudia, 40
Ratcliffe, Carter, 217
Ray, Man, 176
Reagan, Ronald, 36–37
Reich, Steve, 94
Retallack, Joan, 88
Richter, Gerhard, 207–10, 214
Riley, Terry, 94
Rilke, Rainer Maria, 1, 16–17, 100
Rimbaud, Arthur, 1, 107
Roberson, Ed, 181
Robeson, Paul, 27, 126
Rockwell, Norman, 211
Rodin, Auguste, 204
Roethke, Theodore, 141
Rorty, Richard, 62
Rose, Charlie, 174
Rose, Jacqueline, 166
Rosenberg, David, 23
Rosenblum, Robert, 212
Rosenthal, M. L., 177
Roth, Philip, 34–35
Roubaud, Jacques, 188
Rumsfeld, Donald, 212
Ryman, Robert, 93, 203

Sainsbury, Hester, 177
Salinger, J. D., 126
Salisbury, Harrison, 21–22
Saltzman, Lisa, 207

Sandburg, Carl, 176
Sargent, John Singer, 211
Sartre, Jean-Paul, 1
Saussure, Ferdinand de, 167
Schell, Jonathan, 54, 243
Schjeldahl, Peter, 214
Schnabel, Julian, 215
Schuyler, James (Jimmy), 162, 224
Seeger, Pete, 126, 127
Shawn, Wallace, 2
Shelley, Percy Bysshe, 1, 178, 180
Sherman, Cindy, 214
Shklovsky, Victor Borisovich, 167
Shostakovich, Dmitry, 55
Silliman, Ron, 63
Sillman, Amy, 215
Simpson, O. J., 139
Sloan, Mary Margaret, 177
Smith, David, 197–206
Smithson, Robert, 118–19, 199
Spahr, Juliana, 40
Spicer, Jack, 105
Steffy, Richard, 122
Stein, Gertrude, 2, 10, 42, 76, 93, 104, 161, 177, 241
Steiner, George, 165–66
Stella, Frank, 214
Stern, Howard, 212
Stern, Robert, 39n
Stevens, Peter, 197
Stevens, Wallace, 18, 34, 37, 71, 78, 104, 107, 117, 154, 172, 176, 177, 178, 180, 190, 201, 206, 210, 239
Stevenson, Peter, 207
Stevenson, Robert Louis, 126
Stewart, Susan, 17
Storr, Robert, 212
Sylvester, David, 206
Sze, Sarah, 215

Tallman, Warren, 177
Tamny, Martin, 235
Tardos, Anne, 230
Taylor, Ted, 24
Thoreau, Henry David, 25, 243
Toulmin, Stephen, 38–39
Towers, Robert, 31
Trinidad, David, 181
Tripp, Linda, 139
Trow, George, 126
Tucker, Ellen, 236–37

Vendler, Helen, 104
Vermeer, Jan, 55
Vogelsang, Arthur, 46

Waldman, Anne, 222
Waldrop, Keith, 188
Waldrop, Rosmarie, 187–88
Warhol, Andy, 93, 209, 211, 223
Weinberger, Eliot, 177
Weiner, Hannah, 89
Welish, Marjorie, 181
Wendy, Sister, 10
Whitman, Walt, 33, 34, 76, 93, 94, 107, 130, 161, 165, 167–75, 179, 180
Widmark, Richard, 126
Willard, Marian, 204

Williams, Roger, 188
Williams, William Appleman, 236
Williams, William Carlos, 34, 176, 177
Willis, Elizabeth, 222
Winthrop, John, 97
Wittgenstein, Ludwig, 38, 78, 188
Wittig, Monique, 166
Wordsworth, William, 19, 179, 237
Wyeth, Andrew, 211

Yeats, William Butler, 1, 24–25, 126, 144

Zorach, Marguerite, 177
Zorach, William, 176
Zukofsky, Louis, 186

Grateful acknowledgment is made for permission to reprint the following copyrighted works:

Selections from *The Collected Poems of Wallace Stevens*. Copyright 1954 by Wallace Stevens and renewed 1982 by Holly Stevens. Used by permission of Alfred A. Knopf, a division of Random House, Inc.

Excerpt from "Lunar Baedeker" from *The Lost Lunar Baedeker* by Mina Loy. Copyright © 1996 by the Estate of Mina Loy. Reprinted by permission of Farrar, Straus and Giroux, LLC.

"Chanting At The Crystals Sea, Part 6" from *Frame Structures* by Susan Howe. Copyright © 1974, 1975, 1978, 1979, 1996 by Susan Howe. Reprinted by permission of New Directions Publishing Corp.

Excerpts from "Letter 3" and "Letter 7" from *At Passages* by Michael Palmer. Copyright © 1995 by New Directions Publishing Corp. Reprinted by permission of New Directions Publishing Corp.

Excerpt from "Lecture on Nothing" from *Silence: Lectures and Writings* by John Cage. © 1961 by John Cage. Reprinted by permission of Wesleyan University Press.

Excerpt from "In Cold Hell, in Thicket" from *The Collected Poems of Charles Olson—excluding the Maximus Poems*, edited by George F. Butterick. Copyright © 1987 Estate of Charles Olson. Copyright © 1987 University of Connecticut. Used by permission of University of California Press.

Excerpt from "A Blessing in Disguise" from *Rivers and Mountains* by John Ashbery. Used by permission of the author.

Selections from *Paul Celan: Collected Prose*, translated by Rosemarie Waldrop. Copyright Rosemarie Waldrop 1986. Used by permission of The Sheep Meadow Press, Riverdale, New York.

Excerpt from the introduction to *Tales from Ovid* by Ted Hughes. Copyright © 1997 by Ted Hughes. Reprinted by permission of Farrar, Straus and Giroux, LLC.

Excerpt from "Love Sick" by Bob Dylan. Copyright 1997 by Special Rider Music. All rights reserved. International copyright secured. Reprinted by permission.

Selections from *Letters Home by Sylvia Plath: Correspondence 1950–1963* selected and edited by Aurelia Schober Plath. Copyright © 1975 by Aurelia Schober Plath. Reprinted by permission of HarperCollins Publishers Inc.

Excerpt from "Of Being Numerous" from *Collected Poems* by George Oppen. Copyright © 1975 by George Oppen. Reprinted by permission of New Directions Publishing Corp.

Excerpts from "Introduction to the World," "Q," and "The Quietist" from *Selected Poems* by Fanny Howe. Copyright © 2000 Fanny Howe. Used by permission of University of California Press.

Selections from *Forces of Imagination: Writing on Writing* by Barbara Guest. Used by permission of Kelsey St. Press, Berkeley, California.

Jacket art by Joe Brainard used by permission of John Brainard, Executor of the Estate of Joe Brainard.

Printed in the United States
by Baker & Taylor Publisher Services